Informing Communities
The Role of Libraries and Information Services

Edited by

MARGARET KINNELL

CSG Publishing 1992

COMMUNITY SERVICES GROUP
—— of ——
The Library Association

CSG Publishing
c/o Remploy Limited, London Road, Newcastle,
Staffs. ST13 1RX

ISBN 18731 85 01+

British Library Cataloguing-in-Publication Data:
A catalogue record for this book is available from the British Library.

Editor's Acknowledgements

There are many individuals who have supported the publication of this book, the first in CSG's publications programme, and an important focal point of CSG's 10th anniversary year. The CSG Marketing Group deserves particular mention; Howard Matthew and Andrew Green, Chair of CSG, have given enthusiastic guidance and support throughout the project. Tina Dunn and the staff of Remploy Bookbinding made my task as editor a pleasureable one; their help during all the stages of preparing the book was invaluable. To them, and to the contributors, thank you.

Margaret Kinnell
Loughborough, June 1992.

List of Contributors

PAUL CATCHESIDE — Principal Assistant Director, City of Liverpool Libraries and Arts Department.

PAT COLEMAN — Director of Library Services, Birmingham City Library Service.

PAT DARTER — Librarian, Equal Opportunities Commission.

CAROLYN DATE — Librarian-in-charge of Domiciliary Services, East Area, Dorset County Library.

JOHN DAVIES — Director of Leisure Services, City of Liverpool and former Director, St. Helen's Metropolitan Borough Council.

DEBORAH GOODALL — SEALS Project Officer, West Midlands Regional Library Service, Birmingham.

ANDREW GREEN — Assistant County Librarian: Information Services, Libraries, Arts and Archives Department, Staffordshire County Council.

KEVIN HARRIS — Head of Information, Community Development Foundation.

MARGARET KINNELL — Senior Lecturer, Department of Information and Library Studies, Loughborough University.

SALLY KNIGHT — Patient Information, Health Information Service, Lister Hospital, Stevenage.

ALAN MACDOUGALL — Director of Library Services, Dublin City University.

OWEN MCDOWELL   Development Officer, Sheffield City Council.

BERYL MORRIS   Management and Training Consultant, Hudson Rivers, Woodford Green, Essex, and former Head of Cultural Services, London Borough of Newham.

DAVID TOZER   Joint Co-ordinator, Centre for Environmental Information, Cheam, Sutton, Surrey.

BOB USHERWOOD   Senior Lecturer, Department of Information Studies, University of Sheffield.

Contents

Foreword

Mark Fisher, M.P.

We live in a society which is underpinned by information, in which both work and leisure time increasingly depend on intelligent technology. Access to information, for individuals and communities, and for business and commerce, is therefore vital.

This book will play an important role in getting this message across, and in shaping the library and information services of the future. *Informing Communities* will increase our understanding of the potential and importance of our public libraries, and the key role they have to play in transforming Britain into an intelligent and well informed democracy.

The contributors to the book make clear, that as we move towards the millennium, libraries will face the challenge of diversification. Whilst their primary function of book loans must be protected and enhanced, libraries must grasp the opportunity to provide new and wider services; establishing databases, forging links with Europe and increasing specialised services to the elderly, the disabled and to industry.

We need the widest discussion on these issues. Information is the key to our future, and this book will make an important and timely contribution to that debate.

House of Commons
May, 1992.

Introduction

Whether library and information services are seen as radical agitators, or reactionary pillars of the establishment, they have a significant role to play in improving the quality of life of citizens—in both the scope and breadth of the services provided. Library and information services offer a broad range of services from a wide range of generalist and specialist organizations covering factual information, referral, advice, counselling and advocacy.

Informing communities: the role of libraries and information services is written to give managers an overview of the range of services providing information, advice and counselling. It is not meant to be a practical guide on how to provide a certain service—although managers will find much that is relevant to help them manage and develop their services. It is intended rather to give an overview of how other organizations have provided a service to either a specific client group, geographical area or interest group. The book should therefore be especially useful to senior managers who are, or who have recently become, responsible for managing a multi-disciplinary unit, managing services which are a different specialism from their own or who have to seek active co-operation from a variety of agencies and organizations to provide a service.

Students and people newly involved in providing library, information and advice and counselling services, or who are keen to explore co-operation, will also find the book of value in giving an overview of such services. In addition, there are insights into how to effect multi-disciplinary and inter-agency working.

A number of common threads, phrases, terms, attitudes and concepts run throughout the book and a number are worth highlighting. These key concepts are information; access—physical and attitudinal; people, including staff and those in the community; 'citizen action'; communication; co-operation; joint working and community liaison. No library, information, advice or counselling service is effective if attention is not paid to these key concepts. Adherence to them is to be found throughout the book from the varying standpoints of the writers.

Information services have developed rapidly as society has become more complex and success is only achievable if one has the right information and advice to make an informed decision. The identified and stated information needs of a variety of groups in the community, e.g. people from cultural minorities, people with disabilities, unemployed and low waged people, women, one-parent families, etc., coupled with the economic need for co-operation and collaboration between the public and voluntary sectors, has led to a great many of the initiatives cited and the beliefs held. None of the initiatives, services or strategies in the book have been created for their own sake because they are 'a good thing' or because they will bring honour to the initiator. All exist to provide a better service to the customer, whether focused on race, gender or disability, or on people with particular needs or interests, services such as health information or arts facilities. There is also the need to establish the context in which such services can flourish, through activities such as strategic management, the provision of equal opportunities and training.

The book's remit is deliberately wide, with each of the writers contributing from a specialist perspective whilst at the same time relating their chapter to the broader picture. The contributors offer experiences from a number of different public library authorities and other organizations, including: Dorset County Library, City of Liverpool Libraries and Arts Department, Sheffield City Council, the Equal Opportunities Commission, the Centre for Environmental Information, the Community Development Foundation, St. Helen's Metropolitan Borough Council Community Leisure Department, and the Lister Hospital Health Information Service.

In Chapter One, Bob Usherwood provides an overview of the development of community information concepts, and considers the main theoretical issues which underpin the book. A major consideration is the concern that citizens have free access to information, and this is dealt with further in Chapter Two by Kevin Harris. There is not only the principle of making all information, or nearly all information available to everyone. Also of concern is the practical recognition that some constraints on access will remain—how to remove or reduce these is the role of the information provider.

Carolyn Date discusses in Chapter Three how people with disabilities can be helped to access information for their particular needs; physical as well as intellectual access is of concern. The broad nature of equal opportunities in a library and information context is considered in Chapter Four. Services need to be as responsive as possible to the changing customer base and Beryl Morris looks at the implications for selecting stock; developing information and other services; the promotion of library services and staff training in communities with a shifting demographic mix. A further aspect of providing for equality of opportunity, the provision of information services to meet women's needs, is discussed by Pat Darter in Chapter Five. There is a distinction between the various provisions for women that exist under the law and their wider information needs, and both aspects are covered in this chapter.

The information requirements relating to environmental

issues, which have become of increasing significance since the 1980s, are assessed in Chapter Six by David Tozer. Integral to the 'green' explosion has been an outpouring of information, much of it without a clear structure. This chapter provides an overview of the provision of environmental information and also indicated how information providers should set about deciding what to gather, how to store and catalogue it and make it available, and to whom. The question of to whom information should be directed, and at what level has become of particular significance in the health information field. In Chapter Seven Sally Knight examines the need for health information, its general importance for the population at large and the specific importance for individuals when they become ill. The changing relationship between patients and their health professionals as a consequence of access to information is also discussed.

In Chapters Eight and Nine the link between public libraries and the arts and the role played by fiction provision within communities are discussed. Paul Catcheside stresses the importance of this wider perspective for community provision, with individuals in the community being given the opportunity to pursue their own artistic, literary and intellectual interests. Deborah Goodall and Margaret Kinnell consider specifically the importance of fiction provision for enriching the lives of individuals and of their communities.

Managing the complexity of community information provision is discussed more fully in the final three chapters, which bring together many of the points raised in individual chapters. In order to co-ordinate community information, organizations need to co-operate. Public libraries, academic institutions, advice centres, voluntary groups, businesses and many other organizations maintain regular contact. In Chapter Ten Owen McDowell examines how such co-operation has developed and provides three case studies from one city. Above all, co-operation and other activities require a strategic framework, and in Chapter Eleven John Davies discusses a strategic management approach to providing ever more effective community information services. The training and development of staff inevitably lies at the heart of effective service delivery, and in Chapter Twelve Alan MacDougall provides both the rationale and the framework for a successful staff development programme.

In her Conclusion, Pat Coleman draws together many of the arguments and issues raised in the book, and also offers her own perspective on community information provision.

This book is the first in the Community Services Group's new publishing programme and will be followed by a variety of others on a range of topics in the coming months and years. Despite the social and economic changes over the past 10 to 15 years great inequalities remain in society. These inequalities are heightened for people who for one reason or another are unable to take full advantage of opportunities. Such people are disadvantaged because of their gender, race, disability, unemployed or low waged status, or socio-economic situation. The Community Services Group has as its prime objective increasing such people's access to the services to which they have a right.

Published in the Community Services Group's tenth year, I am proud as Chair to write the Introduction to this book since the topics covered represent not only the key concerns of CSG itself but also those people working across the country in information, advice and counselling organizations whether for local authorities, health authorities, central government or voluntary organizations. As Assistant County Librarian: Information Services in Staffordshire, I have a responsibility for leading such initiatives within the library service and for seeking co-operation with other agencies. While Staffordshire has experience of a Library and Information Plan, local information and advice networks and rural information provision, it has much to learn from the experience contained in these contributions.

I am sure this will be true for everyone who reads this book.

CHAPTER ONE

COMMUNITY INFORMATION

Bob Usherwood

Community Information

It is traditional, as well as wise, to start a contribution of this kind by defining terms. However, the title of this chapter on 'Community information' contains two terms, two concepts, which are far easier to describe than define. There are at least 90 definitions of 'community' and I suspect there are almost as many views as to what is meant by 'information'. Despite these difficulties a number of people have attempted to define community information (CI). These definitions range from Alan Bunch's prosaic 'Community Information is more a state of mind than system' to the 'official' utterances of professional groups and government departments.

The most quoted and generally accepted definition is still that which appeared in the Library Association's seminal paper, *Community information services—what libraries can do*. This defined CI services as those:

> which assist individuals and groups with daily problem-solving and with participation in the democratic process. The services concentrate on the needs of those who do not have ready access to other sources of assistance and on the most important problems that people have to face, problems to do with their homes, their jobs and their rights.[1]

The main themes of that statement can still be found in more recent definitions of purpose. Sheffield City Libraries, for example, state that:

> Community Information and Enquiry Services are concerned with helping people solve problems by providing access to quality information in order to enable them to make appropriate decisions on factors affecting their everyday lives.

19

Services are targeted at those least able to help themselves, not only to enable them to overcome crises, but to encourage individuals to achieve and exercise their own democratic rights. This includes encouraging active involvement in personal development in the areas of leisure and recreation.[2]

On the other hand, some public libraries have apparently considered doing away with the term community information. Nottinghamshire, for instance, in a recent management document argued that:

the term 'Community Information' should be discontinued and . . .this aspect of the library's provision should be known henceforth as 'Public Information' [on the grounds that] the term 'community information' is one which holds little meaning for anyone but library professionals. In the light of the many changes to community information provision in recent years. . . a change of name is needed if the revised system is to be accepted with enthusiasm by library staff.[3]

However, in some parts of the authority 'community information' is still the preferred term by members of staff, whilst others in the county attempt to distinguish between 'information about a community and information for a community'. Such debates notwithstanding, the term is still to be found in the Office of Arts and Libraries (OAL) recent publication on *Setting objectives for public library services*. This sees the library as 'the focal point for information about and for its local community, including information to support the democratic process'.[4]

It is perhaps worth stressing at this point that, despite the importance of the Library Association definition and the OAL statement, community information is not only, or even primarily, a library function. It is an activity which involves a wide range of organizations and many different forms of communications media. Some would argue that the concept can be traced back to 'the Settlement House Movement in the 1890s which recognised the need for skilled information services in extremely deprived neighbourhoods'.[5] Later, others promoted the idea of a general advice and information service but relatively little happened until 1939 when the first Citizens Advice Bureaux (CABx) were set up to help people cope with the problems of war-time Britain. These were an early example of information services designed to assist individuals with daily problem solving. By 1943 there were 1060 such outlets 'dispensing free advice on any matter to members of the public'.[6] Today there are 1346 outlets, including 712 main Bureaux, operating throughout England, Wales and Northern Ireland. They provide a service of information, advice, referral, counselling, advocacy and feedback on social policy. In 1990/91 the CABx dealt with over seven million cases; they are staffed by a mixture of paid managers, trained voluntary interviewers, and organizing and support staff.

Although some librarians had always played an important part in their communities it was not until the late 1960s and early 1970s that the library profession started to take its social responsibilities seriously. As part of the general social progress of the times library professionals began to consider the library's social commitment. In the USA writers such as Mary Lee Bundy suggested:

> three strategic information functions for the public library: reducing barriers to access to already existing information, collecting much needed information which does not now exist; and effecting the widespread dissemination of crucial information not now being distributed.[7]

In Britain the British Library instigated a research programme concerned with the provision of community information. The Library Association document quoted above was one result of this; another was the Community Information Project (CIP). This was set up in 1977 and rapidly established itself as a national resource for advice and information services. In 1989 CIP merged with the London Advice Services Alliance (LASA) to provide a stronger basis for research, social security information, development and policy support. In 1990 CIP changed its name but not its initials so as to become LASA's Consultancy, Information and Policy Unit.

As other contributors to this book demonstrate,

community information sources can be said to include governmental and other national bodies, local authority services, and a vast range of neighbourhood and local organizations. National organizations supplying community information include Relate, Citizens Advice Bureaux, The Consumers Association, Liberty, The Equal Opportunities Commission, The Race Relations Commission and so on.

At the national level, the government is a major source of information of potential value to the community. This is disseminated through such means as Department of Health leaflets, employment and training material, publications and advertisements. Some recent government publications, such as *The Parents' Charter,* have been widely criticised on the grounds that they are party political propaganda promoting Conservative policies rather than neutral sources of information. Such criticism indicates that national and local government must beware of the danger of crossing the thin line between giving information and promoting a political point of view. Under recent Conservative governments, government information officers have become increasingly worried about the way 'the boundaries between acceptable and unacceptable information provision were being crossed'.[8]

There are ethical issues too to be faced by those managing and running community information services. I have dealt elsewhere with those facing public librarians,[9] and the questions of privacy, confidentiality and responsibility to the client should be regarded as equally important by staff in other types of agencies. Campaigning agencies, like governments, also have to take care lest they sometimes blur the distinction between giving information and advice and proselytizing a point of view.

At the local level there are groups of various kinds; self help groups, welfare groups, minority groups, pressure groups, representative groups and others. All of these can play a vital role in the community information network of a neighbourhood or area. So too can public libraries, local radio stations, voluntary agencies, clubs, and council departments.

In addition, people themselves are, in many cases, very important sources of information. In communities with a strong oral tradition, information is most frequently spread by word of mouth. It is recognised that, even in specialist areas such as legal information, 'informal sources such as neighbours or the person in the pub. . . may be the most used of all.[10] A fact taken on board by at least one American public library which has published a *People to people index* to link topics with named individuals in the local community. In a similar fashion BBC Radio Sheffield's Helpline provides 'In touch with living'. This is a service provided by people with disabilities to help people newly disabled to benefit from their experience. Thus, through the project's publicity material it is possible to trace the name and phone number of a 'wheelchair user' and an 'amputee'. However, as Kempson observes, 'there is evidence that people are not always satisfied with the information they receive through. . . informal channels [and] a number of reasons why the traditional oral means of acquiring information are becoming inadequate'.[11]

Other contributors to this book will enable the reader to come to grips with a wide range of sources of information and advice, but before looking at the individual services it is worth considering some of the reasons behind this growing interest in community information.

Clearly, the need for information has become greater as society has become more complicated, both in terms of coping with the everyday business of living and at the level of considering and deciding about the great national and international issues. In particular, the British welfare state, or what remains of it, is highly complex with a range of departments overseeing different benefits and services. To quote from a report on Information and Advice Provision in Sheffield:

> There is a range of departments administering different benefits and services; at the last count there were no less than 45 means tested benefits. This leads to a maze of rules and criteria which governs entitlement and whole alphabets of forms to fill in; and it you don't get the right one you may lose your entitlement or at best have to start the process all over again.[12]

Although the detail may have changed since that was written, the general situation has not. In addition, the position of the client or potential client is not helped by a social security system which seems increasingly to be designed for the one per cent who might abuse it rather than to help the 99 per cent who need to use it. As the National Association of Citizens Advice Bureaux (NACAB) reports 'the regulations and administration of social security continue to cause difficulties for CAB clients'.[13] For instance, the Social Security Act which came into operation in 1988 resulted in a huge increase in inquiries to advice and welfare agencies.

Earlier, in the 1960s and 1970s, there had been a great deal of legislation aimed at helping the disadvantaged sections of our society but even then welfare lawyers were warning that:

> the ceaseless outpourings of legislation concerning the rights and liabilities of the poorer sections of the community can achieve little, unless there are enough trained advisers to bring home its meaning to those for whom it is primarily intended.[14]

The fear and ignorance of the law implied by that quotation are just two of a whole range of barriers that exist between some individuals and the information they need. In addition there is the negative role of the tabloid press which, for example, persecutes those living with AIDS and labels and stereotypes welfare claimants as 'scroungers'. As a result of this kind of press coverage people may not take up benefits through a fear of being stigmatised, or worse.

Provision of information is one thing but *effective* access to it is quite another. For many with the greatest information needs, access may be impaired by physical, psychological, educational, social, linguistic, technological, cultural, economic and other factors. The problems of the client or potential client attempting to use a service are often underestimated by information professionals. The client is often revealing personal and psychologically damaging details about her or his private circumstances. Others may be frightened by authority or perceive agencies to be too bureaucratic, 'posh' or whatever. In addition, potential clients may have had bad experiences on previous visits to other organizations and this may cause them to bring negative expectations through the door of the CAB, Neighbourhood Advice Centre, or public library.

Those wishing to use community information services will come from a wide range of socio-economic, cultural, educational and other backgrounds. This can affect the effectiveness of an interaction between an information worker and a client, and workers need to be aware of this. The recent BBC television programme *Crosstalk* demonstrated the problems that can be caused by the cultural mismatch of non-verbal and other signals. It is available from the BBC and is recommended as a training aid. The level and complexity of the language used in community information services both in face-to-face encounters and in publications can also create a barrier between the client and the information that she or he needs.

Furthermore, information, in common with many other resources in British society, is unequally distributed. Moreover a lack of information may in itself be a cause of further inequalities. Those who don't know, don't get. As John Ward has observed:

> We need only to look at the available statistics on low take-up of welfare benefits, the ineffectual use of the health services by certain social groups . . . to conclude that restricted opportunity to get and use relevant information is one of the major causes of deprivation.[15]

The Sheffield report quoted earlier makes a similar point; it states:

> Securing benefits is also difficult because of the resistance of bureaucracy

to claimants. . . It is often true that with the backup of an advice worker's technical knowledge a claimant has a much better chance of success than if it were unsupported.[16]

In fact, the government's own statistics show that at benefit appeals only 30 per cent of applicants without representation succeed, as opposed to 48 per cent of those who are represented; while the London Advice Services Alliance (LASA) reports that 'in 1990-91 93 per cent of cases where [its] Appeal Team members were involved ended happily for the claimants—who received a total of £132,611.90 in benefit awards'.[17]

It is true that over the years there have been a number of official efforts to help the individual obtain his or her rights. Indeed, as long ago as 1942, Beveridge advocated establishing advice centres in Social Security offices, while, more recently, reports on the work of local government such as Skeffington, Maud and Bains have stressed the importance of open government and public participation in local decision making. Such participation requires that citizens have effective access to information if it is to be anything more than a public relations exercise. The Local Government (Access to Information) Act which came into force in 1986 was a very small step in the right direction but much more remains to be done.

There can also be little doubt that the current economic situation has increased the need for information and advice. To take one all too obvious area, the rise in unemployment has increased the demand not just for information on employment prospects, training and welfare benefits; it has also increased the pressure on agencies dealing with such things as physical and psychological stress, family and marital problems, child abuse and so on. The excellent television series *Boys from the black stuff* graphically demonstrated the multi-faceted nature of the problems resulting from unemployment. Unfortunately, that fictional situation is all too often repeated in real life.

Aspects of work, or the lack of it, feature on many of the lists of information priorities to be found in the various reports of community information projects. The type of information requested via community information services provides a clear indication of the kinds of problems people are facing. The latest report from NACAB lists the following categories of enquiries; social security; consumer and debt; employment; housing; property and land; family and personal; administration of justice; taxes and duties; local information; health; enquiries about bureaux; travel; transport and holidays; education; immigration and nationality; communication; national and international; leisure. Recent years have seen 'social security queries topping the inquiry list at most advice centres'.[18] Most also report an increase in recession related problems such as debt and mortgage repossessions.

Of course, many of these issues cut across one another and for practical purposes it is often unreal to place them in compartments. This has sometimes posed problems for more traditionally organized agencies, but at the same time there are numerous examples of information and advice professionals co-operating and adopting a very positive response to community problems. There are, for instance, those libraries and other agencies that have dealt with the aftermath of disasters such as Hillsborough, Hungerford and the Kings Cross fire. Broughton,[19] Palmer[20] and others have demonstrated how public libraries and other services have responded to such events. It is now recognized that when disaster strikes, the 'restoration of essential services, especially power, information and communication' comes very high on the list of community needs.[21]

Amongst information professionals we have seen since the mid Sixties an increased awareness of the importance of relating library services to the needs of the local community; alongside this has been the growth of the consumer movement. In the 1970s the National Consumer Council undertook a review of advice services which led to a report entitled *The fourth right of citizenship*. This influential document stated:

> people will not be able to get their due as citizens of present day society unless they have continuous access to the information which will guide them through it, and where necessary the advice to help them translate that information into effective action; and unless they get their due they are unlikely to recognise the reciprocal obligation that all citizens have to society.[22]

As that statement suggests, provision of community information and advice is part of the local democratic process. The Lord Mayor of Sheffield recognised this nearly half a century ago when he said:

> If power is to be used by the people, it must be exercised with knowledge and judgement. This implies not only education and self-discipline, but knowledge of affairs; knowledge of the manifold activities carried out by the people's representatives in their own city.[23]

Many of the most important information requirements are about local issues, issues such as housing, employment, education and shopping. Also, much of the political unrest one observes at 'grass roots' is often the result of a lack of access to basic information. In many situations individuals and communities need information before something happens; for instance to help them influence proposed legislation. Unfortunately, as recent events demonstrated, local and national governments are not beyond withholding information in order to stifle debate and discussion. Freedom of information issues will be considered further in Chapter Two but one might at this point question the real value of citizens' charters in a country that prevents its citizens from obtaining adequate information on a whole range of issues connected with their everyday life. Indeed, as John Ward wrote recently, 'without the right to information and advice, the other rights are liable to be hollow shams'.[24] I have discussed this elsewhere,[25] so suffice it to say that librarians, CABx and other information workers and their clients are currently hindered by all kinds of restrictive legislation and procedures.

In different types of community some issues, and thus some types of information, will take on greater importance. Rural communities and those communities that contain a high percentage of people from ethnic minorities are obvious examples. *The right to know* (1978)[26] and Clough and Quarmby's study, *A public library service for ethnic minorities in Great Britain* (1978) are early examples of professional concern with regard to such matters.

The right to know reviewed rural advice and information services and identified the particular needs and issues facing rural communities. Provision was found to be variable, to say the least, with the poorest counties being those with fewest advice services. The report advocated greater co-operation amongst advice agencies and argued that a rural advice network be set up. A few years later the village contact scheme was developed and a CIP guide was produced entitled *Village contacts.* This attempted to provide a model of advice-giving which aimed to fill the vacuum left by the disappearance of the local schoolteacher, parson, chemist and other figures to whom rural communities had traditionally turned for advice and information.

Clough and Quarmby felt that 'people from... ethnic minorities... are often more sorely in need of information than any other section of the community' and identified the need for:

> a determined effort to collect information of interest and value to the ethnic minorities from a wide range of sources including related local government services, health services, community organizations and national organizations.[27]

In many areas a sophisticated information network already exists. A student of mine from a few years back reported on the Sheffield scene as 'one large and glorious incestuous underground network'. A network incidentally that had grown up without the help of librarians or information scientists.

What one might call the 'professionally correct' response to these different types of information agencies and their needs is still the subject of some debate. The Library Association report identified a continuum of information and advice work. This started with the provision of straightforward information and progressed through explanation, advice, practical aid, active referral, mediation and advocacy to campaigns. However, over a decade later there is still some discussion within the information professions about what community information work is and which parts of it different agencies should undertake. Some public librarians for example still worry about 'where the boundaries lie around what the Library Service can provide and wants to provide.'[28]

Much of the literature[29] advocates a pro-active stance but recent research for a student dissertation at Sheffield University found that librarians were still reluctant to give advice in practice and that:

> all those interviewed rejected advocacy out of hand with varying degrees of horror and amusement. "Definitely not!" was a fairly typical response.[30]

As Stanley observes, in their day to day work: 'libraries [sic] may... be falling short of the Library Association's own recommendations made by the working party on CI in 1980.[31]

Not only then is there some debate about what community information work actually *is,* but there still remains some doubt on the part of some practitioners over which parts of it they should embrace. However, Bundy warned twenty years ago about the consequences if:

> libraries continue to proffer weak, ineffectual, and basically insulting service, no matter what excuses.

She concluded that:

> The irradication of poverty and the future of people are far too important to be left dependent on any institution's willingness to transform itself.[32]

For those in need, access to information by itself is often not enough to solve a person's problems. Very often the information has to be linked to action and this may require the involvement of a variety of community groups, self help organizations and the like. The kinds of organizations described in the Channel Four series 'Whose town is it anyway?' as 'centres for change'. Centres that can empower people and give them the confidence to deal with bureaucracies—'the effects of the cuts and an increasingly grim and unrelenting officialdom that turns a cold shoulder to the poor.'[33]

Moreover, there are many who feel that those workers who are involved with the provision of information to solve problems should also seek to influence the social policies that can cause or ameliorate those problems. Polly Toynbee recently described a CAB gathering in the following terms:

> Motions at their annual conference. . . consisted almost entirely of political issues to be directed at Parliament.[34]

The question we need to ask is how far and in what ways should community information workers seek to influence the development of social policies and services? It is, of course, the second aim of the Citizens Advice Bureaux 'to exercise a responsible influence on the development of social policies and services both locally and nationally.' In recent times this activity has not always found favour with the government of the day. In 1984 the Conservative Minister Sir Gerald Vaughan criticised CABx for being too left wing while just three years ago a Department of Trade and Industry report gave:

> a veiled warning to NACAB which issued a critical report on the Government's social security changes and took the Government to court for delays in benefits payments.[35]

What though is an information worker to do when, as one of my CAB friends says, her 'clients end up in cardboard boxes in the bus station as the result of government policies'. Is it not the role of responsible information organizations to point out to government and others the inconsistencies of policies which at one and the same time advocate care in the community and Poll Tax capping? Certainly NACAB has a vigorous research department which deals with policy analysis and reviews issues affecting the development and delivery of CAB services. Its current priorities include community care and legislation.

In their day to day work community information agencies and their workers accumulate a vast amount of evidence with regard to the impact and effectiveness of social services and policies. Such information can and should be used as part of the organization's own 'management information' to ascertain, for example, the success or otherwise of referrals. Equally, it can and should be used to inform government and others of the difficulties or opportunities resulting from legislation. The Advice Services Alliance, for example, is currently keeping a watching brief on the controversial proposal to franchise legal advice.

As in many other areas of information work the new, or not so new, technology has a part to play in the provision of community information. Indeed there are those who predict that hypertext will be 'the norm for the handling and dissemination of public information'.[36] However, in general terms, community information has not attracted information technologists to the same extent as business and other forms of information provision which are perceived to be more profitable. One notable exception is Gareth Morgan, the founder of Ferrett Information Systems. His company specialises in the production of software dealing with a wide range of welfare benefits. Products include Helper-PC which deals with family credit, Poll Tax rebates and related issues, and Maximiser which calculates family credit, housing, income support and other benefits, Ferret also provides up-dating packages to take account of changes in government legislation and benefit entitlements.

There are also many examples of local databases which list local clubs, organizations and often council services. For instance, the London Borough of Sutton has developed 'Sutton Link'. This uses public access terminals in the

Borough's libraries and also has a dial-in facility which allows the service to be accessed from suitably equipped home computers. Devon County Library's Public Information In Rural Areas Technology Experiment (PIRATE) investigated not only locally created databases but the use of telecommunications networks linking libraries in different parts of the county. Further details of its activities are to be found in a two-part British Library report.[38]

Theodore Roszak in his splendid book, *The cult of information,* writes of the importance of putting 'members of the public in touch with groups and agencies that can help with daily matters of livelihood and survival'. He goes on to state:

> This is not the kind of information one finds in most commercial databases; and . . . the library can make it available to those who cannot afford to own a computer.[38]

So too, if they are financed adequately, can CABx, Housing Aid Centres, community law centres and other agencies. There are now a number of examples of technology being used to help information and advice workers and their clients. For example, The National Council for Voluntary Organizations uses DataEase on a network while the Resource Information Service has developed Select-A-Hostel. This is a computerized indexing tool designed to enable advice workers make more effective use of the temporary bed spaces available for London's growing population of homeless people.

Looking to the future, at least one colleague of mine believes that expert systems have a part to play in the provision of community information. In fact there are already a number of examples to be found in the field of medical diagnosis and legal information. These deal with topics such as retirement pensions, the British Nationality Act and loans and savings. Travelling far down that road however could present information workers with some interesting legal and ethical problems. Who is accountable, for instance, if a machine gives somebody inaccurate information and/or bad advice? In addition, as one of my students said, most perceptively: 'a machine can't see somebody cry'. Technically it probably can, but its response is likely to be less empathetic than that of a trained counsellor or librarian.

The good community information worker will establish a rapport and effective relationship with the client. This is done by giving her or him full attention. This is by *active* listening which means concentrating on the client while at the same time the adviser suspends his or her own concerns. It means 'tuning in' completely to the client's feelings and then reflecting back what they are saying and feeling. Active listening involves paying this kind of close attention, paraphrasing the client's concerns and then asking open questions that will move the encounter forward. It also means being aware of how easy it is to respond in a way that can be perceived as unaccepting by the client.

In common with any other organization a community information service needs to be managed. The objectives of such organizations should reflect the needs of the particular communities they serve. It is necessary therefore to profile the community and to be aware of local perceptions and priorities. However, while many matters should be decided locally, it is possible to identify some general issues regarding the management and organization of community information and advice services.

Not the least of these is resource allocation. There can be little doubt that the recent squeeze on local authority budgets, together with the abolition of the Greater London Council and the Metropolitan Counties, has had an adverse effect on many community information agencies. In London, for example, those organizations funded by the London Boroughs Grant Scheme (LBGS) found themselves in serious difficulties both as the results of cuts and from the failure of LBGS to set a budget for 1991-92 until well into the financial year. Many agencies are facing increasing demand at a time of decreasing resources. Some of the larger organizations have attempted to raise income through providing training or other services to others in the field. Others are looking to the private sector for funding. In public libraries the pressures to 'charge' and/or to generate income may mean that profitable or cost recovery activities such as business information may be resourced at the expense of socially useful CI services.

The financial path that is taken will depend to a large extent on the support or otherwise of local and national politicians. This is true not only of those services that are run by local authorities but also of those independent units that receive grants and which might come into conflict with the local authority departments or policies. Now, more than ever before, community information services need to be promoted so that politicians, users and potential users develop positive attitudes towards the concept. To this end, in 1990 a number of advice agencies joined together to host receptions at the House of Commons, and to organize fringe meetings at the major political conferences so as to draw politicians' attention to the work of community information agencies.

Staff attitudes are also important, especially where workers are being asked to develop new skills and services. Traditional librarians have sometimes had difficulty in adjusting to CI service provision while even in the specialist agencies, such as the Citizens Advice Bureaux, there has sometimes been a tension, which has not always been creative, between those holding different views on the aims and objectives of the service.

Such attitude problems can sometimes be overcome by training, as will be discussed in depth in a later chapter. Training that should ensure that staff know the aims and objectives of the service and have the professional, personal and technical skills required to run it. Education and training for community information and advice work is carried out by a number of organizations. Community information is included in some courses leading to professional qualifications in librarianship and community work whilst other courses are provided by specialist organizations such as the Child Poverty Action Group, the London Advice Centres Alliance and Shelter. Adult eduction providers such as the Workers Educational Association, local education authorities and the Open University also offer courses which are of value to information and advice workers. NACAB, in particular, has programmes and training resources, including trigger videos, which are of interest to many who work in the field.

Training is one area which lends itself to co-operation and indeed much can be gained if there is a degree of co-operation in the provision of community information services in a particular locality. There are a number of examples of successful schemes such as the Lambeth Umbrella Group, The Peterborough Information Group and the London Advice Services Alliance. There are local variations as to what such groups do but in general they can help avoid expensive duplication of services and can increase the effectiveness of individual agencies. Co-operative schemes can achieve this through such things as the joint use of premises, joint training programmes, joint publicity and promotion, integrated referral systems and the financing of research and publications of use to all members of the group. The development of Library and Information Plans in many areas of the country has given some impetus to this kind of co-operation.

The aim of such ventures should be to develop a co-ordinated and comprehensive policy for information and advice services in a particular area. This may be easier to state than achieve because there can be problems. In some places, for example, there have been disagreements over who is, or who is perceived to be, in charge. Equally, there is potential for conflict between groups with different aims and objectives or over the division of a limited financial cake. Moreover, where local authorities are involved there may be a suspicion on behalf of some of the smaller or more radical groups that they may lose their independence.

Co-operative or otherwise, a community information service must be evaluated in terms of its stated goals and objectives. There is an area for future research here. There is a need to examine not just what the services are actually doing and what they cost but also the impact of such services on the people and communities they purport to serve. We need to develop techniques to evaluate the success or failure of a service in the context of its stated or implied social and/or community objectives. Such information can be used to plan and improve the future development of a service.

In general terms the future, as ever, offers both threats and opportunities. As I have written elsewhere the new technology may help or hinder the citizen in gaining access to information.[39] Politicians have it in their power to pass legislation that will increase or decrease the citizen's right to information and/or increase the gap between the information rich and the information poor. The community itself will no doubt change. In Britain, for instance, we know that the population will include more elderly people. We cannot be as sure about its collective attitude but we can hope for the demise of what *The Observer* called, the 'estate agent tendency',[40] caught in the ideological time-warp of the 1980s. Whatever the future holds it is unrealistic to expect that problems will disappear. People will still need help, information and advice. Information professionals of all kinds will still be required to play a part in the continued development of community helping systems.

References:

1. LIBRARY ASSOCIATION, *Community Information: what libraries can do.* London: LA, 1980.

2. SHEFFIELD INFORMATION AND ADVICE SERVICES WORKING PARTY. *Report on information and advice provision in Sheffield.* Sheffield: SIAC/NCC, 1980.

3. STANLEY, D. *Local   and   public   information   provision   in*

Nottinghamshire: a comparison with other authorities and with best practice. University of Sheffield, Unpublished MA Dissertation, 1990.

4. OFFICE OF ARTS AND LIBRARIES. *Setting objectives for public library services.* London: HMSO, 1991. (Library Information Series No. 19).

5. REID, J. *Education and training for community information and advice work,* Sheffield: University of Sheffield, Department of Information Studies, 1982 (Occasional Publications Series No. 1).

6. CITIZENS ADVICE BUREAUX, *Service notes.* CAB, 1989.

7. BUNDY, M. L. Urban information and public libraries: a design for service, *Library Journal,* Jan. 15, 1972, 161-169.

8. JENKINS, E. Assistant Secretary IPCS in correspondence with author.

9. USHERWOOD, B. *The public library as public knowledge,* London: Library Association Publishing, 1989.

10. HARTLEY, R. J. *and* WILLIAMS, J. Legal information for living: the role of information technology, *In:* J. Meadows *ed. Information technology and the individual.* London and New York: Pinter, 1991.

11. KEMPSON, E. Information for self-reliance and self-determination: the role of community information services, *IFLA Journal,* 12(3) 1986, 182-191.

12. SHEFFIELD INFORMATION AND ADVICE SERVICES WORKING PARTY. *Report on information and advice provision in Sheffield.* Sheffield: SIAC/NCC, 1980.

13. NATIONAL ASSOCIATION OF CITIZENS ADVICE BUREAUX. *Annual Report, 1990-1991.* London: NACAB, 1991.

14. SMITH, C, *and* HOATH, D. C. *Law and the underprivileged.* London: Routledge and Kegan Paul, 1979, xiii.

15. WARD, J. Who needs to know? Identifying information needs in the community, *In: Nationwide Provision and Use of Information. Aslib, IIS, LA Joint Conference, 15-19 September 1980, Sheffield, Proceedings.* London: Library Association, 1981, 126-131.

16. SHEFFIELD INFORMATION AND ADVICE SERVICES WORKING PARTY. *Report on information and advice provision in Sheffield.* Sheffield: SIAC/NCC, 1980.

17. LONDON ADVICE SERVICES ALLIANCE. *Annual Report 1990-91.* London: LASA, 1991.

18. Ibid.

19. BROUGHTON, S. Crisis aftermath—a role for the public library? *Public Library Journal,* 4(4), 1989, 85-89.

20. PALMER, M. North Wales coast flood disaster, crisis information provision, *Public Library Journal* 6(2), 1991, 33-39.

21. RAPHAEL, B. *When disaster strikes: a handbook for the caring professions.* London: Unwin Hyman, 1990.

22. NATIONAL CONSUMER COUNCIL. *The fourth right of citizenship: a review of local advice services—a discussion paper.* London: NCC, 1977.

23. LAMB, J. Sheffield's Civic Information Service, *Municipal Review,* Oct, 1948, 154.

24. WARD, J. Foreword *In: London Advice Services Alliance. Annual Report 1990-91.* London: LASA. 1991.

25. USHERWOOD, B. *The public library as public knowledge,* London: Library Association Publishing, 1989.

26. NATIONAL COUNCIL OF SOCIAL SERVICE. *The right to know: a review of advice services in rural areas—a discussion paper,* London: NCSS, 1978.

27. CLOUGH, E. *and* QUARMBY, J. *A public library service for ethnic minorities in Great Britain.* London: Library Association, 1978.

28. JAMES, I. *The Clwyd Welfare Benefits Unit, Public Library Journal,* 4(6), 1989, 134-137.

29. BUNDY, M. L. Urban information and public libraries: a design for service. *Library Journal,* Jan 15, 1972, 161-169.

MATTHEW, H. *C.I.—a manual for beginners.* Newcastle-under-Lyme: Association of Assistant Librarians, 1988.

McGREGOR, J. C.I.: the library's role, *Tendril,* 2(1), 1980, 11-18.

30. STANLEY, D. *Local and public information provision in Nottinghamshire: a comparison with other authorities and with best practice.* University of Sheffield, Unpublished MA Dissertation, 1990.

31. Ibid.

32. BUNDY, M. L. Urban information and public libraries: a design for service, *Library Journal,* Jan 15, 1972, 161-169.

33. TOYNBEE, P. It is easy to see how their success was built on a spirit of refusal to take any nonsense from the bureaucrats, *The Guardian,* 17, 1, 1983, 10.

34. Ibid.

35. DEAN, M. Power switch proposed for citizens' bureaux, *The Guardian,* 7. 1. 1989.

36. NELSON, T. H. Managing immense storage, *BYTE,* 13(1), 1988, 225-38.

37. DOVER, M. *Public information in rural areas technology experiment, Phase 1,* London: The British Library, 1988.

38. ROSZAK, T. *The cult of information.* Cambridge: Lutworth Press, 1986.

39. USHERWOOD, B. Shadows on the screen. Information technology—some questions in need of discussion. *Audiovisual Librarian,* 10(1), 1984, 25-29.

40. McGHIE, J. *and* HARRISON, D. Estate agent tendency hands over the keys, *The Observer,* 15 Mar, 1992, 22.

CHAPTER TWO

FREEDOM OF ACCESS TO INFORMATION

Kevin Harris

Freedom of Access to Information

Introduction

People can be excluded from sources of information in a great variety of ways. They can be barred in one avenue but gain access through another. The same barrier to information can comprise a number of combined factors such as wealth or geographical location or education. People can inhabit a cultural climate which disinclines them to seek out and exploit information for their own ends. And they can exist within a structure of social administration which formally and vigorously resists attempts to establish a principle of 'freedom of information'.

The issue of 'freedom of access to information' comprises two levels. The first is theoretical: the principle of making all information, or nearly all information, available to everyone. The second is more practical: it is the recognition that certain constraints on access will remain whether or not this principle is accepted and embedded in legislation and policy. This chapter is not about the first, theoretical issue: that is to say, it is not about 'freedom of information' as conventionally, and widely, debated. The question it will address is, 'What factors promote or inhibit the access to information of people in communities?'

To answer this question we must first address three definitional issues that it raises. These have to do with:
(i) what we mean by 'people in communities';
(ii) what we mean by 'access'; and

(iii) why it matters that people have such access in the first place.

I shall then discuss briefly the question of physical access and intellectual access; before considering a number of issues to do with the context in which people become, or fail to become, informed. My principle argument is that providing full access to information means much more than just facilitating physical accessibility: it also means confronting such issues as 'awareness', the institutionalization of knowledge, and the capacity of people to produce their own information. This chapter is intended to demonstrate the complexity of such contextual questions, and indicate some of the interrelationships which have to be taken into account if we are to avoid damaging over-simplifications.

In this chapter the term 'information' is used to refer to information which is made available or transferred either formally or informally, tangibly or intangibly.

People and Communities
When people are categorized, or categorize themselves, in 'communities', how does this differ from the categorization of the same people in business or in schools or whatever? An individual may be, say, a small business owner, part of a family, a consumer of public services, and contribute in the community sector, for example, through the organization of school fundraising events. At any time the individual is always, to a greater or lesser degree of activity, part of the local community. He or she may also consider themselves part of other 'communities', e.g. as defined by race, age, sex, sexual orientation, disability, special interests and hobbies, and so on.

So we are dealing with a complex, nebulous notion in considering 'people in communities': and to those factors suggested above we should add the notion of 'neighbourhood life', which tends to refer to a more narrow locale than 'community'.

This is not the place for an extended debate on these concepts: but it is useful, for the purposes of 'informing communities', to consider the degree of formality of activity in different kinds of community. Thus in personal and household activity, information exchange occurs in an extremely informal context; within the neighbourhood, elements of formality begin to be more evident (e.g. courtesies, discretion) although without formal organization. In a local committee, for example, of a tenants' group, we find slightly more formality again. We can compare these degrees of formality with, say, a community of business people or diplomats, who may adopt very formal conventions of behaviour which influence strongly the accessibility and transfer of information.

In the notion of 'people in communities', I suggest, we find a context for information which is characterized by diversity and flexibility. In much of this context, activities take place at the most informal level—chance meetings at the corner shop, parents chatting at the school gates, work colleagues talking in the pub, and so on. But we also find a degree of formal organization: for example among those community agencies such as advice agencies, which are required by their funders to prepare business plans and by extension require detailed records and projections of their activities.

The principle of networking is often fundamental to information flow in all these kinds of context, and I shall discuss this below.

Access

'Access' is not a neutral concept. It does not refer simply to a condition which is passive—an 'approach' or 'admittance' to something. The term 'access to information' carries with it the implication that access can be broadened or restricted, permitted or denied. In other words, it implies action, either on the part of the person seeking access, or on the part of a person empowered to allow access. Because information is so often a basis of power, and disempowerment is so often characterized by lack of information, access to information is a political issue. The idea that access to information can be neutral, that information is some passive resource waiting for people to use, is politically naive and amounts to collusion in the processes which perpetuate disadvantage.

There is a further point here, to do with the purposes of access. Emphatically, this debate is not just about access to information for problem-solving and decision-making. Provision for this kind of practical need—such as that provided by advice agencies for example—is demonstrably inadequate; but there is a danger that in focusing upon it we overlook the importance of information as a resource for development. The availability of a wide range of diverse sources of information is fundamental for healthy communities, so that information surrounds people and can be 'happened upon' and can be used to stimulate ideas and initiatives. If we deny this role for information—as a kind of compost in which individuals and communities can flourish, rather than as a kind of pesticide which can be sprayed onto social blemishes—we are guilty of restricting human potential for social, economic, community and personal development. Thus 'access to information' means access to resources irrespective of expressed need.

Freedom of Access to Information

If we accept the implication that freedoms are innately desirable insofar as they do not infringe other freedoms, then the key issue to be addressed here is the degree to which access to information is a principle which justifies concerted promotion. There are two aspects to this which I want to discuss here: the first concerns the relationship between one freedom and another; the second concerns the community development perspective on the 'information society'.

Unfortunately and inevitably, freedoms tend to infringe upon each other. This point has been well-demonstrated by

Simon Lee in his book *The cost of free speech,* in which he points out that

> . . .free speech is not free, it is not the ultimate right, it is not an absolute right, it is not self-evident. Not only can it be trumped by other rights, such as privacy, it can even be outweighed by utilitarian arguments as to the general welfare of society, such as national security, under the terms of the European Convention.[1]

We must be clear, in considering freedom of access to information, that the principle cannot be outlined in a vacuum. Thus we may find that it can only be applied as far as, say, freedom to be protected from racist hate literature. Lee rightly suggests that the complexity of the interrelationships between such different freedoms has barely been acknowledged. More understanding and debate is called for, and librarians and information workers should be involved prominently, with other interested parties.

Information has been described as the currency of democracy. It follows that access to information is fundamental to democracy, since inaccessible information is not informing anyone. And since access is not neutral, but calls for action, if we are concerned to promote democracy then we must promote access to information actively.

What appears to characterize the 'information society' is not the prevalence of information technology, but the effect of that technology, in combination with other factors, in increasing the information-intensiveness of the everyday lives of citizens and in the workplace.[2] Certainly the work of most community and voluntary agencies is becoming more and more information-intensive.

> This reflects a general social trend, but can also be attributed to government policies which have placed greater reliance on market forces and principles in the area of social policy; and a more general trend towards decentralising public responsibility for economic development and human services to the local level. Arising from these national policy changes are strong financial pressures on the community and voluntary sector, and a growing emphasis on public-private sector partnerships, which have necessitated higher levels of efficiency, flexibility and competitiveness. In this context, the information requirements of the sector have risen and become more complex—in terms

of contract bids and reports, financial accounting, consumer research, public relations and advertising, and so on.[3]

From the community development perspective, two key points arise: firstly, freedom of access to information is not a 'given' but an issue to be contested; secondly, information-handling is a crucial literacy and a fundamental aspect of access. In this new context of information work, the act of 'informing communities' and of communities informing themselves becomes critical. Information is an essential ingredient in community development; and community development is an essential factor in working towards participative democracy. The capacity of local communities to cope with economic and social change depends heavily on access to information; and if communities don't function, other policy measures will fail.

Physical and Intellectual Access to Information
A classroom exercise to identify factors which might prohibit access to information could be quite enlightening. Many people from privileged backgrounds (being articulate, literate, self-confident, with access to telephones, contacts among professional advisers of various kinds, and experience of using formal bureaucracies and information services) have difficulty recognising the ways in which access can effectively be denied by factors associated with the institutionalization of information. Here are some examples, intended to demonstrate the range of such factors.

Geography, topography and architecture. The location of a reference library at the wrong end of town can restrict access; its location at the top of a building is likely to be a disincentive to use, whether or not there is a lift; people with physical disabilities are still denied access to many buildings where pertinent information is held; people in rural areas (particularly in less-developed countries) are typically disadvantaged in terms of physical access to collections of resources; and so on.

Cost. As the trend towards the commodification of information proceeds apace, it is clearer than ever before that access to information can be denied through the application of market principles.

Language, in two senses: inadequate knowledge of the dominant spoken language can marginalise people severely; they can also be excluded by being subjected to incomprehensible use of that language.

Technology. As more and more information services and sources become available only in machine-readable form, those without access to the technology can quickly find themselves in the 'information gap'. Technologies other than computers can also be exclusive. A poorly publicised example concerns access to the telephone network: as alternatives to the telephone are in decline (traditional neighbourhoods, local offices, the postal and public transport systems), access to the telephone network becomes vital and policy measures are needed to promote such access.[4]

Bureaucracy. The requirements of any kind of administration, for records to be kept, easily breeds a bureaucratic culture in which access can be denied or restricted. For example, 'junior' staff may not be allowed to release information from files, but authorised staff may often be unavailable.

The 'user interface'—by which I mean the interface between service and consumer: for example, the appropriateness of opening times, the intelligibility of computer screen displays, or (a noticeable modern phenomenon) the inability of some organizations to staff their switchboards adequately, so that the enquirer cannot get beyond a continually ringing telephone.

What such examples show is that access is hugely complex. It requires awareness, action, and opportunity if individuals and communities are to counter the gravitational force of the institutions which provide and channel most of our information. In the following section I explore further the context of access, and consider the questions of the use of information which arise.

The Context of Access Information

People living and working in communities tend to have very unstructured information environments. In community groups and local development agencies the formal provision of information tends to have low priority. Often this is because, in under-resourced circumstances, information cannot be shown to be of direct relevance to their objectives. When you're dealing with the reality of poverty, ill-health, or unemployment, against other severe constraints, it is hard to justify the kinds of investment, for uncertain return, which information demands. What we are concerned with here, after all, is the kind of environment 'where the absence of information is a constant minor irritant rather than a major concern.'[5] For people in households, the same tends to apply, except that the minor irritant is not constant but occasional and may be unpredictable. This means that there is a natural inertia in the home and neighbourhood environment for systematic approaches to information. It's also the case that, in circumstances of poverty and hardship, freedom of access to information can be perceived as an irrelevance: as J. K. Galbraith has argued, 'nothing so condemns to silence and submission as a total absence of money and audience.'[6]

The connection between information, and the uses which individuals and community groups might make of it, is often tenuous, as James Halloran has noted:

On any given subject a person may possess the necessary information, but many factors may intervene between the information and what may be regarded as the related action. These intervening factors might include physical, financial and geographical barriers, inappropriate attitudes (even when the appropriate attitude is present there may be others pushing in the other direction— attitudes do not exist in isolation), and lack of skill, competence or opportunity to translate the information into the appropriate social action.[7]

This is a key aspect of the provision of information: it reflects the fundamental truth of Mooers' law—that people will not use an information service when they perceive it to be less inconvenient to go without the information than it is to get hold of it. The context of access to information for communities is suffused with the logic of Mooers' law and its extension, that access may be meaningless without use. Making it possible by legislation to check personal records, if you know about the records, know about the legislation, and take the trouble, is just one small aspect of freedom of access; and one which tends to favour the articulate who have time, energy and resources to pursue their rights. The Local Government (Access to Information) Act and other policy measures designed to 'unblock' public and personal data, are only a part of what is required to clear the site for free and open access to information of all kinds. Other conditions, such as copyright law and the commodification of information, constitute strong and complex forces working in the other direction.

The context for the use of information in communities is unfavourable. People tend to lack time, resources and skills to identify, locate and exploit information which is not immediately available to them. It follows that any momentum for freedom of access to information will be difficult to sustain because the benefits to be reaped are so hard to demonstrate. Access to information may depend more than we acknowledge on an appreciation of the social location of information, and I shall consider this in the next section.

In what follows I explore briefly two concepts— deinstitutionalization, and information capability—which I believe have an important role to play in promoting freedom of access to information. Both of the principles described are essentially community development principles.

The Institutionalization of Knowledge

Over recent decades, commentators have begun raising awareness of the institutional nature of public library and public information services, and the negative effects implied. The modern traditions of community information and outreach grew out of this awareness. William Martin, in an outstanding book published in 1989,[8] reviewed and analyzed the issue of institutionalization; and discussed the principles of deinstitutionalization and the options for libraries. He identified three areas where institutionalization has set in: these are buildings, organizational structures (bureaucracy), and attitudes. Martin rightly stressed the last of these, since change in the others is hard to bring about without changes in attitude.

Libraries as institutions tend to become self-serving and inhibitive of social change; they tend to erect barriers to protect their own interests and to represent stability at the expense of accessibility and flexibility and responsiveness. A comparison with community work may be helpful: community workers operate within a profoundly anti-professional ethos. There are some disadvantages to this, but it is a key aspect of deinstitutionalization because they know that formalized organizational behaviour, norms and values become dominant and disempowering. Institutions tend to have a kind of centrifugal force which binds to the centre and invalidates that which is on the periphery, thus effectively denying access.

There should be no doubt that institutionalization is a major factor in restricting access to information. It seems to be related to professionalization—the curious preoccupation of librarians with status—and the rather silly notion that information work is the same as information science. Be that as it may, we should recognize that it is not just the institutionalization of formal services which is at issue, but the institutionalization of knowledge in general within society. Ivan Illich has noted how people can become dependent on having their knowledge produced for them:

This cognitive disorder rests on the illusion that the knowledge of the individual citizen is of less value than the 'knowledge' of science. The former is the opinion of individuals. It is merely subjective and is excluded from policies. The latter is 'objective'—defined by science and promulgated by expert spokesmen. This objective knowledge is viewed as a commodity which can be refined, constantly improved, accumulated and fed into a process, now called 'decision-making'. This new mythology of governance by the manipulation of knowledge-stock inevitably erodes reliance on government by people.[9]

There is a crucial issue here, concerning the social origin and social location of information. We need a model which 'assumes human beings to be capable of initiating actions rather than merely serving as reactive targets of persuasion.'[10] With the notion of access to information, in the context of 'informing communities', we risk further institutionalization of knowledge, if we fail to confront the imbalance between people's own knowledge and that which is produced for them. It follows that we need structures which support the presentation of communities' own knowledge, for example through public meetings, pamphlets and leaflets, resource centres with desktop publishing, public libraries providing access to bulletin boards where agencies can upload records of their experiences and views, the use of databases and multi-media to provide statements by marginalized groups, and so on. In such ways it is possible to make the experience of people in communities more visible, to make their voices more audible, and their knowledge more valid. There are less likely to be problems of access to locally-generated information and knowledge, of course; but demand for access to other kinds of information which is produced *for* citizens could well increase, because 'it is almost a truism that the more data you provide to people, the more they want.'[11]

A revaluation of what counts for knowledge may well be overdue, as the western tradition of scientism is in decline, and 'softer' values are promoted within such powerful social movements as feminism and environmentalism.

Nonetheless, the resistance to accepting the non-scientific expression of experience as 'knowledge' is profound: consider, for example, the difficulties we have as a society aligning the testimonies of abused children with those of medical and forensic 'experts'. And the new technology, which promises so much in terms of access, may hold dangers, as Edis Bevan notes:

> ...the knowledge of people at the periphery of power is often tacit, and much can be lost through attempts to verbalize the information or to formalize the procedures. Ordinary people can have a good understanding of their needs and their local situation without also having the ability to express these verbally. With the introduction of computerized systems the danger is that only the information that is easily categorized will be collected and that this information, being available in a highly prestigious form, will outweigh other and possibly more relevant information sources.[12]

Again, this is problematic from the point of view of providing access: it requires the information worker at local level to reduce the traditional dependency on exclusively formal sources, and to include *informal* sources of experience and knowledge as potentially valid from the community's perspective.

This is where networking can be seen to be important. Networking takes place when people establish and maintain contact to support one another in their activities and to exchange information. As the *IT and communities report* notes, the importance of networking among local development agencies is well-established,[13] and there are good reasons for this. But it has to be remembered that the traditional networks are often not efficient enough or extensive enough to satisfy the new kinds of information requirement. For example, in communities faced with the shutdown of a dominant employer, economic development strategies—business start-up, credit unions, anti-poverty strategies, job clubs, and so on—require a wide range of interrelated information from sources beyond the local; and they require such information to be woven in to the local context, via the networks.

Providing access to information at local level depends heavily upon networking, and therefore on the development of credibility and on the principle of sharing. Weak networks in a community *may* be an indication of severe under-supply of information: but providing a wealth of information will not necessarily strengthen the networks. Thus the vitality of local networks is fundamental to promoting access within communities.

Information Capability

In the 1970s it was fashionable to proclaim that 'information is power'. This was a useful slogan at the time, although clearly false: many people have plenty of information and hardly any power. Nor does it seem to be the case that 'knowledge is power'. Nonetheless, it is worthwhile reflecting on the nature of the relationship here. Power can be related to information but when someone has such power, they have a particular kind of information: it's information which is of interest to others but denied to them. Thus we might call it 'unshared' information. Furthermore, when someone has power which is information-related, it seems to me that they have three other factors in their favour: firstly, information awareness; secondly, the ability to exploit the information; and thirdly, the opportunities to exploit the information. In other words, they have what I have called 'information capability'.[14]

Information capability refers to the capacity of an individual, group or organization to acquire and use information for its own ends. If a community has such a capacity, we would expect to find an array of groups and agencies with an awareness of information sources relevant to their concerns, with established contacts with other organizations holding resources, and with individuals and procedures geared up to using the information that they acquire.

Many people have difficulty recognizing that they have an

information need. When we refer to 'information awareness', it would seem that what we mean amounts to overcoming this difficulty. As Joyce Epstein has noted,

> . . . it is a very sophisticated leap from merely not having information to being aware that there is something you do not know, that knowing it will help solve your problems, and that therefore you need information.[15]

Information awareness is the ability to recognize that problems may be solved and that development (personal, community, economic and social) may be achieved by accessing and using information. Everything we know about the importance of information handling in society suggests that the lack of this ability may be highly restrictive.

The second part of the equation is physical and intellectual access to information, but as James Halloran points out, library and information workers tend to over-stress this element at the expense of the others:

> As much attention should be given to the conversion and utilization of information as to its provision. Yet, currently, simple provision seems to be the sole concern—even the obsession—of so many in these professions.[16]

There is an obvious training and educational issue here for the library and information profession.

The third element in information capability is exploitation of information. This can take many forms: being able to match discrete pieces of information; gaining access to resources and information channels—word-processing, photocopiers, desktop publishing, bulletin boards, and so on; assessing who else might benefit from the information or best be able to use it; and having or making opportunities to exploit it.

Information capability is a vital attribute of organizations involved in social change. It should be noted that part of its potential lies in offering a *positive* understanding of 'information poverty'. Information poverty implies low levels of awareness, inadequate access, and undeveloped ability to exploit information. If we speak in terms of capability, rather than poverty, we avoid labelling and promote the notion that there is a capacity which can be built up. Information handling skills are closely related to information awareness and confidence, and hence to the general problem-solving and development potential of a group or community. Information workers have a fundamental role to play in promoting this capability and in promoting awareness, education, training, support, and access to information.

Conclusion

It can be argued that the reality of informing communities is of low awareness of the potential role of information, unmanageably high volumes of potentially relevant material, and poor understanding of how information might fit into the context of community action and social change. At the same time, the levels of unperceived and unexpressed need for information are almost certainly increasing at challenging rates.

Throughout this chapter I have been sketching a broader than usual understanding of access to information, and arguing for an appreciation of the context in which access is possible. We have to move beyond the issues of physical and intellectual access, to some more fundamental questions concerning the relationship between information and power. For example, we need to recognize that the free flow of information is felt by some to be a euphemism for the perpetuation of existing inequalities. This is a valid challenge, and it obliges us to consider the kinds of information to which we want to provide access, including the three main categories: public and 'unshared' information; personal data; and information produced by the community itself.

In spite of many demonstrable improvements in recent years, there remains an arrogant assumption among information providers in the UK public sector that 'we know what's best for you and if you need it we'll give it to you'; and the complementary users' perspective, that 'if it's important for us they'll tell us.' Too much disempowerment and disadvantage flows from this cultural compliance, and information workers are open to accusations that they collude, through a preoccupation with physical and intellectual access at the expense of information awareness and use. But the skills and experience are to hand, among information workers: the development of information capability among communities is our responsibility.

References

1. LEE, S. *The cost of free speech.* London: Faber, 1990, 25.

2. LYON, D. *The information society: issues and illusions.* Cambridge: Polity Press, 1988. MOORE, N. *and* STEELE, J. *Information-intensive Britain: an analysis of the policy issues.* London: Policy Studies Institute, 1991.

3. *Press enter: Information technology in the community and voluntary sector: the report of the IT and Communities Working Party.* London: Community Development Foundation, 1992, 1.

4. *Telecommunications policy for the 1990s: submission to the DTI review.* London: Community Development Foundation, 1991.

5. STREATFIELD, D. *and* WILSON, T. *The vital link: information in social services departments.* Sheffield: University of Sheffield, Joint Unit for Social Services Research, 1980, 1.

6. GALBRAITH, J. K. Finding freedom in a world of poverty, *Guardian,* 27 August 1991, 15.

7. HALLORAN, J. Information and communication: information is the answer, but what is the question?, *Journal of Information Science,* 7, December 1983, 162.

8. MARTIN, W. J. *Community librarianship: changing the face of public libraries.* London: Library Association, 1989.

9. ILLICH, I. *Tools for conviviality.* Glasgow: Fontana, 1975, 100-101.

10. DONOHEW, L. *and* SPRINGER, E. R. Information seeking versus information diffusion: an alternative paradigm, *Community Development Journal,* 15(3), 1980, 213.

11. HAKIM, C. Free access to public data, *The House Magazine,* 23 October 1989, 19.

12. BEVAN, E. B. The task for a new professionalism, *Information technology and the human services.* Chichester: Wiley, 1988, 335.

13. *Press enter: Information technology in the community and voluntary sector: the report of the IT and Communities Working Party.* London: Community Development Foundation, 1992, 4.

14. HARRIS, K. Information and social change in the 1990s. *International Journal of Information and Library Research,* 3(1), 1991, 75-85.

15. EPSTEIN, J. *Providing information about urban services.* Shankill, Co. Dublin: European Foundation for the Improvement of Living and Working Conditions, 1987, 11.

16. HALLORAN, J. Information and communication: information is the answer, but what is the question?, *Journal of Information Science,* 7, December 1983, 162.

CHAPTER THREE

COMMUNITY INFORMATION FOR PEOPLE WITH DISABILITIES

Carolyn Date

Community Information for People with Disabilities

Librarians who are attempting to provide community information which is relevant to people with disabilities will have additional factors to consider than with some other user groups. It will not be enough to establish how to identify useful information and how to obtain, store and retrieve it, as unless the material is in places and formats which can be used by people with disabilities it may well be virtually useless for the very people for whom it is gathered.

Access

Libraries which intend to provide community information for people with disabilities will therefore need to be accessible with adequately trained staff, i.e. the user must be able to get in and communicate with the staff. For many people access means providing a ramp for people in wheelchairs, but in reality this is only the beginning. Libraries need to be as user friendly to people with disabilities as possible, with attention given to layout, furniture and equipment, lighting, guiding and staff training. Obviously, libraries and library services vary in size and resources, but much can be done to improve the physical environment—in many cases without spending vast sums of money. For example, rearranging the furniture, using spot-lighting, or taking advantage of redecoration programmes, can make major improvements at little extra cost. Other more expensive changes may have to be part of a long term strategy if alteration to the fabric of buildings is required.

Once an individual with a disability has gained access to the building, the next obstacle they could face may be in communicating with the staff. Can they make their needs known if necessary? Training in disability awareness will be a key factor in staff effectiveness in this area of library work, and its importance cannot be overstated. Library staff need the skills which are necessary in order to communicate properly with all library users. Care in the community, social policy and legislation mean that library staff will increasingly be faced with people with disabilities using libraries as community facilities and resources. The performance of library staff can be improved with some basic training in disability awareness so that they may offer the same assistance to people with disabilities as they do to other library users. Also, investment in disability awareness training or equipment, such as Minicom[1] which assists communication with people who have a hearing impairment, can help to overcome some deficiencies in library buildings in the short term, as well as making the library and information skills of library staff more accessible to people with disabilities. Information on Disability Awareness Training can be found in *Hospital libraries and community care*[2] published by the Library Association, or from the Disabled Living Foundation.[3]

When librarians have begun to address the barriers of physical access and communication with staff, there are still other problems to be aware of and consider, such as unhelpful formats and any necessary equipment. Material for people with disabilities may not be accessible in certain formats. One of the more obvious examples is that printed material, even in large print, may not be useful to a person with a visual impairment, and as Braille is only mastered by 10 per cent of registered blind people it may not be a suitable alternative, even assuming it is available. More publishers and other organizations have become aware of this problem and it is sometimes possible to obtain audio versions of print material. Additionally, organizations such as Calibre[4] will record material on request for individuals, provided that the blank audio cassettes are supplied. Although it is not possible to obtain alternative formats for most material at present, library staff should be aware that such services exist, and know which organizations help with transcriptions. At the very least, staff should know where to go within the library service for advice on such specialist services.

Equipment to assist people with disabilities to use inaccessible formats can be expensive. One of the better known types is the Kurzweil Reading Machine[5] which currently costs between £7,000 and £10,000 depending on the size and model. Although the number of speech synthesizers in libraries grows constantly, in reality it is unlikely that most library users will have access to such equipment in the near future. Other equipment such as closed circuit TV is more common, but requires promotion and properly trained staff in a suitable environment in order to be successfully exploited. This is also pertinent for the provision of other low vision aids, and advice should be sought from the Partially Sighted Society.[6]

Networking for Information
Community information for people with disabilities may be available in printed, taped, braille or computer database form, depending on the topic. However, the greatest amount of information is still only available in print format and may be difficult to identify, obtain and organize in libraries. Identifying such information may be difficult because much of it may be informally produced, of an ephemeral nature and not distributed via networks that librarians are familiar with or use. Therefore providing this type of information

requires considerable involvement in the community, establishing communication links with professionals in the NHS, in Social Services and paid and unpaid workers in voluntary agencies which offer services to, or represent the interests of, people with disabilities. Networking in this way will offer opportunities for obtaining informal publications and information about groups and their activities.

Another essential strand in providing appropriate information is to ask people with disabilities directly which services they would like to see or would find useful in libraries. This can be done in a number of ways. Canvassing relevant organizations which could be identified by the library service itself, the local Citizens Advice Bureau, umbrella organizations for all community groups such as Councils for Voluntary Service, or organizations which involve or represent people with disabilities. Group members could be invited to libraries individually or collectively to give views on current access and provision. 'Wheel In's' and Focus Groups can provide valuable assistance on information needs and will also help to foster good communication between library managers, staff and users. These dialogues also provide the library service with an opportunity to highlight or promote current services which may be of particular interest to such individuals and groups. One extremely important point about consulting in this way is that the library service must respond to information that it receives through these activities or give reasons why they have not, otherwise credibility will be lost within the community.

It may be stating the obvious to note that the person responsible for policies on provision and the establishment of identification, organization and maintenance systems should be clearly identified within the library service structure. This individual, or team, may be a Reference or Information specialist, Community Services Librarian, Domiciliary or Special Services Librarian. Whoever is selected, there must be liaison between library colleagues with community links as well as general encouragement for all staff to look out for suitable material. Many ephemeral items will be free or cost very little, but where publications have to be paid for straightforward reimbursement systems should be established to encourage 'serendipity' purchases whenever suitable items are encountered. As material published by voluntary or community groups will rarely be published in large quantities they have to be obtained in adequate supplies for service points as soon as possible, with bureaucracy kept to a minimum. Regular visits to alternative bookshops will provide opportunities to identify and purchase material Alan Bunch once termed 'citizen action' as well as survival information to aid everyday living.[7]

Organizing the Information
Deciding how much to keep and how to organize the information you have obtained should be guided by what the intelligence gathering in the community has identified. As with all community information, it is vital that the collections are manageable, properly maintained, up to date, and relevant. Collections must be suitable for all service points; staff should understand the organization methods used, and collections should be simple to use with attention given to access as mentioned above. A key factor in organization will be the acknowledgement that much useful information will be in the heads and informal systems of community activists and networks. For this reason it may be preferable for the library service to collect specified areas of information, to act as a gateway to more detailed information and to develop an efficient signposting service to relevant national and local resources.

People with disabilities have suggested the following categories for community information collections, although emphases will vary with different geographical areas:—

General information services for people with disabilities.
Aids and equipment.
Benefits.
Carers' information.
Education.
Employment.
Health and Social Services.
Housing.
Leisure.
Mobility.

Appropriate material should be gathered in different formats if at all possible. Where audio versions are available they should be obtained and reproduction equipment with headphones made available. All information should be dated on receipt if it is not noted on or in the material.

The following sections include suggestions on suitable material which could be included, as well as useful publications which are currently available. They are not intended to be exhaustive.

General Information Services for People with Disabilities

This category should attempt to include major national and local information providers and how to contact them to obtain services and information. Providers should also include media sources. Many library services subscribe to the Disabled Living Foundation (DLF) and the Royal Association for Disability and Rehabilitation (RADAR),[8] thereby receiving their information services and other publications. These two excellent organizations aim to merge in 1992 and this will bring together two of the most useful information sources for people with disabilities. Both organizations actively promote social, economic and political interests in an attempt to improve the quality of life for people with disabilities. The DLF subscription, £100 at present, provides the basic file of information with bi-monthly updates. Most libraries would find this publication useful, but it is essential that the files are updated even though it can be time consuming, to maximise the resource. A RADAR subscription provides Factsheets on a wide range of topics including Access, Holidays, Mobility, etc., as well as two journals—the *Bulletin,* a monthly information service on relevant topics, and *Contact,* a quarterly periodical with in-depth articles on current issues. Useful guides for newly disabled people and their families are RADAR's *If only I'd known that a year ago...*[9] and Bernadette Fallon's *So you're paralysed.*[10] Age Concern Factsheets can be obtained for a modest subscription which includes an updating service. Help the Aged[11] also produce relevant information and in 1991 established SENIORLINE, a telephone helpline for elderly people, many of whom will have information needs relating to health and disability.

Local contacts for national organizations should be noted, especially local branches of organizations such as DIAL, the Disablement Information and Advice Line.[12] Local Access guides, directories or information leaflets about where to go for information or advice should be included and new editions actively sought. In some localities, as in Liverpool and East Sussex, community information is produced on tape by community groups, and the local Talking Newspaper Group may be useful in this context. The Talking Newspaper Association UK[13] produces a Guide to Tape Services and also operates a subscription service for audio versions of newspapers and periodicals, which can obtain relevant information. This information, and the nearest access point, should be included. Most library services subscribe to NACAB, the National Association of Citizens Advice Bureaux,[14] and receive their information service. Reference to the information provided by this service and where it can be located in the library would extend the scope of this section.

Some journals are produced in larger type. Examples of these are *Look Forward*[15] and the *Big Print* newspaper,[16] published quarterly and weekly respectively. The RNIB[17] can supply information on titles produced in Braille. Any journals stocked by the library service should be included in this information, especially if they are housed elsewhere in the building. These might include publications such as *Disability Now*,[18] *Contact*, *In Touch Bulletin*,[19] *Soundbarrier*,[20] *The Carer*.[21]

Television and radio programmes which give relevant information and coverage should be included here, e.g. Radio 4: 'Does he take sugar' and 'In touch', Central TV: 'Link', Channel 4: 'Same difference', BBC 2: 'See hear', BBC 2: 'In four'. Days and times should be given, in large type. General books on information and services available are necessary; these could include Darnborough and Kinrade: *Directory for disabled people*,[22] the *Voluntary Agencies Directory*,[23] *A-Z of disability*,[24] and the *In Touch handbook*.[25]

Databases which could be of interest are DLF Data, a computerized information service giving details of more than 2000 aids, RNID Prestel Frame 1625,[26] Wavelength Axis,[27] and Volnet.[28] Subscriptions at present vary from £150 to £1000, and so the availability at service points will depend on financial and staffing resources.

Aids and Equipment

When you know where to look you will find a wide range of information about aids and equipment. This may be bewildering and result in unnecessary expense for individuals looking for an item to assist them in a particular task or activity. The essential point to make in this section is that advice from qualified professionals, such as Occupational Therapists (OTs), can help to identify the appropriate aid for the task. Many horror stories exist about unnecessary expenditure on inappropriate aids made without the benefit of suitable guidance. An OT colleague in either the NHS or Social Services Department, or member of an appropriate voluntary organization will probably be willing to draft a statement to this effect. There should also be a reference to the Health and Social Services section which gives information on how to make a referral for OT services.

The DLF Information Service referred to earlier is an essential resource for this section. The subscription, presently £100, provides an updated information resource on individual aids, equipment and suppliers. It is provided in an easy to use format in ordinary print, but will not be accessible to people with a visual impairment. At DLF headquarters in London a permanent exhibition of aids and equipment is maintained, and visitors may try aids and seek advice if they so wish. DLF Data, established in 1991, is an exciting development giving computerized access to information on more than 2000 aids to daily living. RADAR also produces useful publications, again in printed form, which must form the core information for this section. Another organization which may have local contacts is REMAP[29] which assists in designing and producing one-off aids for individuals.

Disabled Living Centres (which may have a different name i.e. Centre for Independent Living), have been established in many areas, and provide exhibitions of aids and other related advisory services. They may be funded by health and social services authorities, jointly or separately, or by independent organizations. A list of DLC's which can be obtained from the DLF or RADAR, should be included in large print, giving contact information. Many commercial organizations which produce aids have promotional literature and product lists. The Boots Company, one example, produce a brochure giving their product range. These publications should be included in this section, along with other local specialist equipment suppliers, as a useful source. Many of the privatized public utilities i.e. British Telecom, British Gas, and local Electricity companies, produce literature on aids and adaptions available to customers with disabilities. Obtaining supplies for community information collections should not be difficult via local showrooms or managers with responsibilities for services for customers with disabilities.

Other suitable publications for this section are *How to get equipment for disability* compiled by Michael Mandelstam in 1990 for the DLF, and the Equipment For Disabled People Series[30] which has individual volumes on:-

Communication
Clothing and dressing
Home management
Outdoor transport
Wheelchairs
Gardening
Disabled mother
Incontinence and stoma care
Personal care
Hoists and lifts
Walking aids
Housing and furniture
Disabled child.

It may be more useful for users of the collection to find the different volumes placed in the appropriate section, e.g. 'Outdoor transport' with 'Mobility material'. Careful inspection of the material may suggest an obvious placement, or consulting with people with disabilities on the most useful approach in such cases will also be helpful.

Benefits

Benefits available to people with disabilities usually relate to mobility, attendance, invalidity, income support, independent living fund and community care grants. Grants and allowances are also available in relation to employment. Providing up to date and accurate information on benefits requires a secure organizational framework. Library staff do not generally receive training in this area, and many library authorities would not wish their staff to acquire such skills. As the range, number, qualifying criteria, restrictions etc., of benefits can change relatively frequently, the library service will need to establish a policy on the role that staff are expected to fulfil on this topic. Staff must know how to respond to enquiries for advice rather than information, and the individual authority's boundaries must be known and understood by all staff. For many authorities it may be preferable to establish a reliable system of updating stocks of leaflets and checking information held in libraries with other properly trained workers in the community.

Many areas have a Benefits Agency (BA) Information Officer, or similar, who can be approached for assistance in establishing thorough and reliable systems for setting up and maintaining files of benefits, grants and allowances for people with disabilities. Some information is available in different formats and there may even be a specialist contact or helpline for these benefits, as well as the BA Freephone number. Any guidance notes made available by the Benefits Agency should be included with the leaflets on individual benefits. Telephone lines such as the ones mentioned above may be frequently engaged, and therefore other useful advice organizations should be listed. These might include the Disability Alliance,[31] Disablement Income Group,[32] DIAL groups etc., with local contacts where possible. Another organization which trains its members in benefits advice is the Citizens Advice Bureau which has offices in most areas, and can be contacted by telephone for help. Lists of local post offices and Benefits Agency offices would also be relevant. Most of the public utilities mentioned earlier produce leaflets on how to cope with bills as well as how to arrange for adaptions to appliances.

One of the most useful publications in this field is the Disability Rights Handbook,[33] published annually by the Disability Alliance.

Carers Information

The National Health Service and Community Care Act 1990[34] emphasized the need for more support for carers of people with disabilities in the community. As a result, a number of initiatives and programmes to help carers or to provide more information to them have been established by Health Authorities and Social Services departments, jointly or separately.

Published information on day care and domiciliary facilities, statutory and voluntary, should be available from Social Services departments who will be obliged by the Act to work closely with all organizations providing such services in the community. Information on respite care, if not yet available, will have to be gathered from the two major caring agencies, the Health Authority and the Social Services Department. Both agencies are sure to have officers working to support carers, in order to respond to the demands of the Act. They will be useful sources of information, although initially some reticence may be experienced in geographical areas where funding is poor for services. However, carers have a right to this information which should be easily available to them. A number of Care Attendant Schemes exist, such as Crossroads[35] or the Leonard Cheshire Family Support Scheme;[36] these may have local branches and contacts. Health authorities have a number of little known services, such as night sitters and other medical services made available at home during the night hours and weekends. Amazingly, some doctors seem unaware of the range of services available to help carers, which is unfortunate as the doctor may be the primary source of information for carers regarding services and support.

One of the most prominent support groups for carers is the Carers National Association,[37] and details of the national and local contacts should be filed. Any other local or national helplines of organizations which provide a listening ear should also be included as carers often feel guilty, isolated and exhausted by their caring role. Nancy Kohner has written a book called *Caring at home*[38] which could be included in this section, along with other publications such as *The caring trap,*[39] and *24 hour care.*[40]

Education

In all areas the Local Education Authority (LEA) is responsible for the provision or arrangement of appropriate education for all children up to 19 years of age. The 1981 Education Act,[41] reinforced by provisions in the 1988 Education Reform Act,[42] encourages the mainstreaming of children with special needs in ordinary schools. Assessments of children with special needs can be requested by the LEA or by the child's parents, and if necessary a Statement of special education needs will be made outlining how appropriate provision will be made. Parents may appeal if they are dissatisfied with the Statement of intended provision. LEAs' prospectuses and policy statements will include relevant information on this issue and should be included in this section, with information on procedures.

Colleges of further education increasingly have special courses or bridging courses which are aimed at school leavers with special needs. Local careers offices can offer specialist advice and will usually have leaflets giving useful information. If not, careers contact information should be obtained and included.

Local Training and Enterprise Councils (TECs) will also offer courses and training for people with disabilities or special needs and will be willing to supply relevant information. Information on adult education which is relevant could be useful here, e.g. lipreading, British Sign Language, computer courses.

Other organizations who give advice or produce useful information are: the Voluntary Council for the Handicapped Child,[43] ACE—the centre on Aids to Communication in Education,[44] the Advisory Centre for Education,[45] SKILL the national bureau for students with disabilities[46] and the Disabled Students Committee.[47] RADAR produces a factsheet and *The educational implications of disability*,[48] which should be included.

Employment

The Disabled Persons Employment Act 1944[49] obliges enterprises with more than 20 employees to recruit people with disabilities who are registered as disabled, as 3 per cent of the workforce. One of the best sources of information and local services will be the Disablement Resettlement Officer (DRO) at the local job centre or employment office. A number of leaflets, often giving information on different conditions, e.g. hearing impairment, mental illness, people with learning difficulties, will be available, as well as equipment loans and adaption grants available to employers. Additionally, information on Assistance With Fares To Work schemes, Sheltered Placements, Sheltered Workshops and Homeworking should also be available. DROs will also have information on courses available for rehabilitation and work experience, as well as information on recruiting people with disabilities and help available to employers in order that they may retain an employee who has become disabled. Local careers offices may also have useful information available from a specialist member of staff.

Organizations which offer advice and assistance on this topic are the DLF, RADAR, Association of Disabled Professionals,[50] the Employment Service,[51] Opportunities for Disabled People,[52] Disabled Graduates Careers Information Service[53] and the Shaw Trust.[54]

RADAR produces 22 factsheets for employers and employees and an information pack called *Into work*.[55] The DLF publication *Computers and accessories for people with disabilities*[56] will also be useful in this section. Both organizations also have publications relating to homeworking.

Health and Social Services Information
One of the particular problems faced by newly disabled people or patients discharged from hospital is that no-one tells them anything, or perhaps not enough to point them in the right direction for information or support in the community. This issue will be addressed in Chapter Seven, and there is no need to elaborate further, other than to state that signposting information is particularly important in this area. Staff training and guidance is also important, in order that the right response is made to requests for advice or the interpretation of information. Health information for library services could be considered to fall into four categories:-
Specialist information services.
Support groups and helplines.
Services available.
Library service information sources.

  Specialist information services such as the Help for Health Trust,[57] Lister Health Information Service,[58] Healthpoint[59] and College of Health[60] should be listed with hours of operation, contact information and any other useful publications. The Help for Health Trust, for example, produces factsheets on specific conditions, from Acupuncture to Women's Health, which include useful information on local and national support groups and publications. Subscriptions for services such as Help for Health can provide for the use of information databases, but this would only be considered for properly staffed and resourced service points. Bob Gann has produced a Health Care Consumer Guide[61] which could usefully be included, although it is not specifically directed at people with disabilities and may need to be duplicated elsewhere in a library's stock. The College of Health, a health care consumer body, can give information on the nearest Healthline which makes available taped health topics for the public to access via telephone. Information on alternative medicine sources should not be forgotten.

Many library services compile a community information database which gives details of most local organizations. Signposting information should be included here to direct enquirers to where in the library service they may gain access to specific information on self-help, campaigning and support groups, directly via a terminal or in printed material. Such groups invariably hold or have access to greater or more relevant information for people with disabilities who may not be aware of the existence of such organizations.

Services available through the National Health Service or Social Services should include a 'who provides what' section. For example, how and to whom to apply for domiciliary chiropody, eye tests and dental treatment within the NHS. Every Family Health Services Authority (which replaces the Family Practitioner Committee) publishes lists of doctors, dentists, opticians etc. Information on how to apply for a home help, the RNIB Talking Book Service,[62] occupational therapists' assessment or interpreting services for people with hearing impairment from local social services departments, should also be included. Under the National Health Service and Community Care Act, social services departments are obliged to make more information available regarding their services and therefore will have published information and leaflets available, perhaps in different formats. Lists of social services contacts for special services, such as visual and hearing impairment, are also important.Many Social Services departments produce guides to services which will be useful for this purpose. Another publication which Social Services departments are obliged to produce is a Community Care Plan and these will be readily available and should be stocked in all public libraries for consultation purposes.

This section should also contain information on how to make complaints about the NHS or Social Services departments. Again Social Services departments are obliged to publicise complaints procedures, and a leaflet will be available from local offices. A useful publication called *Patients' rights*[63] can provide relevant information with regard to the NHS. The address and contacts for the local Community Health Council should also be kept with this information, as well as published information on how to gain access to personal medical records—Community Health Councils are themselves a useful information resource.

Information material is still predominantly in print form, and reference material which is considered useful in this context can be identified elsewhere in this publication. Specific titles which may be useful for this collection could be the *BMA complete family health,*[64] the *BMA guide to medicines and drugs,*[65] with either *Black's medical dictionary*[66] or *Butterworth's medical dictionary,*[67] if a new edition is available. It is important not to underestimate the library's lending stock for providing helpful information to people with disabilities. Many libraries, for example, stock material such as *Learning to live with MS,*[68] *The food intolerance diet book,*[69] and *Living with epilepsy.*[70]

Housing

Many people with disabilities live in their own homes with the assistance of aids, adaptions, care attendant schemes, friends, family and other carers. Existing homes can be adapted to meet the needs of people with disabilities and this may involve ramps, grab rails or major building work to produce a suitable living environment. Funding for adaptions would normally be provided by the local housing authority, as improvement grants which can cover as much as 75 per cent to 90 per cent of the cost, according to need. Social Services departments should make assessments and assist people with disabilities to obtain adaptions, and they may even provide smaller adaptions via their OT services. If rehousing is a possibility, local authorities do provide accommodation which has been designed for people with disabilities although it is often in short supply.

Some housing associations, such as Raglan[71] and Shaftesbury,[72] specialise in suitable housing for people with disabilities, although again demand is high and availability low. Organizations such as the Richmond Fellowship, which gives support to people with or recovering from mental illness, may have an establishment in the locality, and Social Services Mental Health Teams should know where they are. Local contacts and addresses should be included in the file wherever possible, including references to the local Citizens Advice Bureau and any local housing action groups. Age Concern publishes factsheets[73] on other issues including housing, as well as a booklet—*Housing options for older people,*[74] and booklets to aid choices to be made about residential care. RADAR and the DLF also produce publications and factsheets which are relevant for this section. There should also be reference to care attendance schemes and the 'carers' section. Social Services departments should be able to provide information on housing associations and adaptions.

Leisure

Leisure interests which people with disabilities may wish to pursue range from reading books to abseiling, in just the same way as with other members of the community, but one of the most frustrating aspects of living with a disability must be the difficulties experienced when trying to gain access to activities and facilities which other people take for granted. Thus going to the cinema, theatre, public library, sports centre, stately home or going on holiday can present the most formidable challenge or may even be impossible. Whether interests are pursued within special interest groups or special organizations catering for people with disabilities will very much depend on the attitudes of able bodied people or the fortitude and determination of people with disabilities. Awareness is improving slowly in leisure centres, entertainment establishments and holiday companies but many physical barriers to access still remain. However, this section could be substantial if reasonable efforts are made to obtain relevant material.

Information providers and local and national access guides will be useful and should form the core stock. RADAR produces a number of guides on different topics:—

Arts centres and creative opportunities for disabled people
Countryside and wildlife for disabled people
Directory of airline facilities for disabled people
Holidays in the British Isles
Holidays abroad
Spectators access guide for disabled people
Sports centres for disabled people.[75]

RADAR also publishes holidays factsheets, as well as information about the National Key Scheme,[76] which gives locations of toilets that are suitable for people with disabilities and are accessible by using a special key. Most local authorities and other organizations produce local access guides to facilities, as do national organizations such as the National Trust.[77] Supplies of a wide range of leaflets can be obtained from local authority publicity or tourism departments. National organizations often provide information, special accommodation or holidays for people with disabilities. MENCAP,[78] for example, provides information and holidays for people with learning difficulties and their families, and produces a substantial amount of literature on the subject. Access guides to London and other large cities are available for purchase and should be included here—or reference made to where they are held. Local organizations which exist to provide holidays or leisure opportunities for people with disabilities will range from special Scout or Ranger groups to horse riding and water skiing activity groups. Most of these organizations will produce information about their activities and these can be traced or tracked down with the help of other groups for people with disabilities.

One of the most comprehensive information providers other than RADAR and the DLF is the Holiday Care Service[79] which gives information on all aspects of holiday making from travelling arrangements, escorts, accommodation to nursing care while away. There are also enabling organizations such as SHAPE[80] and the more obvious organizations such as The National Listening Library[81] and PHAB, Physical Handicap and Able Bodied,[82] which encourages integration of people with disabilities.

Mobility
Being able to make short or long journeys individually or by using accessible transport is the key to independent living for many people with disabilities; this is underlined by the fact that public transport must be accessible by 1995. A number of useful information packs and leaflets which would be suitable for library use can be obtained from a number of sources. Any section on mobility should include a reference to the 'Benefits' Section or, preferably, have duplicate leaflets on relevant benefits. Useful information packs can be obtained from MAVIS (Mobility, Advice and Vehicle Information Service).[83] The pack includes Department of Transport publications as well as a range of other information and fact sheets:—
Door to door.
Ins and outs of car choice.
Exemptions from Vehicle Excise Duty.
How to get a driving licence.
How to return to driving.
Fitting of hand controls.
Pedal guards.
Cushions.
Check list for comparing models.

How to obtain an orange badge.
Mobility allowance.
Motability.
Various services, e.g. Tripscope.
Lists of assessment centres and car adaption specialists.
Disabled drivers' motoring clubs.
RADAR mobility factsheets 1-10.

MIS (Mobility Information Service)[84] also provides useful printed material.

Other information to include here will be local community transport schemes such as Dial-a-ride or Voluntary Transport schemes, with contact information, together with any local branches of the Disabled Drivers Association or the Disabled Drivers Motor Club. British Rail and most of the Airport Authorities produce guides for travellers who are disabled, and large print route maps can be obtained from London Underground. Also, motoring organizations publish appropriate guides, e.g. the *AA Guide for the disabled traveller.*[85]

All the information suggested above could form the core stock for the sections listed earlier in this chapter. In the interests of empowerment other sections might be added. For example, a legal section could include various reports, papers, consultation documents, and responses to the many legislative changes. The DLF, RADAR, MENCAP and MIND[86] would be fruitful starting places for identifying suitable material and information on the legal rights and aspirations of people with disabilities.

Library Service Roles
Changes in legal and social policies coupled with the more determined attitude of people with disabilities to share in the community's 'wealth' will result in stronger demands that their needs be met. Librarians must be part of the response to those needs, acting as information providers and gatekeepers to more detailed sources. For people with

disabilities in the community this can best be done by library staff truly being part of that community, sharing and participating fully in networks outside static service points. In some areas library staff are participating in information groups involving other statutory and voluntary agencies with the aim of promoting available resources to each other and informing the community. Although library resources are often limited, some library staff seem professionally 'disabled' by their reluctance to relinquish their more passive custodial role, or 'handicapped' by their inability to share their expertise and resources with all those people in the community to whom it actually belongs.

References

1. MINICOM. Teletec Ltd., Exchange House, 494, Midsummer Boulevard, Central Milton Keynes MK9 2EA. Information on systems and suppliers from the Disabled Living Foundation or the Royal National Institute for the Deaf.

2. GOING, M. edited by Jean M. Clarke. *Hospital libraries and community care.* London: Library Association Publishing, 1990.

3. DISABLED LIVING FOUNDATION, 380/384 Harrow Road, London W9 2HU.

4. CALIBRE, Aylesbury, Buckinghamshire HP22 5XQ.

5. KURZWEIL READING MACHINES. Sight and Sound Technology, Quantel House, Anglia Way, Moulton Park, Northampton NN3 1JA.

6. PARTIALLY SIGHTED SOCIETY, 206 Great Portland Street, London W1N 6AA or Dean Clarke House, Southern Hay East, Exeter EX1 1PE.

7. BUNCH, A. *Community Information Services: their origin, scope and development.* London: Bingley, 1982.

8. RADAR, The Royal Association for Disability and Rehabilitation, 25 Mortimer Street, London W1N 8AB.

9. RADAR. *If only I'd known that a year ago... a guide for newly disabled people and their families,* rev ed. London: RADAR, 1991.

10. FALLON, B. *So you're paralysed,* 2nd ed. London: Spinal Injuries Association, 1987.

11. HELP THE AGED, St James's Walk, London EC1R 0BE.

12. DIAL UK. Park Lodge, St Catherine's Hospital, Tick Hill Road, Balby Doncaster. DN4 8QN

13. TNAUK, Talking Newspaper Association of the United Kingdom, 90, High Street, Heathfield, East Sussex TN21 8JD.

14. NACAB, 115-23 Pentonville Road, London N1 9LZ.

15. LOOK FORWARD. The Chest, Heart & Stroke Association, CHSA House, 123/127 Whitecross Street, London EC1Y 8JJ.

16. OCULUS. The Partially Sighted Society (ref.6)

17. RNIB The Royal National Institute for the Blind, 224, Great Portland Street, London W1N 6AA.

18. *Disability Now.* Monthly newsletter available from the Circulation Superviser, The Spastics Society, 12, Park Crescent, London W1N 4EQ.

19. *In Touch Bulletin.* BBC, Broadcasting House, London W1A 1AA.

20. *Soundbarrier RNID.* Published monthly by the RNID, 105, Gower Street, London WC1E 6AH.

21. *The Carer.* Carers' National Association, 29, Chilworth Mews, London W2 3RG.

22. DARNBROUGH, A. and KINRADE, D. *Directory for disabled people,* 6th ed. London: Woodhead Faulkner, 1991.

23. *Voluntary Agencies Directory.* 12th ed., London: Bedford Square Press, 1991.

24. SAUNDERS, P. *A-Z of disability.* 1989. London: Croword, 1989.

25. *In Touch Handbook, 1991-92.* London: BBC Broadcasting Support Services, 1991.

26. RNID The Royal National Institute for the Deaf, 105, Gower Street, London WC1E 6AH.

27. WAVELENGTH AXIS, P.O. Box 426, Reading RG6 1QR.

28. VOLNET UK. The Volunteer Centre UK, 29. Lower Kings Road, Berkhamstead, Hertfordshire HP4 2AB.

29. REMAP GB, Technical Equipment for Disabled People, John Wright, Hazeldene, Ightham, Sevenoaks, Kent TN15 9AD.

30. EQUIPMENT FOR DISABLED PEOPLE, Mary Marlborough Lodge, Nuffield Orthopaedic Centre, Headington, Oxford, OX3 7LD.

31. DISABILITY ALLIANCE, First Floor East, Universal House, 88-94 Wentworth Street, London E1 7SA.

32. DISABLEMENT INCOME GROUP, Millmead Business Centre, Millmead Road, London N17 4QU.

33. *Disability rights handbook.* (Annual, with updates). London: Disability Alliance.

34. GREAT BRITAIN. STATUTES. *National Health Service and Community Care Act.* London: HMSO, 1990.

35. CROSSROADS CARE ATTENDANT SCHEMES LTD, 10 Regent Place, Rugby, Warwickshire. CV21 2PN.

36. LEONARD CHESHIRE FAMILY SUPPORT SCHEME. 26/29 Maunsel Street, London SW1P 2QN.

37. CARERS NATIONAL ASSOCIATION, 29, Chilworth Mews, London W2 3RG.

38. KOHNER, N. *Caring at home.* London: National Extension College, 1988.

39. PULLING, J. *The caring trap.* London: Fontana, 1987.

40. *24 Hour Care.* Bicester: Winslow Press, (Telford Road, Bicester, Oxon).

41. GREAT BRITAIN. STATUTES. *The Education Act.* London: HMSO, 1981.

42. GREAT BRITAIN. STATUTES. *The Education Reform Act.* London: HMSO, 1988.

43. VOLUNTARY COUNCIL FOR HANDICAPPED CHILDREN, 8 Wakely Street, London EC1V 7QE.

44. ACE CENTRE, Aids to communication in Education, Ormerod School, Waynfleet Road, Headington, Oxford OX3 8DD.

45. ADVISORY CENTRE ON EDUCATION, 18, Victoria Park Square, London E2 9BP.

46. SKILL, The National Bureau for Students with Disabilities, 336, Brixton Road, London SW9 7AA.

47. DISABLED STUDENTS COMMITTEE, National Union of Students, Nelson Mandela House, 461, Holloway Road, London N7 6LJ.

48. RADAR. *The Education Act 1981: the implications.* London: RADAR, 1987.

49. GREAT BRITAIN. STATUTES. *Disabled Persons Employment Act.* London: HMSO, 1944.

50. ASSOCIATION OF DISABLED PROFESSIONALS, 170, Benton Hill, Horbury, Wakefield, West Yorkshire, WF4 5HW.

51. EMPLOYMENT SERVICE FOR PEOPLE WITH DISABILITIES, Steel City House, Moorfoot, Sheffield.

52. OPPORTUNITIES FOR DISABLED PEOPLE, 1 Bank Buildings, Princess Street, London EC2R 8EU.

53. DISABLED GRADUATES CAREER SERVICE, Reading University, Bulmershe Court, Woodlands Avenue, Earley, Reading Berkshire RG6 1HY.

54. SHAW TRUST, Caithness House, Western Way, Melksham, Wiltshire SN12 8DZ.

55. RADAR. *Into work.* London: RADAR, 1990.

56. DISABLED LIVING FOUNDATION. *Computers and accessories for people with disabilities.* London: DLF, 1989.

57. HELP FOR HEALTH TRUST, Highcroft Cottage, Romsey Road, Winchester, Hants SO22 5DH.

58. LISTER HEALTH INFORMATION SERVICE, Lister Hospital, Coreys Mill Lane, Stevenage, Herts SG1 4AB.

59. HEALTHPOINT, Poole Central Library, Dolphin Centre, Poole, Dorset, BH15 1QE.

60. COLLEGE OF HEALTH, St. Margaret's House, 21, Old Ford Road, London E2 9PL.

61. GANN, R. *Health care consumer guide.* London: Faber, 1991.

62. RNIB TALKING BOOK SERVICE, 224, Great Portland Street, London, W1N 6AA

63. NATIONAL CONSUMER COUNCIL. *Patients' rights.* London: NCC, 1989.

64. *BMA complete family health.* London: Dorling Kindersley, 1990.

65. *BMA complete guide to medicine and drugs.* 2nd ed. London: Dorling Kindersley, 1991.

66. *Black's medical dictionary* 36th ed. London: Black, 1990.

67. *Butterworth's medical dictionary.* London: Butterworth, 1986.

68. PONEY, R., DOWIE, R. *and* PRETT, G. *Learning to live with Multiple Sclerosis.* London: Sheldon Press, 1989.

69. WORKMAN, E., JONES, V. A. *and* HUNTER, J. *The food intolerance diet book.* London: Dunitz Positive Health Guide, 1986.

70. CHADWICK, D. *and* USISKIN, S. *Living with epilepsy,* rev ed. London: Dunitz Positive Health Guide, 1991.

71. RAGLAN HOUSING ASSOCIATION, Wright House, 12/14 Castle Street, Poole, Dorset BH15 1BQ.

72. SHAFTESBURY SOCIETY HOUSING ASSOCIATION, 18/20 Kingston Road, South Wimbledon, London SW19 1JZ.

73. AGE CONCERN FACTSHEETS. Age Concern England, Astral House, 1268, London Road, London SW16 4ER.

74. BOOKBINDER, D. *Housing options for older people.* London: Age Concern, 1991.

75. RADAR. *Arts centres and creative opportunities for disabled people.* London: RADAR, 1987.
RADAR. *The countryside and wildlife for disabled people,* 3rd ed. London: RADAR, 1989.
AIRLINE TRANSPORT USERS COMMITTEE. *Care in the air.* London: RADAR, 1987.

RADAR. *Holidays in the British Isles: a guide for disabled people.* (Annual).
RADAR.
RADAR. *Holidays and travel abroad: a guide for disabled people.* (Annual).
RADAR.
RADAR. *Spectators access guide for disabled people.* London: RADAR, 1986.
RADAR. *Sports centres for disabled people.* London: RADAR, 1989.

76. RADAR. National Key Scheme (NKS) information sheet. RADAR.

77. NATIONAL TRUST GUIDE TO FACILITIES FOR DISABLED PEOPLE. The National Trust, 36, Queen Ann's Gate, London SW1H 9AS.

78. MENCAP. The Royal Society for Mentally Handicapped Children and Adults, 123, Golden Lane, London EC1Y 0RT.

79. HOLIDAY CARE SERVICE, 2, Old Bank Chambers, Station Road, Horley, Surrey RH6 9HW.

80. SHAPE, 1, Thorpe Close, London W10 5XL.

81. NATIONAL LISTENING LIBRARY, 12, Lant Street, London SE1 1BR.

82. PHAB, Physical Handicapped/Able Bodied, Tavistock House North, Tavistock Square, London WC1H 9HX.

83. MAVIS. Transport and Road Research Laboratory, Old Wokingham Road, Crowthorne, Berkshire RG11 6AU.

84. MIS, Mobility Information Service, Unit 2A, Atchham Estate, Upton Magna, Shrewsbury SY4 4UG.

85. AUTOMOBILE ASSOCIATION. *Guide for the disabled traveller.* (Annual). Automobile Association.

86. MIND, The National Association for Mental Health, 22 Harley Street, London, W1N 2ED.

CHAPTER FOUR

EQUAL OPPORTUNITIES

Beryl Morris

Equal Opportunities

Librarians have, to some extent, been aware of equal opportunities issues for a number of years. This is because there has been an awareness that libraries have a duty to serve their publics without regard to race, gender, or religion. This chapter looks at the broad nature of equal opportunities in a library and information context and at some of the practical actions that are being carried out to make equality of opportunity a reality. In particular, it looks at the implications for the selection of stock; the development of information and other services, the promotion of library services and for the recruitment and training of staff.

What are Equal Opportunities?

The term equal opportunities is difficult to define, but usually incorporates a commitment to providing a service without discrimination on the grounds of race or gender. The Industrial Society favoured a simple but easily remembered definition—'to help everyone achieve their potential'—which includes employment, but also access to services and facilities. Some organizations have taken this a step further and include an element of positive action in encouraging groups who have previously experienced discrimination to gain employment, take advantage of services, etc.

The reasons for a concern about and commitment to equal opportunities are many. First, there is a legislative framework which makes discrimination, either direct or indirect on the grounds of sex or race, illegal. The Sex Discrimination Acts of 1975 and 1986 and the Race Relations Act of 1976 forbid discrimination in terms of employment or access to services or information. Although not covered by the legislation, many organizations including a number of local authorities have widened the scope of their equal opportunities policies to include age, disability, sexual orientation, trade union activities or political beliefs.

Another very powerful reason for a concern about these issues in a library context is to ensure that our services are as responsive as possible to the changing customer base. In the last twenty years, the demographic mix has changed dramatically. For example, in the London Borough of Newham, the percentage of ethnic minority groups has risen to more than 30 per cent of the population. At the same time, the proportion of elderly residents has increased and the birth rate is the highest in the UK. This creates different demands on the service, which need to be addressed.

Equal Opportunities is also an important element in redressing the political and social imbalance that has existed for so many years and through this to empowering the public. Finally, many organizations, particulary local authorities, who may be the largest employers in an area, feel that they have a duty to set an example to others.

Although this chapter gives an overview of equal opportunities issues, other chapters in the book look in detail at issues related to women and disability. This chapter therefore tries to concentrate on the needs of black and other ethnic minority communities and the ways these needs are being met to illustrate the points made. It should also be stressed that there is a concentration on public library issues and actions, although other sectors are mentioned where appropriate.

A Brief Review of the Literature

According to Section 71 of the Race Relations Act, 1976, local authorities have a duty to ensure that their functions are carried out in order to:

—eliminate unlawful discrimination:

—promote equality of opportunity and good relations between persons of different racial groups.

In 1982, Ken Young surveyed 40 urban local authorities to ascertain the progress that had been made, and discovered that only a few London boroughs had any tangible results.[1] A number had pledged support to equality of opportunity through policy statements, but there was little evidence of practical actions.

These findings tended to be reflected in public library provision, with a few authorities attempting to develop services in the late 70s while others had not even recognised the need for change. The need for libraries to cater for black and other ethnic minority groups was advocated in 1976 in a report published by the Commission for Racial Equality (CRE). This suggested that if public libraries were to be efficient and comprehensive, as they are required to be by law,[2] new approaches were vital. These included identifying the needs of different ethnic groups as well as working with community and voluntary associations to promote and develop services. The report also gave advice on the selection of stock and the development of information services. There was also a brief discussion of the possibility of using the Home Office's Section 11 funding to assist with staffing. This is a special fund to support staff who provide for ethnic minority groups from the Commonwealth and will be discussed in some detail below.

The CRE's report was followed by a policy statement from the Library Association[3] which also advocated the development of services aimed at different cultural groups and a number of other texts which gave comprehensive ideas for services to specific groups. A particulary useful example is Ziggi Alexander's book on *Library service and Afro-Caribbean communities*.[4] Further guidelines were published by the Library Association (LA) in 1985,[5] and in 1988, the Association published a statement on the recruitment of black librarians.[6] This followed the Association's own equal opportunities statement and deplored the lack of black and ethnic minority staff in libraries, particularly at senior level. Since 1988, there has been a limited number of publications, many concerned with the changes in Section 11 funding which are discussed below. Jo Haythornthwaite gives a useful review of recent literature in the *Journal of Multicultural Librarianship*.[7]

Selection and Presentation of Stock

According to major writers in the field, there is still considerable evidence of racism in the UK despite the legislation mentioned above. In order to counteract this, it is important that the multi-cultural nature of our society is reflected in all aspects of the library service. Even if black and other ethnic minority groups do not form a significant part of the local community, it is essential that different cultures are represented in the stock and the way it is presented. As the CRE suggested in 1976, a library that does not reflect this approach can hardly call itself comprehensive.

The selection of stock for ethnic minority groups has been the subject of much debate between librarians, some of which has been quite acrimonious. Many librarians advocate impartiality at all times while others suggest that the library has a crucial role in promoting anti-racism by rejecting materials that present a negative image of different cultural groups. Certainly, if the library service is to play its part in promoting anti-racism, as is the case in Newham, it is vital that material which presents negative racial stereotypes is rejected. Equally important is the need to have a selection policy that emphasises stock which includes positive images. This is particularly so for books and other materials for children and young people but should also apply to the whole collection.

Collections of material in different ethnic languages are vital if the library is to appeal to different groups in the community. This is especially the case with books and other materials aimed at elderly readers. Leicestershire, for example, has established a collection of large print books in Asian languages with the help of the Public Libraries Development Incentive Scheme.

Many users, however, are likely to prefer books in English as this will be their first language. This makes the balance of the stock difficult to determine and means that having a selection policy is vital. Dual language texts are also important as are translations of books in languages that reflect the local community.

In the past there has been a tendency for collections aimed at ethnic minority groups to be isolated from the rest of the service. The use of the Home Office's Section 11 funding for staff to develop these services tended to reinforce this view. However, in April 1992 the criteria for Section 11 funding changed. Support became project based rather than staff based and is intended to aid the integration of services rather than emphasising the differences in cultures. The guidelines for the new arrangements suggest that the library service has a particularly important role to play in the acquisition of English language skills and assisting access to information about employment, education, consumer matters and health.

Section 11 apart, it is important that services and collections aimed at ethnic minority groups are available throughout the library service. This includes having collections of relevant material available on the mobile libraries and through the housebound service. Newspapers and magazines in different languages are an important aid to encouraging a wider community use. Similarly, audio visual material should not be forgotten. Story cassettes and videos in different languages help to attract those who are perhaps less confident with the printed word, and music reflecting the different cultures is important in ensuring that the library appeals to everyone in the community. In Newham, the audio visual librarian has developed an excellent collection of Bhangra music which is proving popular with young Asian residents.

Library services are responding to the changing needs by identifying new approaches to service. Birmingham Library service, for example, conducted a MORI poll of library users which found that take-up by ethnic minority groups was lower than it should be. The Birmingham Public Libraries Strategy Report for 1991/92 therefore states that:

> Meeting the needs of ethnic minority communities must be assimilated more fully into the main stream service delivery patterns... and (the service) recognise that ethnic minority groups now exhibit a much wider range of needs than hitherto.[8]

The report also pledges a major review of the way the service is provided, allied to determining the needs of this group of users.

Ways of identifying the gaps in service provision have traditionally included surveys of users and, perhaps more importantly, non-users. Community profiles have been an important element in determining the needs of the local community and the 1991 Census will be useful in providing up to date demographic information.

Other approaches which help to identify customer needs include customer panels such as those used in Sheffield City Libraries and the London Borough of Newham. These target particular groups of residents and ask a series of questions aimed at determining the use and take-up of specific services. At Newham they are also used to determine whether the approaches to publicity and promotion are effective. Newham has also experimented with the customer forum. This has a dual purpose. It is intended to promote and publicize an aspect of the service such as the libraries or museum, but is also used to encourage feedback from the public. The forums have, in fact, had a mixed success. They have tended to be supported by the same small group of residents and have now been replaced with a series of open days.

Information Services
According to writers such as Alexander *et al* there has been a tendency for Reference and Information services to ignore the needs of black and ethnic minority groups.[9] As early as 1982, they were advocating that libraries should include information on immigration, health and other issues that were relevant to ethnic minority groups. There was also criticism of passive librarians who tended to wait for information to be easily available rather than actively seeking it out. Similarly, there is criticism that many reference collections tend towards an ethnocentric bias. It is obviously important that reference materials such as encyclopaedias, dictionaries, statistical information, etc., reflect the needs of different minority groups. Otherwise, enquirers are likely to receive limited and unhelpful information in response to their needs.

In order for such services to be relevant, it is vital to know the community served. The use of community groups in helping to create and advise on such collections is an important element in making them as responsive as possible. Using local expertise, a number of library authorities have attempted to develop information services aimed at black and other ethnic minority groups, e.g. business information in Tower Hamlets and training information at Newham.

Likewise, First Stop Information Services which are being developed at Enfield and by a number of other local authorities are aimed at providing a point of contact for residents and others. First Stop usually includes information about Council and community services as well as facilities and help available in the area. The use of computer systems has made this information widely available and, in many cases, it is accessible through 'hole in the wall' terminals which allow 24-hour access. A particularly exciting development is the introduction of ethnic language help and advice screens which will be crucial in encouraging use by minority groups.

Publicity and Promotion
Without a well thought out approach to marketing and promotion, many of the initiatives described above will be wasted. Factors to take into account include having leaflets and other publicity materials translated into relevant languages. This is particularly important for services aimed at older people who may have little command of English such as the mobile or the housebound services. Equally important in publicizing services, is the use of positive cultural images which reflect the communities that the library is hoping to serve. Photographs showing cultural diversity can help to encourage use by different groups. It is also important that publicity material is as widely distributed as possible. This includes making use of community facilities such as community centres, shops and voluntary agencies in order to ensure maximum exposure.

Exhibitions targeted at different groups in the community can provide a focus for a number of approaches to service. For example, Newham's library service was recently responsible for devising and promoting an exhibition to commemorate Mahatma Gandhi's visit to East London in 1931. The exhibition has toured the Borough and been displayed in community centres and other cultural facilities as well as in the Borough's libraries. This has helped to attract different groups into the library, and has also provided a focus for linked events such as talks, visits and a sitar recital. In addition, the exhibition has been well publicized and helped to put Newham on the map.

Other approaches include involvement in festivals, e.g. Mela's and religious celebrations as well as exhibitions and displays which can form part of community events. Publicity in the ethnic press is also important. A recent example of a multi-lingual newspaper in East London, *The Deep,* has been very helpful by including information about library developments.

Finally, the library itself needs to be seen as an attractive and welcoming place for people to visit. Many library authorities are refurbishing libraries to make them more accessible. An interesting development is the use of moveable shelves which can make the library a flexible space which may then be used for meetings and performances. Newham libraries have been used for a variety of activities aimed at different cultural groups, including children's theatre and workshops, exhibitions of ethnic art and artifacts and information and advice sessions for small businesses. These help to attract people into the library and demonstrate that the library service has changed and now offers something for them.

Staffing Issues
Recruitment and selection
Finally, the recuitment, training and development of staff is an important aspect of making equal opportunities happen. The Library Association's Equal Opportunities Policy Statement was published in 1987. The statement endorses the LA's commitment to 'combat discrimination in its various forms and to actively promote equality of opportunity within the library and information community.'[10] The LA sees its role as publicizing initiatives, stimulating debate and acting as a pressure group for change.

As part of this commitment, the Association carried out a major monitoring exercise in 1988.[11] The survey illustrated that 73 per cent of the membership was female, that very few women had reached senior positions and that

99

the proportion of LA members from ethnic minority groups was far lower than the national average. The Library Association's monitoring exercise suggested that the staff in libraries are not representative of the population as a whole. This not only creates difficulties in providing a service which meets the needs of different communities, but also deters staff from ethnic minority groups from applying.

The LA's statement on the employment of staff from black and other ethnic minority groups has already been mentioned. Following the LA's statement, two conferences sponsored by the British Library were held to try to address the issues involved. The conferences identified some of the strategies such as positive action approaches that could be used as well as identifying topics for further research.

Verena Thompson in a recent article in *Library Management* describes some of these approaches in detail.[12] They include making libraries the sort of places that people want to work in, but also targeting the selection procedures to attract different groups in the community.

First, it is important to undertake a profile of the workforce which will identify not only the number of people employed, but also their grades and salary level. For example, a survey of staff in Sheffield City Libraries found that 84 per cent of employees were female, but that only 6 per cent were graded at SO1 or above. A similar concern applies to the lack of ethnic minority staff in senior library positions.

Having identified the employee make-up, some of the approaches used to attract staff from different groups are as follows. Using existing links with schools, colleges and Compacts to create a positive image of the library and librarianship which will encourage recruitment. Similarly, putting on open days or exhibiting at careers' conventions can help to promote library work to different groups. Hertfordshire Libraries, for example, commissioned a series of photographs showing the range and variety of library work which was displayed throughout the county and helped to attract potential applicants.

Positive action approaches can also be successful. These include targeted advertising in papers such as the *Voice* and *Everywoman,* and the use of positive images in advertisements and statements that stress that different groups such as women and ethnic minorities are under represented and are particularly welcome to apply. Rosemary Raddon, in a comprehensive article in *Public Library Journal,* [13] suggests a number of other positive action approaches to selection. These include making a knowledge of an area or particular ethnic group part of the person specification and including community groups in the selection procedures.

Although the equal opportunities legislation prohibits positive discrimination, i.e. the selection of a person because of their gender or ethnic origin, if a post offers a personal service to a specific ethnic or gender group, a Genuine Occupational Qualification (GOQ) can apply. These are permissible in law and include specifying gender or ethnic origin if this is deemed essential. For example, an Indian restaurant can advertise for an Indian waiter, but not an Indian cook. If a GOQ is claimed, the relevant section of the Act must be quoted in the advertisement.

It goes without saying that the selection procedures should be free of bias. Considerable work has gone into this area and many employers, especially local authorities, have a comprehensive recruitment manual as well as insisting that everyone involved in the selection of staff undertakes appropriate training. Most local authorities use a combination of job description and person specification to make the initial selection. Many also use practical tests as well as the interview in the belief that this is more objective. Newham also specifies that questions at interview must relate to the candidate's ability to do the job rather than their hobbies or personal interests. Rod Evans provides a useful overview of the importance of equal opportunities in recruitment and selection in *Library Management*[14] and in *Training & Education,* Madeline Cooke describes attempts by Leicestershire Library Service to increase the numbers of staff from Asian and Afro-Caribbean backgrounds.[15]

The strategies used included monitoring the ethnic origins of the workforce, establishing recruitment targets and monitoring the effect on the recruitment itself. Advertisements included the phrase 'knowledge of the cultures and languages of communities served, while not a requirement could be an advantage', and appeared in relevant publications. Leicestershire also set aside one trainee post a year and encouraged graduates from an ethnic minority background to apply. The trainee was also supported during their librarianship course at Loughborough. At the same time, six Section 11 posts were established which catered for the needs of specific communities. Madeline Cooke states that the cost of these initiatives was high, but that they did result in a greater proportion of staff from ethnic minority backgrounds.

Training
Training for equal opportunities is also crucial. This includes training for service delivery; the selection and recruitment training mentioned above and training for members of minority groups to help them to take advantage of the opportunities available.

Gillian Burrington's comprehensive article on equal opportunities and staff training[16] provides a useful introduction to this area. She advocates general equal opportunities training which raises the issues, followed by courses aimed at helping staff to be more sensitive to the needs of different groups. Sheffield City Libraries, for example, includes equal opportunities in its induction courses, so that staff are aware of its importance from the start. Race and disability awareness training are also important as many aspects of discrimination such as language and stereotyping are unintentional. As with all forms of equal opportunities training, race awareness training needs to be handled very sensitively. Margaret Kendall's chapter on training for multi-cultural library work in the *Handbook of library training practice,* Volume 2, gives a very useful list of approaches including ways to improve communication, stock selection incorporating international writing, recruitment issues and dealing with racism.[17] Training should not of course be restricted to staff at lower grades. Managers at all levels should receive awareness training to ensure that policies also recognize and take account of equal opportunities issues.

Training for staff from under-represented groups is also important. The legislation does allow for this form of positive action which helps to give staff from different backgrounds the skills and confidence to progress their careers. According to Raddon, induction training is essential in order to help staff feel they belong to the organization.[18] This needs to be followed by training aimed at helping black and ethnic minority staff to recognise their skills and experience and to gain confidence. Many employers offer targeted training aimed at minority groups and also encourage staff to attend qualification and management courses.

A major concern within library and information work is the difficulty experienced by those who wish to gain qualifications but have limited eductional attainment or no 'A' levels. Although there are a number of part time degree courses, they tend to be lengthy and not always very accessible in terms of geographical location. Two initiatives which may be helpful in redressing the balance include the growing acceptance of credit accumulation and, in particular, credit for experiential learning at a number of institutions of higher education. This allows a candidate to count prior learning against a course of study and can help reduce the time it takes. Secondly, the Polytechnic of North

London has developed an access course which is aimed at helping black and ethnic minority groups gain entry to their librarianship courses. Staff need to be made aware that most higher education institutions are concerned to enhance their recruitment through access initiatives, and are especially sympathetic to well motivated adult learners.

Other approaches that help to develop skills and confidence in staff include co-operative training and, in particular, a chance to exchange ideas and experience. Secondments, exchanges and other approaches are also important in helping staff to recognise their abilities. Staff appraisal, too, assists staff in identifying their training needs, but this needs to be sensitively handled to ensure that the appraisal is not threatening. Finally, as stated before, there has been a tendency for community librarians to be isolated from the mainstream of library work. It is crucial for their own development as well as for the service, that they are fully involved and integrated with general library activities.

Finally, on a negative note, there is a tendency on library and information courses to reduce the emphasis on community librarianship in order to concentrate on information technology. This means that most graduates are ill prepared for working in a community context and there may not be adequate in-house training to provide the necessary skills and confidence.

Conclusion

This chapter has tried to present an overview of issues to be addressed in providing equality of opportunity through the library service, looking specifically at services for ethnic minority groups. The chapter scratches the surface of what is a crucial and exciting aspect of library provision but has also tried to include examples of good practice where appropriate, as well as references which allow the points made to be followed up. There is considerable evidence of excellent work in providing services for ethnic minority groups, but there is also a long way to go.

References

1. YOUNG, K. An agenda for Sir George, *Policy Studies,* 3(1), 1982, 54-69.

2. GREAT BRITAIN. STATUTES. Public Libraries Act and Museums Act. 1964 London: HMSO, 1964.

3. COMMISSION FOR RACIAL EQUALITY, *Public library services for a multi-cultural society.* London: CRE, 1976.

4. ALEXANDER, Z. *Library service and Afro-Caribbean communities.* London: Association of Assistant Librarians, 1982.

5. LIBRARY ASSOCIATION. *Library and information services for our multi-cultural society.* London: Library Association, 1985.

6. LIBRARY ASSOCIATION. *Recruitment of black librarians.* London: Library Association, 1988.

7. HAYTHORNTHWAITE, J. Multicultural librarianship: a bibliographical overview, *Journal of Multi-cultural Librarianship,* 3(3), 1989, 99-104.

8. BIRMINGHAM PUBLIC LIBRARY SERVICE. *Public libraries strategy report 1991/92.* Birmingham: Birmingham City Council, 1992.

9. ALEXANDER, Z. *Library service and Afro-Caribbean communities.* London: Association of Assistant Librarians, 1982.

10. LIBRARY ASSOCIATION. *Equal opportunities policy statement.* London: Library Association, 1987.

11. LIBRARY ASSOCIATION. *Membership monitoring report.* London: Library Association, 1988.

12. THOMPSON, V. Recruitment of library workers from black communities, *Library Management,* 12(2), 1991, 15-19.

13. RADDON, R. Black and ethnic minority staff: issues of recruitment and training, *Public Library Journal,* 2(4), 1987, 62-67.

14. EVANS, R. Equal opportunities in recruitment and selection, *Library Management,* 12(2), 1991, 4-14.

15. COOKE, M. The recruitment and training of library and information workers of ethnic minority background, *Training & Education,* 4(3), 1987, 45-52.

16. BURRINGTON, G. Equal opportunities and staff training, *Library Association Record,* 92(5), 1990, 364-367.

17 KENDALL, M. Training for library work in multi-cultural Britain, In: *Handbook of library training practice,* Aldershot: Gower, 1990, 17-48.

18. RADDON, R. Black and ethnic minority staff: issues of recruitment and training, *Public Library Journal,* 2(4), 1987, 62-67.

CHAPTER FIVE

WOMEN'S RIGHTS

Pat Darter

Women's Rights

Introduction

I should perhaps start by saying that I feel a slight unease that it is still thought necessary to treat women as a separate and special category when in fact, as 52 per cent of the population, we could with some justice claim that it is we who should set the norm. However, if one is going to be classified as a minority and therefore deemed to be in need of special treatment I see no reason whatsoever for not taking full advantage of that situation and exploiting it.

The approach that I therefore intend to take is that I shall first of all discuss the various provisions for women that exist under the law. In other words, the somewhat narrow but essentially legalistic definition of 'women's rights'. However, beyond that I will expand into not only the information sources which cover these legal rights but also the needs of women for information in a much wider context.

The formulation and implementation of a book selection policy, either for a library authority as a whole or for one particular service point is also crucial to the way in which I have approached this chapter. One practical outcome of such a policy should be that anything published by what I would term a mainstream publisher—in other words the books listed each week in *The Bookseller* or appearing on the approval lists of any library supplier—which is either of interest to or aimed specifically at women is subject to the same critical appraisal as any other item, and not just dismissed out of hand simply because it is a 'woman's book'. This is of course an enormous assumption on my part, and one which perhaps deserves a whole chapter to itself, but it does have the advantage of allowing me to draw some parameters around the scope of this chapter. Neither shall I be covering major reference works or the more academic publishing, which would fall within the area of 'women's studies'.

Bearing in mind the reduced budgets on which everybody operates these days, I shall cover the ephemeral and fugitive material. The pamphlets published by small voluntary groups and the 'freebies' from the bigger organizations, the alternative sources of information and advice. The very things which in my terms are what community information is all about but which, because of their very nature, are all too often seen to be 'difficult' because they do not fit easily into the neat patterns that we like to impose on our libraries.

The Equal Opportunities Commission and the Sex Discrimination Acts

At the beginning, I made a distinction between legal rights and the wider need for information, and so to start with considering the law the most important pieces of legislation are:—

—The Equal Pay Act 1970 (as amended by SI 1983 no. 1974)

—The Sex Discrimination Acts (SDA) 1975 and 1986.

The SDA 1975 covers three broad areas of discrimination—employment, education and consumer affairs but, most important of all, it set up an enforcement agency, namely the Equal Opportunities Commission (EOC) which has the duty of ensuring that the provisions of the Act are fully implemented. Just to digress briefly, it should be pointed out that there is only one other piece of UK anti-discrimination legislation with an enforcement agency and this is the Race Relations Act 1976 which established the Commission for

Racial Equality. In Northern Ireland there is a parallel Sex Discrimination Act/Equal Pay Act overseen by the EOC for Northern Ireland and the Fair Employment Act which is enforced by the Fair Employment Agency. This question of an enforcement agency is an important one because it is due to the lack of any such body that our legislation regarding disability is largely ineffectual.

The SDA makes discrimination between men and women unlawful and in doing so defines two types of discrimination:—

a) direct discrimination which arises when a person is treated less favourably than another on the grounds of his or her sex.

b) indirect discrimination which involves the application of conditions which if applied to all would in practice favour one sex more than the other.

As far as employment is concerned, this means that an employer cannot discriminate in the arrangements made for recruiting and engaging new employees, nor in the treatment of existing employees as far as promotion, training, transfer or even redundancy and dismissal. Training may be given on a single-sex basis but it can only be in areas where it can be proved that very few members of that sex are currently employed.

In education it is the duty of all co-educational schools, colleges and universities to ensure that there is no discrimination in the provision of facilities or in their admissions. It is however permissible to offer single-sex teaching in subjects where research has shown that in this way better results have been attained e.g. teaching girls mathematics or science. Similarly, the Careers Service must not discriminate in the advice and assistance offered to school leavers.

The remaining area of consumer affairs covers a very wide range of service delivery, of which perhaps the two most important are housing and credit. Here again, it is unlawful to discriminate solely on the basis of the sex of the applicant.

It is also unlawful to place or publish an advertisement, which by its very nature is discriminatory in any of the above areas. Job advertisements for instance should be couched in non-sexist terms, or if the job title could be construed as applying to one sex only, e.g. steward, then it should be made clear that the position is open to both men and women.

As previously stated, the Equal Opportunities Commission was set up under the SDA 1975 and is charged with three statutory duties:—

a) to work towards the elimination of discrimination;

b) to promote equality of opportunity between men and women generally;

c) to keep under review the working of the SDA and the Equal Pay Act and when...necessary draw up and submit...proposals for amending them.

In order to carry out these duties the EOC has a wide range of powers, including:—

a) the power to undertake formal investigations into potentially discriminatory practices which cannot be tackled on the basis of individual complaints;

b) the ability to provide financial and legal support to individual cases;

c) the power to issue codes of practice. (Although not legally binding these can be used as evidence to an industrial tribunal).

From this it will be seen that as far as upholding women's rights is concerned the role of the EOC is crucial. As a result it could justifiably be called the most authoritative source for information on women's rights. To back up this claim it publishes a wide range of guidance booklets, all of which at the time of writing are free and are listed in a regularly updated Publications List. In addition, it produces a series of research reports which together with the *Annual Report* and *Women and Men in Britain* (a statistical digest) are published by HMSO. They can all be traced through the

Daily List and Annual Catalogues.

For advice on specific instances of (alleged) discrimination, the appropriate section of the EOC is an obvious starting point but for more general help there is the Information Centre which, with a stock of c.22,000 volumes and over 350 current periodical titles, is the largest collection of information on women's rights in this country.

Employment

In addition to the Equal Pay Act and Sex Discrimination Acts there are also important rights set out in a number of Employment Acts— notably The Employment Protection (Consolidation) Act 1978 and the Employment Act 1989. This is without doubt the most well documented area of women's rights. Much of the documentation comes from trade unions who in the past have had a somewhat ambivalent attitude to women, but especially in the current era of falling union membership all have now realised that some of their members are women and that they need to do something in order to attract and retain this important segment of the workforce. Both the Trades Union Council and individual unions produce a wide range of pamphlets and guides which in addition to basic employment rights also cover such topics as sexual harassment and non-sexist language—two areas of increasing concern to working women and certainly in the case of sexual harassment the subject of an increasing number of successful cases. The Institute of Personnel Management have also produced a range of codes of practice covering such topics as recruitment and redundancy, as well as one specifically on equal opportunities and more recently on age discrimination; single copies of these are free.

Management and Training

These are a further two areas where there is increasing interest, both on the part of women themselves and by their employers. The Pepperell Unit of the Industrial Society and

Catalyst (formerly Women and Training Network), together with its Scottish equivalent Training 2000, put on a wide range of courses in this area. Although membership of both organizations is expensive they do send out mailings listing their forthcoming courses. Another group working in this area is Women in Management and they have a number of regional sub-groups, all of which would be only too pleased for a library to publicize their activities.

Maternity Rights

Over the last few years this has become an increasingly complex area. At the risk of gross over-simplification, the basic legal position is that a woman needs to have worked for 26 weeks to qualify for maternity pay but in order to qualify for the right to return to work she needs to have worked full time for the same employer for two years. The relevant social security leaflets are needed here and again various unions also issue guides for their members. The Working Mothers' Association also publishes some very helpful information to guide women through the maze of regulations, as does the Maternity Alliance. A number of successful cases have now been pursued through the courts in which it was possible to prove that the woman had been dismissed simply because she was pregnant.

Childcare

It is by now widely agreed that one of the most important factors in preventing women from taking up work to the extent that many of them would wish, is the appalling lack of childcare facilities in this country. Social Services Departments should be able to provide listings of all local nurseries and may even provide lists of child minders too. As far as setting up such facilities is concerned and also for general information on maternity and childcare issues The Working Mothers' Association can again provide much useful help.

Education

For many people, education is an on-going lifelong process and once beyond school or college leaving age this can only be satisfied by adult education classes, Workers Educational Association courses, or if convenient the extra-mural department of the local university. A whole range of subjects is available here, from the academic women's studies and women's history courses, the work orientated assertiveness courses and management training, to the non-traditional; for instance the vitally practical area of car repairs for women. Brochures and prospectuses from all local colleges are easy to obtain and in the more commercial climate operating at present, colleges are only too anxious to boost their student numbers. Incidentally, women wishing to return to college on a full or even part-time basis often have difficulty in obtaining finance for this, so both staff and readers need to be aware of the existence of directories listing educational grants and trusts even if the physical location of such books is separate from the community information collection.

Social Security

This is quite literally a very mixed area, including as it does a number of actual exemptions to the Sex Discrimination Act and other areas in which the law is, to say the least, unclear or in a state of flux; for instance the present confusion and uncertainty surrounding the whole question of pensions and retirement age. However, a number of legal victories have been achieved, particularly as far as married women are concerned, in respect of certain social security benefits. So again, a good collection of Department of Social Security and National Insurance leaflets setting out the position as far as entitlement and claiming is concerned are a vital part of the collection. If further help is required on finding a way through this particular maze, the address of the local Welfare Rights Office is essential.

Health

A major provider of services as far as women are concerned is the National Health Service. So librarians need to look to the area or district health authority for a list of well-women clinics. The Health Education Council also produce a number of leaflets relating to women's health and in addition maintain a register of local initiatives in this area. Another useful organization is Women's Health (formerly the Women's Health and Reproductive Rights Information Centre) who produce inexpensive leaflets covering the whole range of women's health problems and needs. As far as legislation is concerned this is very limited and covers very specialised issues. The only two of any note are the Abortion Act 1967 (which does not apply to Northern Ireland) and the Human Fertilisation and Embryology Act 1990.

Marriage and Personal Relationships

Health problems can of course arise from the stress of a relationship that is not working so it is desirable to collect the names and address of local counselling services such as Relate. For more extreme problems libraries should have the address of the local Women's Aid group; for obvious reasons a librarian will not be given the address of the refuge but at least libraries should know how to put women in touch with it. There are a number of relevant pieces of legislation in this area. In England and Wales the Matrimonial and Family Proceedings Act 1984 reduced the time limits on the presentation of divorce proceedings and also set out new guidelines for financial settlements. Similar measures apply in Scotland under the Law Reform (Husband and Wife) (Scotland) Act 1984 and the Family Law (Scotland) Act 1985. The legal position of children born outside marriage was also clarified in the Family Law Reform Act 1987 and the Law Reform (Parent and Child) (Scotland) Act 1986.

Black and Ethnic Minority Women

If there is a high proportion of ethnic minority groups living in the area, then it is important to ensure that in the general outreach programmes to these groups the needs of women are not forgotten. There are certainly particular needs as far as the Asian Community is concerned. Older women, for instance, may have language problems and therefore be isolated in the home and for all ages it may be necessary to think in terms of women-only activities and services; so lists of women who can provide medical and other personal services are a useful part of any resource collection.

Voluntary Organizations

In terms of women's groups it is very easy to think just of new feminist groups but of course there are a number which have been around for a great many years—The Women's Institute, Townswomen's Guilds, Business and Professional Women and The Soroptimists are all well-known examples of this. At a national level the Women's National Commission publishes a comprehensive list of women's organizations. From both this and regular scanning of the local newspapers, it should be possible to find out the names of all the groups that meet in an area together with the secretary's name and the date and place of their regular meetings.

Local Government

Many local authorities have set up Equal Opportunities Units, and a number even have a specially designated Women's Officer. It should go without saying that this is a group of people with whom one should work very closely. To set up a good two-way flow of information can be very beneficial—to the library in being a short-cut route to accessing much local information and to the Unit as a means of publicizing their activities and also in providing information on a wider scale. The National Association of

Local Authority Women's Committees acts as a co-ordinating network for their activities.

These days library budgets are very tight indeed as far as newspapers and periodicals are concerned, but if it is at all possible libraries should subscribe to *Spare Rib* or *Everywoman*. Both are now widely available, and as well as providing an interesting read they are both full of useful information for anyone building up a resources bank. *Equal Opportunities Review* is probably outside the scope of all but the larger reference libraries but its authoritative reporting of case law as well as general articles across the whole spectrum of discrimination make it a standard work in the field. It may be that a local women's group do in fact produce their own newsletter: these are by no means as common as they once were, but if librarians are fortunate enough to have one in their community then that must be an essential purchase for the women's collection and will be invaluable in giving listings of local groups, events, etc.

Libraries and Resource Centres
It is in many ways a sad reflection on the services which public libraries are perceived as providing that a number of libraries have been set up for women quite independently of the library network in this country. Consequently, an additional problem with these libraries is that of funding so that although set up with the best possible will and with every good intention they are all now struggling to exist. A number of these libraries is listed at the end of this chapter, but if intending to visit it is essential to telephone to confirm opening hours. Even the best known of women's libraries—the Fawcett—is now beset with financial problems and is no longer able to offer the range of help and assistance that they would wish.

The Way Forward
Given the problems outlined in the previous paragraph there

is obviously a gap in the market which public libraries should fill. The need for information has not diminished, in fact if anything, given the complexity of many of the laws and regulations which I have listed, that need is greater than ever. As citizens we all need to be well informed, for women as the major influence on succeeding generations it is even more important.

Contacts

Catalyst, Hewmar House, 120 London Road, Gloucester GL1 3PL.

Equal Opportunities Commission, Overseas House, Quay Street, Manchester M3 3HN.

Equal Opportunities Commission for Northern Ireland, Chamber of Commerce House, Great Victoria Street, Belfast BT2 2BA.

The Fawcett Library, City of London Polytechnic, Calcutta House, Old Castle Street, London E1 7NT.

The Feminist Archive, Trinity Road Library, St. Philips, Bristol BS2 0NW.

Feminist Audio Books, 52 Featherstone Street, London EC1Y 8RT.

The Feminist Library, 5 Westminster Bridge Road, London SW1.

Glasgow Women's Library, 50 Hill Street, Garnethill, Glasgow.

Institute of Personnel Management, IPM House, Camp Road, Wimbledon, London SW19 4UW.

The Maternity Alliance, 15 Britannia Street, London WC1X 9JP.

National Association of Local Authority Women's Committees, The Pankhurst Centre, 60-62 Nelson Street, Manchester. M13 9WP.

The Pepperell Unit, Robert Hyde House, 48 Bryanston Square, London W1H 7LN.

Training 2000, St. George's Studios, 93-97 St George's Road, Glasgow G3 6JA.

Women Artists Slide Library, Fulham Palace, Bishop's Avenue, London SW6

Women in Management, 64 Marryat Road, London SW19 5BN.

Women's Aid, P.O. Box 391, Bristol BS99 7WS.

Women's Health, 52 Featherstone Street, London EC1Y 8RT.

Women's National Commission, Government Offices, Horse Guards Road, London SW1P 3AL.

Working Mother's Association, 77 Holloway Road, London N7 8JZ.

CHAPTER SIX

ENVIRONMENTAL ISSUES

David Tozer

Environmental Issues

Introduction

The latter part of the 1980s witnessed an explosion of 'green' awareness and activity. With it has grown a demand for environmental information.[1] Although general media attention has subsided following its peak around 1988-9, the environment remains one of the prime concerns of people.[2] The environment has become an issue which people and organizations in all walks of life need to address in order to sustain the planet, which is unable to speak up for itself.

From the planet's perspective, there is a need to place that concern on to everybody's agenda; people require access to accurate, easy to handle information, and the ability to exploit and act upon it. In this sense the environment cannot be regarded as a separate sphere of information for sectional interests. The pressures for information have come from many sources such as educationalists, decision-makers, voluntary groups, business and the general public.

A publishing boom has emerged, with new publishers like Green Print. New magazines such as *Green Magazine* and *Conservation Now!* have appeared. A plethora of directories and 'How to. . .' practical guides have appeared in books,[3] consumer guides,[4] pamphlets,[5] leaflets (e.g. in supermarkets) and pull-out features in specialist and popular magazines.

The growth of various new organizations has paralleled this trend. New national and local environmental groups (e.g. Women's Environmental Network, and Ark) have appeared, together with more local branches of national campaign groups. Groups and individuals have established, or are trying to establish, green resource centres; regional environmental networks have been set up; the number of databases has mushroomed as has the growth in the number of environmental consultants.[6] New techniques such as environmental auditing and product life-cycle analysis have been developed as have study materials to meet the needs of the National Curriculum. Yet, as one commentator has remarked, 'we have never had so much environmental awareness together with so much destruction'.[7]

Integral to the 'green' explosion, has been an outpouring of information from a variety of recent initiatives and services to meet the demands and perceived needs. This has emerged with no clear, systematic or structured direction, co-ordination or framework. Indeed, the field of environmental information provision is characterized to a large extent by numerous, autonomous, voluntary, often grassroots, initiatives aided by non-institutionalized networking. There has been an innovatory and pioneering spirit about these developments which involves not simply the dissemination of information, but also the spreading of ideas.

This chapter serves two purposes. First, it provides an overview of the provision of environmental information in terms of the needs, problems, targeted audiences and the variety of means by which information is provided, disseminated and made accessible. In doing so, it focuses on the broad public sphere, but reference is also made to particular sectors, e.g. business, education. Secondly, through examining the experience of one organization, the Centre for Environmental Information in Sutton, it highlights how some of these aspects can be addressed to make information an aid to environmental benefit.

Overview

Finding the information

It is widely recognized that environmental information provision should be led by the needs of the inquirer. However, this raises as many difficulties as it offers directions. It is not an obvious or easy task to define the needs of the public and its various sectors, or specific groups and their interests.

Friends of the Earth divide their standard responses to information requests between children, adults, teachers and international. Ostle (1991) identified twelve 'types' of people based on the studies and concerns expressed by interviewees in her research. She also suggests a different approach with four categories of people mirroring the bandwagon effect of environmental concern. They are 'innovators' (the first act), the 'environmental majority' (those that come to share the concerns), the 'tailenders' (those that come to express concern but take no action) and the 'unconcerned' (the disinterested, apathetic). This perspective has clear implications for strategies of information provision and targeting.

In view of the *ad hoc,* almost organic way in which many initiatives in the field have emerged, it is not surprising that Norman, Rennie and Fleming discovered that no previous research existed on the provision of environmental information to the public.[8]

For users, it is vitally important to know who to approach, or at least know how to identify the appropriate source or organization. Despite the plethora of organizations providing environmental information, this can be a difficult and frustrating process. Directories provide a valuable role in this respect, while the Environment Council has produced a leaflet, *Starting points for environmental information,* giving details of organizations that provide a general inquiry service. Signposting for users by such means is an invaluable service, but it begs the question of how easily the inquirers can find the signposts in the first place!

Once the inquirer has discovered the source, the 'hands-on' accessibility of that information by personal visit, telephone, post, computer terminal etc, then becomes critical. Furthermore, users need to be confident that the information is up to date, accurate and useful. They may also face conflicting information from different sources on a particular issue.

There is a clear need to ensure that the needs of inquirers and the 'user friendliness' of information are adequately matched by what the providers have or seek to provide. Ideally, a choice of formats at an appropriate level needs to be available for different people to enable them to take the next steps. For instance, a simple leaflet may be more suitable for somebody who is uneasy with computers. The need for evaluation by service providers is self-evident in this respect.

Providing the information
A key question for providing organizations is what should their specialisms be in terms of subject coverage, media, resources, target audiences etc. Such an enormously wide field as the environment creates problems of how to respond to a range of inquiries in terms of their relative degree of generality, specificity, and depth. Part of this consideration revolves around the definition of 'environment(al)' and its multi- or trans-disciplinary character. The third edition of the *Directory for the Environment* included organizations of the peace movement because of the links between nuclear weapons and energy issues, but did not include those of the mind/body/spirit movement or solely green commercial organizations even though many would regard such subjects as part of the green perspective. Others may also feel that definitions of the environment should include animal rights and complementary medicine.

At a practical level, providers have to decide what

information they want to gather, how they intend to store and catalogue it, how they are going to make it available (either directly or by referral), and to whom? Providers also need to know where those subjects they do not cover are handled and be able to refer inquirers to them. For those organizations unable to give an adequate response themselves, this seems vital. This means that recipient organizations also have to be geared up to deal with referrals.

Providers are often faced with a vast quantity of information, and projects have been known to sink amidst the sheer volume of it. The collection of masses of information can become disproportionate to its value and usage. The tasks of systematic cataloguing, data entering, updating, maintaining databases, filing etc. are time consuming and the effort and cost involved should not be underestimated.

Another practical choice needs to be made between following a 'low-tec' route that is perhaps paper-based with filing cabinets, book shelves, leaflet racks etc., and adopting a 'high-tec' approach employing information technology and developing databases. The latter approach faces the high costs frequently involved in new technology. The key aspect, however, is not technology but information management and accessibility, so that the former serves the latter and not vice versa.

The funding of services, and by whom, is another key aspect. Providers need a secure financial base with continuing funding. Many initiatives rely on grants from public funds, trusts, or sponsorship. This may, however, lead to accountability veering towards the funders rather than the public.

An alternative to attempting to provide information on commercial grounds is problematic. It may be appropriate to charge certain sectors, e.g. business, but this is not necessarily feasible for students and voluntary groups. Charging also raises ethical questions of whether or not people should be denied access to information which enables them to take better care of the environment if they are not in a position to pay for it.

In view of the ecological crisis, it is arguably not sufficient just to inform, rather, material should empower users to contribute to a more caring and responsible ethos towards the planet. An archival, storage approach may house important studies or research, but it may do very little to enable people to take action for the environment. An emphasis should be given to information in formats that are more motivating and action orientated. When answering requests, organizations need to ensure that they include 'what you can do' type information. Just knowing of the seemingly ever-worsening plight of the rain-forests, for instance, is of little practical value in itself.

Despite this emphasis, a major difficulty is knowing how effective in terms of motivation and practical action the provided information has been. Follow-up and assessment research needs to be undertaken to evaluate the effectiveness of that information with the inquirer.

Steps Forward

The practical problems that arose in the environmental information field, such as co-ordination between organizations, targeting, duplication, updating of common core data, prompted the formation of the Environmental Information Forum. This began in May 1989 before becoming formalized under the auspices of the Environment Council in October 1990. It is not a centralist body, but rather facilitates co-operative working, with specialist groups looking at particular areas of concern and provides invaluable networking opportunities by disseminating news of projects, activities, and the research undertaken by member organizations.

The Environmental Information Forum, (called the Environmental Information Committee until January1992), has four broad objectives in its terms of reference:

i. To raise awareness of members of the Forum and users as to existing and planned data sources and information services in order to promote their use, prevent unnecessary duplication and facilitate information exchange.

ii. To provide a framework for co-ordinated development in this field, for example by encouraging standardization of core data provision and the development of a centralized updating and revision facility.

iii. To identify the key users of environmental information services and the most appropriate means of reaching them and their requirements, with an emphasis on making information more accessible to users.

iv. To promote the regional networking of information providers and to encourage better links between national and regional levels.

Another organization, the ECO Environmental Education Trust has commissioned research projects to look at ways of addressing some of the concerns. A better understanding is now beginning to emerge from active practice and the limited amount of research to date.

In her survey of library users in Barkingside, Ostle found that people (especially the less concerned) felt motivated by simple, practical information.[9] The Department of the Environment's recent leaflet, *Wake up to what you can do for the Environment,* scored highly in this respect. An element of self-interest was also found to be important, rather than simply appealing to 'the greater good'. If people can see that by cutting electricity use they can cut their bills, they will then have a stake in the environment.

In the face of perceived powerlessness and inability to make a difference, Ostle concludes that the effectiveness of personal contributions needs to be stressed. She supports the idea that people's existing attitudes and concerns should be channelled rather than trying to redirect them to areas they are less concerned about. At the same time, people need reassuring that others do care and take action; are made aware of successful campaigns; given concise, non-technical information and educated on the limits of science as a tool for solving problems.

At a local level, there is an increasing demand for information that is not always readily available. Local environmental issues and information tend to be the main demand by the general public, e.g. recycling, planning. Global issues such as global warming, acid rain, tropical rain-forests etc. tend to be the focus for younger people and often tied to school projects.

In their comparative study of the London Boroughs of Wandsworth and Southwark, Norman, Rennie and Fleming found that local government departments and voluntary environmental groups were principally contacted for information. Public libraries received some enquiries, but had surprisingly limited resources for answering them. More general bodies such as the Citizens Advice Bureau were rarely contacted. Very little referring occurred with each organization trying to answer as best they could from within their own resources and there was little evidence of co-ordinating plans to meet demands. In addition, the general service available to the local populace varied markedly between the two neighbouring boroughs.

This study concluded that, in general, the 'older the person and the less educated, the less interest they have in environmental issues', whilst younger, educated people are most concerned, with children being very interested but probably the least well catered for.[10]

The Council for Environmental Education (CEE) is currently researching the needs and resources for children in relation to teachers and youth workers, whilst the National Educational Resources Information Service (NERIS) supports the teaching of the National Curriculum by providing, either on-line or by CD-ROM, a guide to resources and ideas that are available. Although American based, an annotated bibliography of children's books is also available. [11]

Several writers have found voices expressing a need for an organization providing a national, general environmental database which could meet a high proportion of inquiries. [12] For others, there is a perceived need for some kind of umbrella organization as it is difficult for them to know which of the many environmental organizations to contact. [13]

Two initiatives may help fulfil this need. First, the Science Reference and Information Service (SRIS) of the British Library launched an Environmental Information Service in 1989 as a centralized access point of information using several on-line databases to serve all sectors, e.g. students, business, government. The service is free for quick inquiries such as checking names and addresses, but a charge is made for longer, more complex inquiries. SRIS is also due to publish a practical guide to sources of environmental information. [14]

Secondly, the Conservation Trust is developing a National Environmental Enquiry and Data Service (NEEDS), whereby its vast database will be accessible without charge to the public at environmental centres and libraries around the country. Using CD-ROM equipment, the Conservation Trust hope that over 200 centres in Britain (eventually including field study centres and tourist centres) will be using NEEDS at the end of its third year, relieving many organizations of the burden of answering information requests. Free CDs of the updated database will be provided quarterly, and a facility will also be provided allowing other organizations to put details of their work into the scheme. From April 1992, four pilot schemes will be operating for six months from the London Ecology Centre, Southampton Environment Centre, Leicester Ecology Trust, and Exeter.

The scheme is to be funded by the Department of the Environment, other grants and sponsorship.

The response from Government

The Government White Paper, *This common inheritance,*[15] recognizes the need to make environmental information available. It acknowledges the contribution of the voluntary sector and regional networks, but the extent to which they are willing to provide active support for initiatives is unclear.

The Government's own commitment to improved information remains ambivalent. Details of schemes like eco-labelling and energy efficiency ratings are unknown and fears exist that they will be ambiguous and confusing as much as they will be informing. Friends of the Earth launched a 'right to know' campaign in March 1991 for the details and amounts of toxic chemicals released from production plants to be made publicly available and have also criticized the inadequacy of the Government's air quality information service. The Government has not adopted internationally recognized World Health Organization standards for air quality designation, and measures a limited range of pollutants.[16] Among large sections of the public there is also a general mistrust and suspicion of information that comes from Government sources or that is perceived to be closely associated with it.

Local authorities also hold or should have an enormous amount of local environmental data to which it can be difficult to gain access, despite the local Government (Access to Information) Act. Such information is often known only to specific officers and sits in their files, unknown to others. Furthermore, while the Act also gave the public the right to seek certain information there was no requirement for local authorities to hold such information. This has now changed in specific areas under the Environmental Protection Act. Public registers are now required for contaminated land, authorizations of air pollution control processes and radiation, for instance.

Now that many councils are keen to pursue green policies, this type of local data could be brought together in a systematic way to form a publicly accessible data bank of local environmental information to provide a valuable resource to its community.

Methods of Service Delivery

A number of methods of providing information have emerged in the period of the 'green explosion'. None of these are necessarily mutually exclusive, for they may be linked or complement one another.

Databases

For the purpose of this review, databases are understood to be those available through information technology (IT). In this rapidly changing technological field, there are no published directories concentrating on environmental databases, although this is due to be remedied.[17] The first conference on computers and environmental information, 'Surviving the Computer Jungle', covering the opportunities and hazards of IT, only took place as recently as November 1991.[18]

De Silva undertook a comprehensive review of on-line and CD-ROM databases available.[19] Both systems are able to offer vast amounts of data, with some holding over a million records, but this can amount to little without potential users knowing what is available, its ease of access, use and cost.

Some databases are directly related to specific environmental issues, while others are more general (e.g. business or scientific) but carry large amounts of environmental data. Although both systems can cater for specialist and multi-thematic databases, de Silva discovered a tendency for CD-ROM to be associated more with the latter rather than the former. CD-ROM was also found to be more favourable for retrospective information search, whereas on-line systems were most likely to expand for day-to-day practical use, e.g. for business, law and news.

Others have found that computer databases were not extensively used by organizations answering public inquiries.[20] Perhaps surprisingly, very few of the 100-120 environmental organizations that de Silva approached used on-line and CD-ROM services, preferring to rely on print and personal contacts instead. Even fewer had regular access, seemingly due to there being comparatively few 'one-stop' or full text databases, poor user support, and the prohibitive costs involved. Southwark Environmental Health Office spent £200 in one morning on British Telecom's commercial database, to find three addresses![21] The cost factor is critical for voluntary and charity organizations who form a major part of the environmental sector and have to operate within limited budgets. Community Computing Network exists to provide assistance and support for organizations in the voluntary and charity sectors in a manner that is sensitive to their needs, capabilities and limitations.

De Silva concludes that 'until improvements in access, help and costs occur both CD-ROM and on-line systems will remain under utilised as powerful enabling resources'.[22] There is perhaps a role for libraries and resource centres to become focal points by providing facilities for these systems to serve a range of groups and interests.

A further development has been the growth of computer networking and electronic mail. One system, GreenNet, provides contact between people via a central computer. This provides bulletin boards on which users can 'pin up' notices, requests, etc. These can generally be accessed according to subject or purpose. This service has proved very useful for conveying news, events and international networking and is utilized particularly by larger and national organizations. This facility does require compatible equipment for access, and it is possible to have public terminals.

To date, grassroots, community access has been underdeveloped, but demand is growing. Manchester Host is a new initiative set up to connect community and voluntary organizations allowing them to contact each other and gain access to the databases and files of other groups. In Hampshire another initiative is occurring through the Greenspace Networking Resources Project. This is seeking to establish self-sustaining networks to support community action in conserving the natural environment. Using Cata-List database software, the first stage is to link principal conservation organizations to develop the system before extending access to voluntary groups, schools, councils, libraries, community centres, country parks, etc. Users will be able to gain access from their own terminal and input or update their own data rather than relying on a central point. Control of the network will be spread among the participating users. Initiatives such as these are helping to create what has been called 'electronic citizenship' or 'electronic village halls'.

Libraries

Although people do look towards libraries as sources of environmental information, they are most likely to provide a generalist rather than specialist service. In fact, in Southwark and Wandsworth, it was found that libraries were not used to the extent expected. Additionally, the study revealed their restricted ability to respond to inquiries due to uncertainty over what was available, lack of resources, staff time, etc.[23]

Similarly, both Kirklees and Adur district councils have recognized the limited ability of libraries to respond in this field. Kirklees attempted to enhance the role of its library service by proposing an Environmental Living Centre, combining information, advice and green shop. In contrast, Adur considered a more autonomous environmental information centre managed by a consortium of local voluntary groups. Both schemes have been deferred due to costs.

Libraries have an undoubtedly important role to play, perhaps with information technology, which may differ from the traditional library service. They do not necessarily have to provide a fully comprehensive service and indeed the Kirklees Community Librarian now feels that the library service can only fill a partial role. Libraries could consider developing partnerships with other organizations and initiatives.[24]

Organizations and voluntary groups
Environmental organizations are continually regarded as sources of environmental information, and in many cases there is a close relationship with environmental education. Some distinctions are, however, possible.[25] For organizations such as Friends of the Earth and Greenpeace who provide information and some specific educational material, it is only secondary to their main task of campaigning. In this, however, the spread of information is at the heart of seeking beneficial environmental change.

Other organizations such as the Council for Environmental Education and the Conservation Trust are more explicitly providing resources for environmental education and project a more 'balanced approach'. Other organizations like World Wildlife Fund for Nature (WWF) attempt to combine both aspects.

Local voluntary groups (often branches of national or regional organizations) are frequently looked to for information, but are not always able to respond adequately. Beyond conveying information about their specific aims, activities and campaigns, they are often being asked to provide a service which is not part of their remit.

Networks
Local voluntary environmental groups undertake an

informal networking process, often as a natural extension of campaigning activities. They will often be affiliated to a national office and are in contact by phone, newsletters, local events, word of mouth with local members, other groups, etc. In the last few years this informal process has been given some channelling with the increasingly common establishment of local Environmental or Green Forums which bring together various groups, individuals and sometimes council officials. They do provide a means of formal information exchange, but exist primarily to develop and implement environmental policies and, meeting perhaps only quarterly, these forums are not a substitute for handling day-to-day general public inquiries.

The development of regional environmental networks has been supported by the National Council for Voluntary Organizations (NCVO), but otherwise their significance is seemingly overlooked by national environmental organizations. The NCVO facilitates a Regional Environmental Network Steering Group, maintains a directory and has held conferences. Regional networks can fulfil an important role as a 'signposting' service. They act as a means of sharing information, increasing co-operation, encouraging community action and liaising with regional and national policy development. However, only two existing networks have staff while the others rely on volunteers and very little funding; this constrains their ability to provide information as well as pursuing their other objectives.

Environment Centres
Unlike libraries 'Environment Centres' are more identifiably specialist organizations, of which three types can perhaps be distinguished. First, there are environmental interpretation centres, commonly associated with visitor centres at tourist sites, where the information helps the visitor's appreciation and understanding of that specific venue but expects little response other than perhaps helping to instil a sense of

environmental respect.

The second type falls into the category of technical aid centres. These are enabling agencies supporting community and environmental action, but tending to focus on the urban built environment. They include Architecture Workshops, Urban Studies Centres and Community Technical Aid Centres. These organizations pre-date the 'green explosion' and their work has been reviewed by the Newcastle Architectural Workshop. The Review evaluated the practical worth of these projects; it concluded that a new conception was needed that would enable communities to participate in making positive changes to the environment. The services such centres would provide include: information and resources, active learning education programmes, training support, advice and aid on architecture, planning, landscaping, technical reports, surveys, etc., to support communities in actively planning, designing and managing their environment. Information and enabling are seen as going hand in hand.[26]

The third type encompasses what may loosely be termed environmental resource/information/green centres where the focus is on encouraging the 'green' dimension of environmental improvement, i.e. the use and conservation of resources that relate more to the impact of human activity and lifestyles, together with the appropriate changes in these.

To support the development of local centres rooted in their communities, an embryonic initiative called 'Centres for Change' has emerged from a conference at Brighton in June 1991. A further conference, held in Birmingham in June 1992, invited a wide variety of resource centres, libraries, campaigning shops, etc. on the basis that the distinction between environmental, third world and peace issues has become increasingly blurred. It allowed participants with an interest in informing and motivating their communities to benefit from exchanging experiences. Details and conference reports are available through the Brighton Peace Centre.

The Experience of the Centre for Environmental Information

The Centre for Environmental Information (CEI), based in Sutton, is one of the most established of its kind in the country. It evolved from a Sutton and District Friends of the Earth Recycling Research Project, administered in 1985-6 through the Manpower Services Commission (MSC) Community Programme. The project produced a comprehensive Local Recycling Guide, a report of proposals for developing recycling initiatives for the local authority, and indentified the potential for an organization with a broader concept.

The CEI became established in July 1987 with the Trust obtaining charitable status in November 1988. The objectives of the Trust are:

i) to build up an efficient environmental information service;

ii) to provide advice and resources to the community on environmental matters;

iii) to promote a greater awareness of environmental problems and the potential for resolving them.

The Centre is primarily grant funded by the London Borough of Sutton and employs two and a half paid staff, receives additional assistance from volunteers and is overseen by a small group of Trustees. There are two main arms of the Centre's work. One is maintaining and making available a range of environmental information resources. The second is providing advice to enable the introduction and implementation of environmental policies and action. This enabling service is largely focused at the local level through 'greening' the council and the community and making that experience available to others around the country. Implicit, is the intention that information is not simply gathered for its own sake, but is seen and utilized as part of enabling action and change by offering advice and linking individuals and/or organizations together.

The local niche of the Centre

The CEI undoubtedly has the broadest range of environmental information available in the locality. A librarian from the Central Library commented during a visit that the CEI had a better range of books and other publications than it stocked and they were more accessibly stored. The Centre is not, however, the sole provider. Although no rigorous analysis has been undertaken of the local situation, the Borough's Ecology Centre, environmental health officers, the Planning Department's 'green team', libraries, and local environmental groups all provide a service to a varying extent with some referral and co-operation taking place between them.

The Ecology Field Centre is an outlet for leaflets, newsletters, etc. of other organizations, with a tendency towards wildlife and conservation subjects. It also hosts a small shop selling 'environmentally friendly' goods, but otherwise does not possess the same depth or range of information as the CEI. Campaigning and raising public awareness on issues as diverse as global warming, tropical rain-forests, can-recycling, diesel fumes, whales, etc. have been taken up by local groups such as Friends of the Earth, Greenpeace, Earth Action, Women's Environmental Network at various times. The local Green Party also makes a continuing contribution to informing the public and lobbying the council. There are also a number of local amenity groups that act as watchdogs and campaign on particular issues such as the loss of parkland.

The Centre for Environmental Information, on the other hand, has a unique niche. It does not conduct high profile campaigns, but has developed a quasi think-tank role to get issues and ideas taken up by the local authority and assists with their implementation. In this way it is making practical use of the information at its disposal by looking to build it into policy and project development.

This practical expression of the Centre's enabling role has helped for example in the drafting and implementation of the Borough's Environmental Statement, conceiving and developing the Sustainable Sutton initiative, sitting on council working parties and supporting other green initiatives. Liaison occurs with particular officers and councillors, although not to the extent desirable.

Through advice and consultancy, this enabling activity extends to other organizations and individuals in the community. Before they became fashionable in books and magazines, the Centre was effectively providing a 'How to. . .' service to a variety of clients. This often requires an individual response which has ranged from helping people to find environmental employment or setting up community recycling schemes to companies trying to 'green' their office. Due to Sutton's green reputation, inquiries are also received from other councils on how to adopt various initiatives. In this light, the Centre is regarded not just as a source of information, but as a repository of experience to be drawn upon. This has also led the Centre staff into providing talks, workshops and seminar presentations for various bodies and events.

The Centre's resources
In general, the Centre has adopted a 'low-tec' approach rather than the 'high-tec' path associated with computerized databases and on-line systems. Although the Centre has a computer and word processor facility, the staff have been wary of becoming dominated by the technology and seek to ensure they use it only for appropriate purposes. The Centre has also found very little need for extensive bibliographies, abstracting or indexing services. If it did need them, they could be obtained from the excellent Central Library in Sutton.

In assembling the information resources, the

'environment' has been interpreted broadly, so that the tendency has been to specialize at being generalists. At the same time, the Centre has avoided acquiring highly scientific and technical reports and studies for which it has no evident demand.

The Centre's resources fall into the following categories:

1. *Files:* The Centre has two large filing cabinets packed with information on a broad range of environmental/green subjects. These are the 'foundation' of the Centre's resources. It has not used a 'ready made' cataloguing system but has evolved its own system over time. This has worked reasonably well, although it is perhaps lacking in logic to the casual outside observer. There are on occasions difficulties in deciding the most appropriate place to file particular items but an effort is made to keep in mind where people would expect to find information, rather than simply where the staff think it should go. They are not always the same! The files are a mixture of leaflets, briefing sheets, press cuttings, pamphlets, conference papers, etc. and are periodically reviewed with the assistance of volunteers. They are widely utilized by staff, users of the Centre and to meet postal and telephone requests from the public, students, business, council officers, etc.

2. *Books and pamphlets:* The Centre has a small library of books, booklets and reports which is cross-referenced with the filing system. Items are usually acquired selectively for their usefulness rather than attempting to obtain everything that is published.

3. *Magazines and journals:* The Centre subscribes to a selection of relevant environmental and green periodicals which have a broad coverage rather than subscribing to every specialist publication that is available.

4. *Leaflets:* The Centre maintains a wide-ranging stock of leaflets bought in from a variety of organizations, e.g. FoE, UNA, Women's Environmental Network, Environment Council, the local authority, etc. It has also produced its own *ad hoc* leaflets adapting material from other sources, but has undertaken very little of its own professional publication due to its limited expertise in design and printing. Where necessary it has sought sympathetic outside assistance.

5. *Exhibition materials:* Although the Centre has not specialized in designing exhibitions, it does possess a cabinet of posters and display sheets on a range of issues used to mount 'home-made' rather than professionally produced exhibitions. To the limited extent that the Centre has mounted exhibitions, very little 'knock-on' effect has been noticeable—which questions the worth of the effort involved.

6. *Videos:* The Centre has a small selection of videos.

7. *Reports:* The Centre has produced a number of its own reports derived from its activities, e.g. greening local councils, and is also able to make selected council reports available.

Copies of the Centre's reference files, booklist, periodicals, Centre reports, key London Borough of Sutton reports and publicity are available on request from the CEI.

Sources of inquiries

Although the Centre exists to meet the needs of the local community, it does receive requests from all over the country. In some cases this is due to the reputation it has established, but also due to the listing of the organization in Yellow Pages and other national directories, leading people to perceive it as the most appropriate place to approach, or at least a starting point in their search.

The Centre has received inquiries from a diverse range of

clients. These have included local authority officers and councillors, teachers, students, business, voluntary groups and the general public, although the Centre has no systematic breakdown to give a precise picture.

A limited indication is provided below for inquiries received by post or phone between April and December 1991 for which information had to be assembled and posted:—

School children e.g. GCSE/A level projects	52
College students	30
Adults (including teachers)	21

By topic these inquiries break down as follows:—

General inquiry on 'the environment'/'what can I do?'	20
Pollution/acid rain	18
Animal welfare/nature conservation	15
Recycling/packaging	14
Green business/office	9
Nuclear/alternative energy/energy conservation	7
Tropical rain-forest	6
Sutton	4
Cars and transport	3
Planning	3
Environmental organizations	2
Global warming	2
Green economics	1

This is far from a complete picture of the Centre's inquiry service. For instance, it does not include simple inquiries that can be dealt with immediately by 'phone, visitors (mostly local) who take away information, or orders for the Centre's reports.

It is surprising, perhaps, that global warming inquiries are not common, and a perception exists that tropical rain-forest inquiries are not so frequent as a year or two earlier. Similarly, nuclear power has declined in popularity.

Targeting

The environmental crisis offers everybody the opportunity and scope to adopt practices in their lives and work whether they are homemakers, council leaders or business executives. Accordingly, the Centre has not restricted itself in who it assists, other than by the limitations imposed by the scope of its resources.

At the same time, significance has been attached to targeting decision makers whose influence and effect are potentially wide-ranging and pervasive. This also supports the enabling aspect to information provision.

Service charging

The Centre has operated a policy of not making payment a condition of the resources' availability, believing that it is ultimately preferable for the information to be accessible and a spur to action rather than to have costs inhibiting its use.

Nevertheless, the Centre has been attempting to increase the generation of its own income and therefore tries to seek some remuneration where feasible. For example, it feels justified in putting a price on its own reports or for particular materials it buys in. Additionally, with commercial organizations and public bodies who are clearly in a position to pay, the Centre also feels able to charge a fee for its service.

For information packs sent to students, a compliment slip is included indicating what it has cost to supply and suggesting they might like to make a donation to cover this. It does not always provide a response, but on other occasions the inquirer sends more than was suggested—a sign, perhaps, of the satisfaction they have gained.

All the Centre's resources are available on loan to users in the local area, based on a trust system with very few losses having been incurred. No charge is made for this facility, but again donations are sometimes received as an expression of appreciation.

Additionally, the Centre provides a photocopying service which is available to those who come to the Centre and this too sometimes attracts a donation above the actual charge.

Effectiveness of the service
The Centre is not a 'drop-in' resource located in a prominent location. Initial contact is therefore usually by telephone or letter from motivated inquirers, rather than casual visits. Whenever practicable, people are then encouraged to visit by appointment, so that they can be assisted more personally. This also allows them to browse through the resources, with direction, so that they can find the most pertinent information for themselves. Quite regularly, people leave having gained far more than they anticipated at the outset and are very grateful for discovering the 'treasure chest' of resources. Teachers, for instance, have gained a sense of relief at finding a single A4 sheet of information around which they can devise a lesson plan. This arrangement of course works best for people within easy reach of the Centre.

When it is impractical for inquirers to visit, information is sent by post and is often 'blind', in as much as requests are not always explicit. This is true particularly of young students who have school projects and blandly ask for 'something on the environment' or 'conservation'. There is an evident need for teachers to give clearer direction to their pupils to enable providers to supply an appropriate response.

Assessing effectiveness
To date, the Centre has not made great efforts to measure the impact and effectiveness of the responses it gives to inquiries. This is partly due to the belief that the monitoring effort involved for a small organization will distract from other work, partly because there are many intangibles involved in addressing the effect of the provided information and/or advice. For instance, although one of the purposes is to encourage more positive action towards the environment,

there may be a considerable time lag before any indentifiable action occurs.

At a more perceptive and subjective level, the Centre generally feels that it is valued and meeting the broad Trust objectives—judging by the letters of thanks, donations, return visits, recommendations it receives and reputation it has achieved. However, an absence of systematic feedback prevents a more precise assessment of its impact.

There have been occasions when people's expectations have been deflated when they realize the Centre is not quite the organization they perceived it to be, e.g. a place of scientific or technical expertise. However, the Centre does strive to give assistance to all even if only by referral to a more appropriate source, sometimes by using the Centre's network of contacts. It is very rare indeed for us to be totally unable to assist.

To really verify the extent of the effectiveness of the Centre's service, a follow-up survey to users would be necessary. A questionnaire need not necessarily be included with the initial response, but could be sent two or three months later when the impact may be easier to judge. Discretion would perhaps need to be exercised in distinguishing between passive information (e.g. associated with school projects) and information that helps inform environmental action.

The CEI as a Model

The Centre certainly believes that its successes and general approach make it a model that could usefully be applied elsewhere. It has definitely been an inspiration to others, judging by over 30 contacts it has received from those considering setting up and/or maintaining similar bodies. Perhaps just as every town and city has a Citizens Advice Bureau, there is a need for some kind of environmental information and resource centre that can be the focus for these resources and a catalyst for enabling practical environmental activity. These would reflect the local circumstances and probably operate under different names.

This approach justifies a primary role for independent, local 'environmental' centres with secure financial and management support. Such a call has come from various sources including local environmentalists, information providers, writers on the subject,[27] and the Newcastle Architecture Workshop. Some feel central government could back its commitments in *This common inheritance* in this way.[28] However, it is vital that any government support does not impose conditions that compromise its independence. In being autonomous rather than an arm of another organization, there is greater scope for activities than might otherwise be possible and this independence needs to be recognized as a much valued aspect of obtaining public confidence.

Norman, Rennie and Fleming provide one note of caution regarding specialist centres, suggesting that those disinterested or apathetic are unlikely to use it.[29] Such people obtain most of their information from television, newspapers and magazines which Ostle suggests is treated more as entertainment rather than motivation.[30] It is the already knowledgeable, motivated and active persons who are most likely to utilize any kind of environmental information centre.

Conclusions

Systematic research on the provision and dissemination of environmental information is still in its infancy and yet, given the urgency of the ecological crisis, the planet needs people to use information for action. From a limited sample, Ostle found a diversity of popular concerns, attitudes and motivations, leading her to conclude that no single approach to environmental information will meet all demands and succeed on its own.[31] Quite clearly a variety of approaches is needed to reach the largest number of people and motivate action. The Kirklees Community Librarian has come to a similar conclusion for establishing an environmental information system in his area, foreseeing a network of local information suppliers with no single mode of delivery and approach. For example, the information needs of voluntary environmental organizations have been recognized as quite different from those of the general public.[32] Existing poor local co-ordination presents new challenges to the statutory and voluntary agencies, challenges which offer opportunities for partnerships, planning, funding, promotion, implementation and evaluation. In some cases, for instance, there could be partnership initiatives linking councils, libraries, voluntary service councils, environmental groups and other organizations.

To date, the initiatives and networks providing environmental information have not been structured, formalized and directed from the top, and this should not in fact be the aim. A more organic development of vertical and horizontal networks connecting different organizations, initiatives and approaches may be more fertile—providing the independence of these initiatives can be assured—and for their development to be controlled by those involved according to arising information needs and demands. This requires a respect for these initiatives and projects from grant funding organizations and sponsors.

If change is ultimately the purpose, then ways of keeping information provision and environmental action together must be foremost and at the interface with the user. This is not to argue that there is no role for specialist environmental information organizations, perhaps serving particular needs, e.g. in the formal education sector, but action and information should not be treated as separate entities. Accessible information needs to be the means for empowering people and communities to change. Forms of action-orientated research and evaluation is a promising direction to pursue. Greenspace in Hampshire is embarking on an unique evaluation of its scheme's use and impact in the community. The old maxim 'information is power', failed, but the maximum 'information is empowerment' has unrealized potential.

Contacts

British Library Environmental Information Service, 25 Southampton Buildings, London, WC2A 1AW, 071-323 7955.

Centre for Environmental Information, 24 Rosebery Road, Cheam, Surrey, SM1 2BW, 081-642 3030.

Centres for Change, c/o Brighton Peace Centre, 28 Trafalgar Street, Brighton, Sussex, BN1 4ED. 0273 620125.

Community Computing Network, c/o Community Computing in Newcastle, 35 Pink Lane, Newcastle upon Tyne, NE1 5DW, 091-261 0317.

Conservation Trust, George Palmer Site, Northumberland Avenue, Reading, RG2 7PW, 0734 868442.

Council for Environmental Education (CEE), Faculty of Education and Community Studies, University of Reading, London Road, Reading, RG1 5AQ, 0734 756061.

ECO Environmental Education Trust, Avon Environmental Centre, Junction Road, Bristol, BS4 3JP, 0272 724936.

Environment Council, 80 York Way, London, N1 9AG, 071-278 4736.

Friends of the Earth, 26-28 Underwood Street, London N1 7JQ, 071-490 1555.

Greennet, 23 Bevenden Street, London, N1 6BH, 071-608 3040.

Greenspace Networking Resources Project, BTCV, North Hill Close, Andover Road, Winchester, SO22 6AQ, 0962 846172.

Manchester Host, 30 Naples Street, Manchester, M4 4DB, 061-839 4212.

National Council for Voluntary Organizations (NCVO), Environment Unit, Regent's Wharf, 8 All Saints Street,

London, N1 9RL, 071-713 6161.

National Educational Resource Information Service (NERIS), Maryland College, Leighton Street, Woburn, Milton Keynes, MK17 9JD, 0525 290364.

Newcastle Architecture Workshop, 6 Higham Place, Newcastle upon Tyne, NE1 8AF, 091-232 8183.

World Wide Fund for Nature (WWF), Panda House, Weyside Park, Godalming, Surrey, GU7 1XR, 0483 426444.

Acknowledgement

My thanks are due to my colleague Vera Elliott for her comments during the writing of this chapter.

References

1. The Friends of the Earth office claims to receive one thousand requests for information a week. Interview with former Director, David Gee, in: *Green Magazine*, 2(11) July, 1991, 31.

2. This was reflected in an extensive public opinion poll, *The Guardian*, 14 September, 1990, 33 and the 1991 *Social attitudes survey.* Professor Ken Young suggests that Britain has undergone a cultural shift with respect to environmental values—'Modern Britain has become somewhat green and may become greener yet. But the process seems to be one of wider permeation rather than one of deepening commitment'. *The Guardian*, 22 November, 1991, 32.

3. BUTTON, J. *How to be green.* London: Century Hutchinson, 1989.
BUTTON, J. *New green pages: a directory of natural products, services, resources and ideas.* London: Macdonald Optima, 1990.
FRISCH, M. *Directory for the environment: organisations, campaigns and initiatives in the British Isles,* 3rd ed. London: Green Print, 1990.
KRUGER, A. *H is for ecoHome: an A-Z guide to a healthier, planet-friendly household.* London: Gaia Books, 1991.
MILNER, J. E., FILBY, C., *and* BOARD, M. *The green index: a directory of environmental organisations in Britain and Ireland.* London: Cassell Educational, 1990.
SILVER, D. *and* VALLELY, B. *The young person's guide to saving the planet.* London: Virago Press, 1990.

4. ELKINGTON, J. *and* HAILES, J. *The green consumer guide.* London: Victor Gollancz, 1988.
WELLS, P. *and* JETTER, M. *The global consumer: best buys to help the Third World.* London: Victor Gollancz, 1991.

5. ELKINGTON, J. *and* HAILES, J. *The universal green office guide.* London: Universal Office Supplies, 1989.

WINGROVE, I. *Greening your workplace: a practical guide for working people and trade unionists.* London: Green Party Trade Union Group, 1991.

6. ENVIRONMENTAL DATA SERVICES LTD. *Directory of environmental consultants,* 2nd ed. London: ENDS, 1990.

7. EVANS, P. *The Guardian,* 6 December, 1991, 33.

8. NORMAN, D., RENNIE, J. and FLEMING, P. *The green maze: environmental information and the needs of the public.* Bristol: ECO Environmental Education Trust, 1991.

9. OSTLE, B. *Qualitative research into environmental information needs in relation to attititudes and motivation.* Unpublished MSc dissertation, City University, 1991.

10. NORMAN, D., RENNIE, J. and FLEMING, P. *The green maze: environmental information and the needs of the public.* Bristol: ECO Environmental Education Trust, 1991, 62.

11. SINCLAIR, P. *E for environment: an annotated bibliography of children's books with environmental themes.* New Jersey: Bowker, 1992.

12. DE SILVA, D. *Online databases and CD-ROMs as sources of environmental information.* Unpublished MSc dissertation, City University, 1991.
NORMAN, D., RENNIE, J. and FLEMING, P. *The green maze: environmental information and the needs of the public.* Bristol: ECO Environmental Education Trust, 1991.
OSTLE, B. *Qualitative research into environmental information needs in relation to attitudes and motivation.* Unpublished MSc dissertation, City University, 1991.

13. A librarian in Southwark stated: 'It would be nice to have a database, and one simple group to approach, even if only for national issues'. In: NORMAN, D., RENNIE, J. and FLEMING, P. *The green maze: environmental information and the needs of the public.* Bristol: ECO Environmental Education Trust, 1991, 46.

14. WOOLSTON, H. and LEES, N. eds. *Introduction to environmental information.* London: British Library Science Reference and Information Service, forthcoming.

15. DEPARTMENT OF THE ENVIROMNENT. *This common inheritance: Britain's environmental strategy.* London: HMSO, 1990, Cmnd. 1200.

16. *Green Magazine,* 3(4) January, 1992, 7.

17. DE SILVA, D. *Online databases and CD-ROMs as sources of environmental information.* Unpublished MSc dissertation, City University, 1991.
A *directory of databases* is due to be published in Spring 1992 by the ECO Environmental Education Trust.

18. A report of the conference is available from ECO Environmental Education Trust.

19. DE SILVA, D. *Online databases and CD-ROMs as sources of environmental information.* Unpublished MSc dissertation, City University, 1991.

20. NORMAN, D., RENNIE, J. *and* FLEMING, P. *The green maze: environmental information and the needs of the public.* Bristol: ECO Environmental Education Trust, 1991.

21. *Ibid.,* 41.

22. DE SILVA, D. *Online databases and CD-ROMs as sources of environmental information.* Unpublished MSc dissertation, City University, 1991, 2.

23. NORMAN, D., RENNIE, J. *and* FLEMING, P. *The green maze: environmental information and the needs of the public.* Bristol: ECO Environmental Education Trust, 1991.

24. Personal communication with Howard Taylor.

25. NORMAN, D., RENNIE, J. *and* FLEMING, P. *The green maze: environmental information and the needs of the public.* Bristol: ECO Environmental Education Trust, 1991.

26. NEWCASTLE ARCHITECTURE WORKSHOP. *National review of architecture workshops: summary of and extracts from the interim report for the Department of the Environment.* Newcastle: Newcastle Architecture Workshop, 1990.
KEAN, J. *and* ADAMS, E. *Local environmental resource centres,* Newcastle: Newcastle Architecture Workshop, 1991.

27. NORMAN, D., RENNIE, J. *and* FLEMING, P. *The green maze: environmental information and the needs of the public.* Bristol: ECO Environmental Education Trust, 1991.

28 DEPARTMENT OF THE ENVIRONMENT. *This common inheritance: Britain's environmental strategy.* London: HMSO, 1990, Cmnd. 1200.

29. NORMAN, D., RENNIE, J. *and* FLEMING, P. *The green maze: environmental information and the needs of the public.* Bristol: ECO Environmental Education Trust, 1991.

30. OSTLE, B. *Qualitative research into environmental information needs in relation to attitudes and motivation.* Unpublished MSc dissertation, City University, 1991.

31. *Ibid.*

32. Personal communication with Howard Taylor.

CHAPTER SEVEN

HEALTH INFORMATION

Sally Knight

Health Information

Introduction

Health information has undergone a fashion change in the last decade. Until recently, the population had not been encouraged to perceive a general need to know in the field of health and had been actively discouraged from knowing anything about 'medicine'. A number of reasons exist, notably paternalism in the medical profession, and case law. Consequently, owing to consumer pressure and rapid changes in the law, the topic is now exploding in an unorganized manner; health information delivery to the public is developing in a variety of ways and attention must be paid therefore to ensure co-operation between information services and agencies in order to avoid duplication, and ensure maximum efficiency, economy and satisfaction for the community. This chapter will examine the need for health information, particularly in the light of its complex history and sudden recent legislation and Government Command Papers, its general significance for the population at large and the specific importance for individuals when they become ill. The changing relationship between patients and their health professionals as a consequence of access to health information will also be discussed.

The Need for Health Information

Health information is an area currently receiving increased

attention at both grass roots and governmental level. The reasons for this are varied. The policies of successive governments have stressed the need for greater personal responsibility and wider consumer choices in health matters, thereby giving even greater impetus to consumers to seek and obtain information. At the same time there is controversy between law makers, health professionals and consumers as to how far these demands should be met. The expectation of the right to knowledge and information in this field, both legally and ethically, is growing as paternalism is fading. As medicine becomes more complex in its technology, treatments and therapeutics, the need for consumers to have access to more information increases in order that they may understand and co-operate with the procedures and agree to treatment. As people are generally living longer and the prognosis of many diseases improves, particularly in the area of chronic illness, the need to be more informed increases so as to enhance the quality of life. The emergence of AIDS has ironically also forwarded the need for information.

There has been a shift of emphasis from perceiving the medical profession as the controlling influence to public realization that socio-economic and environmental factors are equally important to health. This has led from passive patient response to an active demand for fuller participation in health care. The need for information follows this shift of emphasis. There are related facets to be considered in this information process with regard to the fundamental differences between the traditional providers of information (i.e. doctors) and recipients, with potential problems in communication. These problems may give rise to some consumers needing alternative sources of information.

This public realization that involvement in health care is important for individuals' well-being has led to a growth of interest in health education in general, and to self help and education in particular, when specific illnesses have occurred. This is facilitated by information. Information aids recovery, reduces stress, increases compliance with medication and treatment and increases satisfaction with health care.

Due to this more active demand and because expectations are greater, many consumers now envisage that their health care practitioners can provide them with more information. Because health care professionals failed to provide information in the past, many patients may seek this information direct from an alternative source. To meet these demands, available information services have been moving from the public library's reactive service to a more proactive approach. Some public libraries such as the Marylebone Library carry collections of health literature but the major works are based in medical libraries such as Guy's and St Thomas' Hospital Medical School, which frequently have restricted access. Health information services are growing in different ways, as reflected by local initiative, and may not be library based in the traditional sense.

Before one looks at the various types of service it is necessary to glance at history to see why growth is varied and haphazard. Medicine has been, and is, governed by both legal constraints and ethical codes of practice.

Legal Considerations

Until 1984, no legal rights to medical information existed. Even now, such rights as are conferred under the Data Protection Act 1984 and Access to Personal Files Act 1987 are limited. The Disabled Persons Act 1986 decrees that local authority Social Service departments have a duty to provide information about local services to local disabled people. The Access to Medical Reports Act 1988 now allows an individual to have access to (and the right to remove some facts if he so wishes from) reports sent to an employer or insurer. Until 1988 there were but two circumstances in which a patient had a legal right to medical information:

    (i) where there was a contemplated disposition of property,
and
    (ii) where the patient was contemplating legal action for compensation.

In 1981, Edmund-Davies stated that in such cases individual doctors must decide whether or not to act as advisers and if a doctor acts as an adviser then s/he should 'tell the truth as he sees it'.[1] Case law has been known to defend untruths in medicine on the grounds that it was for the patient's own good.[2] Until very recently, doctors needed to tell patients as much or as little as they thought necessary, with the guiding code of practice being the Hippocratic Oath to do the patient no harm. A number of cases tried in law have tested how much the patient needs to know and on studying these it can be seen that a muddled picture emerges. They also point to the fact that 'informed consent' does not yet form part of English law.

Case law such as Bolam v. Friern Hospital Management Committee (1957),[3] Chatterton v. Gerson (1981),[4] Freeman v. Home Office (1984),[5] and Sidaway v. Bethlam Royal Hospital (1985)[6] illustrates that the doctor had acted in accordance with accepted medical practice and was not held to be negligent in a failure to inform. Paradoxically, although judgement was found against the patient in the Sidaway case, one judge did further explore whether the patient had a legal right to information and whether the doctor was under any legal duty to tell of risks involved in treatment. If the law recognizes this right an argument is then left as to whether there is a right to full disclosure or if the doctor can clinically judge the amount of disclosure that can be made to the patients. This remains untested in case law. Further discussion by Lord Scarman led to him defining a doctor's duty as:

> one which requires him not only to advise as to medical treatment but also to provide the information needed by the patient to consider and balance the

medical advantages and risks alongside other relevant matters, such as family, business or social responsibilities of which the doctor may be only partially, if at all, informed.[7]

Health Information and Access to Health Records Act 1990

Statute law, in the form of the Access to Health Records Act 1990, will significantly increase the cause for health information. This Act became active in November 1991. The main provision enables access to a health record or to any part of a health record by:

a. the patient,
b. a person authorized in writing to make the application on the patient's behalf,
c. a person having parental responsibility for a child,
d. where the record is held in Scotland and the patient is a pupil, a parent or guardian of the patient,
e. where the patient is incapable of managing his own affairs, any person appointed to a court to manage those affairs, and
f. where the patient has died, the patient's personal representative and any person who may have a claim arising out of the patient's death.

It will be readily appreciated that, with the enforcement of the above, patients having full access to their health records will in the future (the Act will not allow access to records prior to November 1991) automatically share health information with their practitioner. For some this new right, together with the opportunity to discuss with their health care practitioner what is recorded on their health notes, will be sufficient. It will also facilitate fuller participation between health care staff and patients. It has been conjectured though that this Act will force some doctors to include less detail in the patient's record in order that they will not be held to account for their remarks at a later date. If this happens it could be detrimental for the patient when, for example, another doctor takes over the care of a patient. It also means that the same ground may have to be covered again in subsequent consultations.[8]

Assuming a positive stance to this new legislation, it could be argued therefore that the starting point for health information should be in the doctor's surgery. This is the primary point of contact between doctor and patient. Studies have shown that information can be most effectively delivered by the general practitioner. Patients take more advice from general practitioners, particularly when accompanied by such factors as clinical competence, warmth, ability to empathize and willingness to listen and explain.[9] Doctors, by virtue of their clinical knowledge, are in a good position to diagnose the condition. Their observations and interpretation may enable them to make a prognosis. An important emotive element, possibly on both sides, is introduced into the relationship as this may impinge on the patient's long term morbidity and mortality. Where a trusting relationship exists or can be developed, verbal health information can be most effectively imparted.

When patients require written health information to support the verbal consultation in the general practice setting, studies show that patient information collections placed in the surgery are a successful method.[10] These can be professionally established by librarians and evaluated for usage and success. In this way doctors and their primary health care teams have the information to hand and patients are free to read what they like. The opportunity is then available for the doctor-patient relationship to be enhanced, in that the patient feels there is approval to become informed and feels encouraged to ask more questions in the light of new knowledge gained by reading. A doctor can adapt the information gained, from the general to the specific, and provide emotional support when it is needed.

Ethical Considerations

Patients are frequently heard to complain that they have not been given information by their doctors, but it must be remembered that when a doctor imparts health information the stating of truth within the context of a doctor-patient relationship may prove a threatening disclosure. Traditionally, general practitioners, the prime sources of information, are constrained by their ethical code. The doctor has to temper hard fact to the circumstances and to the personality of the patient being treated—which must be based on a knowledge of the individual as well as the disease. Hence other factors enter the situation.

Total information relating to an individual with a medical condition is arrived at by discovery from observation, history and diagnosis. Specialists who become involved are, at the time of consultation, in possession of partial information about the patient and in such a setting the imparting of restricted information could be misleading.

Clinical practice decrees that doctors must take all steps to find a clinical answer for a patient's condition. Not to do so is in breach of their ethics. Thus diagnosis, prognosis and treatment must be knowledge based. It is then left to the doctor's own discretion as to how much of this specialised knowledge should be imparted to the patient. It is the interpretation of this aspect which can cause problems.

Individuals from lower socio-economic groups may not ask direct questions and often express their information needs differently to others.[11] Doctors then have to be very sensitive in deducing what patients really want (which presupposes patients know what they want). The Royal Commission on the National Health Service study of *Patients' attitudes to the hospital service* (1978) pointed out that what one patient regards as adequate information about his or her condition would not necessarily be so for another.[12] Doctors have to be adept at translating verbal and non-verbal signs and signals about how much a patient really wants to know and when.

In the surgery setting it must be understood that those who give and those who receive information tend to have very different educational backgrounds.[13] Doctors communicate differently with people whom they feel are less educated.[14]

Women tend to be told less information by their doctor and yet they should be more informed, as traditionally women take on the caring role. Women have also been found to be more enquiring, so they should be told more.[15] Both doctor and patient must be prepared to listen and be receptive because when communication flows in one direction only, from doctor to patient, information reception is ineffective. Lack of communication is a common criticism voiced by patients.[16]

An analysis of 336 patient-doctor encounters found that doctors spent very little time providing information and they over-estimated the amount of time they thought they had spent in so doing. Most patients expressed a desire to be told more.[17] Sometimes doctors find the task of information provision distressful or embarrassing. It may be that doctors are not very sure of the information themselves or that they wish to hang on to power by non-communication of information, thus keeping patients in a state of ignorance. They may hold particular religious or moral beliefs which constrain their ability to impart information.

Some doctors feel that there should be compromise in truth-telling in medicine, with the situation being likened to having a problem at home with the electrical system or plumbing.[18] The house owner who does not know much about how the job is done employs a professional to do the work and trusts that the person picked for the job will do it satisfactorily. There are instances quoted in the literature where patients have subsequently thanked the doctor for not having spelt out the horrors of disease.[19] The withholding of health information is governed by three basic attitudes:

1. the doctor must do no harm: informing a patient about, say, a terminal condition may be harmful,
2. the doctor may not be sure of diagnosis and outcome,
3. the patient may not wish to have any information.[20]

These may be some of the reasons why patients feel the need to seek their health information from sources other than their general practice.

There may be another totally different set of reasons causing a patient to deliberately seek health information away from the clinical setting. Some of these reasons could be due to:

1. an inability to retain, or a denial of, what was told at the surgery,
2. an attempt at self diagnosis, and/or prognosis,
3. a desire to seek complementary medicine or self help,
4. the avoidance of communication with their doctor because of shyness, reticence or apprehension,
5. the seeking of knowledge from information providers seen as peers, rather than doctors who may be seen as superior,
6. the opportunity to manipulate or fake illness,
7. the search for an answer to a medical problem where one does not yet exist, and
8. a possibility of the formation of the basis for legal redress when operative techniques or treatments have failed.

Apart from the recent legislation described above it is important that a person knows of risk if they are about to undergo operative procedures. There is little evidence published to date of how patients' perception of risk is changed by being more knowledgeable but it is the experience of health information services that patients evaluate the side effects more than doctors do. There is evidence of a conscious evaluation of risk information before decision making.[21] Two examples are whether to have their children vaccinated against illness like whooping cough, and whether to have antenatal tests like amniocentesis, the latter being a procedure which carries its own risk of abortion.

The Surgeon General's (United States) report *Healthy people* (1980) promotes the knowledge of risk on the premise that the more the general public know the more likely they are to take steps to reduce such risks through education and adaptive life styles.[22] However Freemantle, a doctor who recently underwent major surgery, recounts from his own recent experience and still maintains that:—

> in each case a doctor or surgeon has to judge the intellectual capacity of the patient to that particular patient's medical benefit. If every cut, suture, injection and test is explained to its finite, surely no one would ever agree to anything![23]

Information Sharing and the Changing Relationship Between Patient and Doctor

The power held by the medical profession, because of their knowledge, has been described as:

> an occupational strategy to maintain certain monopolistic privileges and rewards...The professional dominance of certain occupational groups is clearly grounded in the possession of a body of knowledge which is a crucial feature of the exercise of professional power...the medical profession has been relatively successful in maintaining its position within the class structure and the professional hierarchy over the last hundred years by regulating and controlling access to health care delivery.[24]

The sharing of information and the listening approach increasingly used by doctors decreases some of their authority, thus the 'magical' healing and anxiety relieving power is reduced. Those doctors who wish to have influence over their patients, consciously or unconsciously, maintain a degree of uncertainty in their patients. There are those doctors who say that some patients really do prefer to be uncertain and need the safety net of denial.[25] In this way, the doctor remains a powerful figure who refuses to share information with the patient.

The doctor's authority is defined by Osmond as:—

a. sapiental—doctors must know or appear to know more about medicine than their patients,

b. moral—the right to control and direct with concern for the good of the patient, and

c. charismatic—which comes close to magical powers in that patients often do not understand what the treatment is doing to them, only that they are hopefully being healed.[26]

Doctors who sit behind their desks, making them a barrier in the consulting room, are maintaining authority; a simple test of seeing where doctors sit in their rooms shows the understanding patient immediately what the relationship is likely to be. The doctor creating barriers does not make a situation conducive to asking for or receiving information. However, there is an opposite and beneficial effect of a doctor's non-verbal behaviour. The patient who experiences the doctor using the power of touch can establish trust and a mutual sharing of care, which in turn stimulates information sharing at both a practical and emotional level. [27]

Doctors argue that to disclose information to a patient whose illness is terminal may destroy hope and this knowledge may make the patient decide to commit suicide, refuse further treatment or embark on unorthodox medicine. This is not generally correct and patients can display high levels of hope when they are aware of their diagnosis. If, however, the patient decides to refuse treatment, and to turn to unorthodox medicine or even commit suicide it could be argued that it is the patient's right to choose his or her own course of action once in possession of the full facts—even if it seems extreme.

The rise of consumerism in general is making itself felt in medical circles. Patient pressure groups and self help groups are increasing expectation. Indeed, advances in medicine itself have raised consumer expectation to such a degree that people expect to be cured where no cure yet exists. People become desperate and think that if only they search hard enough the information is there somewhere. Gann says that during the 1960s there was a growing realization that further improvements in health may be beyond the reach of current medical research and instead would partly depend on changes in lifestyle. [28] In more recent years, there has been increasing knowledge of the great potential of new research in molecular biology for the understanding and prevention of diseases previously thought incurable. This has changed expectations again. What people have to come to terms with is the way in which this is sometimes achieved and this can be distressing. At the present time, therefore, thought must be given to adding good quality of life to years, not years to life. Information on healthy living has become essential.

With this rise in expectation from the public, the doctor has to provide more information to the patient and to the patient's relatives as they also become more demanding. Mongiardi conducted a small survey which examined the needs of partners of patients admitted to a coronary care unit.[29] Nearly half said that they would have liked more information than they had actually received and the same number again said that they had difficulty in obtaining any information pertinent to the patient.

The picture is slowly changing and the precept that doctor knows best is gradually being replaced by the patient knows best. The solution lies somewhere in between these two polarised approaches. The medical and other health care staff should be adapting to the concept that if the patient wants information and involvement in his own health care then it should be given on a tailor-made basis so that informed choices can be made on true partnership terms.[30] Consumers are also demanding to know more of alternative therapies and in one study at the Centre for Alternative Therapies, patients going there for the first time appeared to be well informed about alternative medicine—most of them having found out about the subject from the media or friends.[31]

Information sharing is power sharing and this diminishes paternalism. It facilitates informed decision making on the part of the patient. However, some doctors could feel threatened by this changing relationship.

Service Delivery

It is highly probable that in the not too distant future multi-media facilities will exist which will enable people to access many of their information needs in the privacy of their own homes through their computers or television screens. This will be particularly beneficial in the field of medicine because so many searches for health information are of an emotive and confidential nature. Meanwhile, service delivery of health information is growing in a variety of ways. Geographical and local needs are important considerations and may, in part, account for the different types of service. Likewise, the background and skills of the information providers are varied—with librarians, information scientists, health educators, nurses and administrators all bringing different talents.

The following describes only a few of the more established services.

Service delivery at the doctor's surgery
The prime location for imparting health information is the general practitioner's surgery and the information process should begin with the general practitioner and the primary health care staff. This being so it would be ideal if the health information librarian can offer service here. There are encouraging signs that this is a very effective method of service delivery. A recent pilot scheme in a general practice in North Hertfordshire shows that a patients' information collection is well received both by patients and health professionals.[32] This includes books, journal articles, video tapes and audio cassettes available for loan to patients and based at the GP's surgery or health centre. Its purpose is to provide health information, at an appropriate level and at the time of consultation, on a range of medical conditions and health topics. Patients are either encouraged to self- select material of their choice, or are directed to specific material by their doctor or another member of the health care team, thus giving the opportunity to discuss any concerns generated as a result of the information provided. It promotes an equal partnership of health and care. Public librarians could seize this opportunity to provide service in the form of patient collections.

This form of delivery is especially timely as general

practices and health centres are becoming more health promotion based with new clinics such as well man, well woman, hypertension, dietetics and asthma being formed to encourage awareness of self health. As a result of the White Paper issued by the Department of Health and Social Security called *Promoting better health,* health promotion facilitators are being appointed.[33] Their remit is to facilitate the free flow of information between all general practice health care professionals and their patients. In some places they are taking over the health education departments. It is advantageous therefore to have up-to-date patient information in the health centres as they become more proactive towards patients. Information may be most effective if it is available immediately at a clinic or during the doctor/patient consultation. The United States established experience of employing patient education co-ordinators shows that the library plays an integral part in the health education process.[34]

The pilot scheme in North Hertfordshire was as the result of the collaborative efforts of the Health Information Service based at Lister Hospital, Stevenage and a local general practice. Funding was provided by Hertfordshire Library Service to purchase approximately 200 books, covering 107 topics. The books were selected jointly by the general practice and the Health Information Service Librarian. A user profile was compiled in advance to reflect likely need. The medical staff, if given the opportunity, are keen to help professional librarians in the choice of book stocks. The Health Information Service Librarian also advised on the stock's simple subject classification, shelf arrangement and cataloguing. A manual of procedures was produced for the receptionist staff who manage the collection, and simple data are recorded. Such a scheme is successful in building a relationship and co-operation between medical practitioners and librarians. It also aids the medical staff in becoming familiar with the level at which the general public read.

Since its inception, patients have been given a questionnaire to assess their usual reading habits. The primary aim was to discover whether they used their public library service and whether or not they generally read on health matters. Of 106 questionnaires returned in a short period it was found that 65 per cent would not have sought the information elsewhere had it not been so readily available in the GP's surgery. Ninety-seven per cent found the books they had read either very useful or of some use. The perceived level of anxiety was raised in 5 per cent of respondents, but reduced in a further 44 per cent.

From this limited evaluation, it would appear that health information delivered in this way does not generate undue anxiety but enables patients to derive useful information on topics which they would not have sought from other sources. As this method of service delivery is considered successful, on the initiative of the Health Information Service Librarian, another nine surgeries in Hertfordshire now have patient information collections. These were facilitated by funds provided from Hertfordshire Library Service, the North West Thames Regional Health Authority, a grant from the Public Library Development Incentive Scheme and various donated funds.

There are a few general practices who offer a patients' library in varying stages of development.[35]

Public library service delivery
Health Point, Dorset. This service is based at Poole Public Library. It has recently come under the managership of the Help for Health Trust.
Hertfordshire Library Service. If a request for health information is made at any public library in Hertfordshire which cannot be serviced from within the library itself then the enquiry is sent directly to Health Information Service, Lister Hospital who then deal directly with the enquirer.

The public library could also foster other community links

with organizations such as Citizens Advice Bureaux, health centres, health education departments, women's health mobiles and the like as an opportunity to place health information. It is incumbent on the public librarian to find such centres in the community.

Where there is a District General Hospital which provides a multi-disciplinary library service to its own hospital community there may be an opportunity for public librarians to co-operate in this service as is the case for example in Lister Hospital, Stevenage and Milton Keynes General Hospital.

Hospital service delivery
Patient & Family Information Centre, Frenchay Hospital, Bristol, BS16 1LE (Tel: 0272 701212) operates from the Outpatients Department of the hospital and provides information to patients, family carers and health care professionals. It is accessible by personal visit, letters and telephone. It has a link with Frenchay Postgraduate Medical Library. Funding comes from voluntary donations and fund raising events.

The Library, Doncaster Health Authority, Medical Library, Doncaster Royal Infirmary, Doncaster, DN2 5LT (Tel: 0302 366666 Ext. 650). This library services all health enquiries from Doncaster Hospital patients, outpatients, and ward staff. The enquiries are received predominantly by personal visit. Since 1990 a Child Health Information Centre has been functioning from the Children's Hospital, Doncaster Royal Infirmary. It aims to provide information to help families cope with the effects of illness and treatment through wider knowledge and deeper understanding. It specialises in books for children on various disease and disabilities, a comprehensive collection of adult books, information and literature on local and national self help groups and organizations, specialist toys and supplier catalogues.

Health Information Service, Lister Hospital, Corey's Mill Lane, Stevenage, Herts, SG1 4AB (Tel: 0438 314333 Ext. 4877 or 0438 315414 or 0438 781092) is a personal service based on over 3,000 files on medical conditions. If a file does not exist on a requested topic then a literature search is carried out both of the lay literature and the medical literature in an attempt to find the information. It is situated adjacent to the medical and patients' library, and is open to all the general public and NHS staff in the North West Thames Regional Health Authority and beyond.

Health Shop, Outpatients Hall, Addenbrookes Hospital, Hills Road, Cambridge, CB2 2QQ (Tel: 0223 216686) operates as a drop-in centre primarily aimed at staff, outpatients, relatives and friends but answers queries from all-comers. The shop acts as a clearing house for health information and has a comprehensive local community information system based on Cambridgeshire Community Database. It is staffed by 12 different organizations from the voluntary and statutory sectors, and hospital departments. This enables inquirers to consult a member of staff who may have a skill for their particular need.

High Street service delivery

Health Matters based at 795 Avebury Boulevard, Milton Keynes MK 3NW (Tel: 0908 691212) delivers its service in the form of a shop front. It is linked to the Medical Library at Milton Keynes General Hospital. It provides a drop-in and telephone information service and has developed a local database of self help groups.

The Health Information Centre at Baxter Gate, Loughborough LE11 1TT (Tel: 0509 611600 Ext. 8364) was established as a shop front to increase awareness in health and related matters to the general public acting as a resource base for health education and health promotional activities in Loughborough. It also provides health promotion information to NHS staff in Loughborough and has initiated an interpreting service for all health related matters to the local ethnic population. The centre holds sessions with health professionals, for example midwifery, dietetics and counselling. In-depth medical enquiries received are referred to Leicester Polytechnic Library.

Health Information Service at Victoria Health Centre, Glasshouse Street, Nottingham NH1 3LW (Tel: 0602 509242) provides free confidential up-to-date information in non medical language on all aspects of health, illness and disability. It has a database of all local self-help groups and also any groups of related interest such as keep fit or alternative therapies. It is open to all health professionals and the general public. The service has links with the Queen's Medical Centre, Nottingham. It is closely allied to the Self Help Team, 20 Pelham Road, Sherwood, Nottingham, NG5 1AP (Tel: 0602 691212) which provides support and information to and about self help groups.

Sunderland Health Information Centre, 223 High Street, Sunderland, SR1 1TZ (Tel: 091 5100249) is open to the public four days a week. Specialist drop-in services are also offered here by self help groups and health professionals.

Service delivery by telephone
The Help for Health Trust is based at Highcroft Cottage, Romsey Road, Winchester SO22 5DG (Tel: 0962 849100). The service is built around the most comprehensive database in the United Kingdom of self help and patient organizations and provides predominantly a phone-in information service to patients and professionals. Help for Health is also used as a drop-in service for the people of Winchester and surrounding districts. The Trust also offers a number of other services such as the HIV/AIDS Information Service and the Wessex Waiting Line. The Acorn Project is another service which is being developed by the Trust. A patient education resource centre is being developed and linked to a hospital ward in St Mary's Hospital, Isle of Wight. Every patient will receive an individual pack of information about treatment and care.

Health Search, Scotland based at Woodburn House, Canaan Lane, Edinburgh EH10 4SG (Tel: 031 452 8666) became operational in 1989 and aims to provide mostly a phone based service to all those living or working in Scotland. It is a computer based system, with regularly updated information on self-help and voluntary groups. In addition, there is a collection of self-help leaflets and booklets.

Information North, Quaker Meeting House, 1 Archbold Terrace, Newcastle upon Tyne, NE2 1DB (Tel: 091 281 8887) is primarily a telephone service covering the North East of England and Cumbria. The service is based mainly on Help Box North which is a subscription data base for information professionals.

Health Promotion Authority for Wales, Brunel House, (8th Floor), 2 Fitzalan Road, Cardiff, CF2 1EB (Tel: 0222 472472) provides a statistical data and library service for health professionals throughout Wales. The service revolves around health promotion theory and practice, life styles and health status of the people of Wales. It also provides a new service, Health Link Wales, for the public, a service based on Help Box which has been adapted for the Welsh locality. It is envisaged that access will be channelled through public libraries and hospitals.

Future Developments
In view of the growing number of consumer health information services in the United Kingdom a network called the Consumer Health Information Consortium has been formed. It aims to develop a national informal network of consumer health information providers for mutual support and to raise public consciousness. This should, in the future, have a role to play in service co-operation. A directory of health information services is being compiled and is to be published in 1992.

Since the publication of the Command Paper issued by the Secretaries of State called *Working for patients* (1989) there has been a shift of emphasis for health information provision. The White Paper states, among other things, that each hospital should now offer

> ...clear information leaflets about the facilities and what patients need to know when they come into hospital.

> ...once someone is in hospital, clear and sensitive explanations of what is happening—on practical matters such as where to go and who to see, and on clinical matters, such as the nature of an illness and its proposed treatment.[36]

Since 1990 there has been a growth of a new breed of health professionals called Health Promotion Facilitators committed, amongst other things, to identifying patients' needs and demands for health promotion services and assisting with medical audit. These facilitators will need information from published literature in order to perform their new tasks.

More recently, publication of the *Citizen's Charter 1991* (Command Paper no. 1599) has generated interest with particular regard to the section entitled 'Charter for Patients'.[37] The Charter includes in its objectives the need for patients to have clear information about options for care or treatments, continuing information about how each case is developing, involvement in patients' own care and treatment, control with a right to give or withold consent to medical treatment, freedom to decide whether or not to participate in medical research and student training and access to information held about them.

It can be seen that the health information provider may have input to all the points mentioned above. In her report to the British Library and College of Health, Kempson made the recommendation that health information should develop nationally in a hybrid form, combining the Lister Hospital Health Information Service and Help for Health.[38] More recently, the Minister of State for Health, in launching the Department of Health's contribution to the Citizen's Charter said the Patient's Charter will build on the NHS Reforms which were themselves designed to extend patient choice, and to ensure that the patient comes first. It is intended that all regional health authorities set up health information services. It is also envisaged that every citizen should be able to telephone or possibly drop into a local information centre—to find out more about local services.

With the shifts in attitudes by consumers as they demand more active participation in their own care, the stance being taken by the Government with their recent statute law and White Papers, and diminishing paternalism on the part of the medical profession, the present time is significant for consumers and health professionals to develop in true partnership so as to achieve maximum benefit from health information. It will be evident that self help and the need to be well informed will take on a greater meaning in the new reformed Health Service. It is incumbent on all health information providers to investigate the possibility of providing a health information service in whatever setting seems to be the most appropriate in their locality.

Addendum

Since April 1992 there has been a significant development for the future provision of health information. The Patients' Charter requires all 14 Regional Health Authorities in England to offer information on such matters as local charter standards NHS services, common diseases, conditions and treatments, etc. A telephone helpline has been established in each region.[39]

References

1. EDMUND-DAVIES, H. E. Truth telling, In: A. S. Duncan, et al. *eds. Dictionary of medical ethics,* 2nd ed. London: Darton, Longman & Todd, 1981, 443-5.

2. What should a doctor tell? *British Medical Journal,* 289, 1984, 325-6.

3. Bolam v. Friern HMC (1957) 2 All ER 118.

4. Chatterton v. Gerson and another (1981) 1 All 252.

5. Freeman v. Home Office (1984) 1 All ER 1036.

6. Sidaway v. Bethlam Royal Hospital (1985) 1All ER 643.

7. SCARMAN, L. G. Consent, communication and responsibility, *Journal of the Royal Society of Medicine,* 79, 1986, 697-700.

8. Personal Communication with S. Rowlands, 1989.

9. PAINE, T. Patients—past and future, *Practitioner,* 228, 1984, 1113-1117.

10. COLLINGS, L. *and* KNIGHT, S. Patient information collections in general practice, *Health Libraries Review,* 7 (3), 1990, 166-168.

COLLINGS, L. et al. Value of health information in the general practice setting, *British Journal of General Practice,* 41, 1991 (in press).

VARNAVIDES, C. K. et al. Health library for patients in general practice, *British Medical Journal,* 288, 1984, 535-537.

11. TATE, P. Doctor's style. In: D. Pendleton *and* J. Hasler, *eds. Doctor-patient communications.* London: Academic Press, 1983, 75-85.

12. ROYAL COMMISSION ON THE NATIONAL HEALTH SERVICE. *Patients' attitudes to the hospital service.* London: HMSO, 1978. (Research Paper No. 5).

13. BRATTSTROM, M. Communication problems in health care, *Clinical Rheumatology,* 6 (2), 1987, 158-161.

14. STEWART, M. Patient characteristics which are related to the doctor-patient interaction, *Family Practice,* 1, 1983, 30-36.

WAITZKIN, W. Information giving in medical care, *Journal of Health and Social Behaviour,* 26, 1985, 81-101.

15. STEWART, M. Patient characteristics which are related to the doctor-patient interaction, *Family Practice,* 1, 1983, 30-36.

16. CLAYTON, S. Prescribing information to patients, *British Medical Journal,* 292, 1986, 1368.

HARTNELL, L. Personal view, *British Medical Journal,* 294, 1987, 1029.

17. WAITZKIN, W. Information giving in medical care, *Journal of Health and Social Behaviour,* 26, 1985, 81-101.

18. BREWIN, T. Truth, trust, and paternalism, *The Lancet,* 11, 1985, 490-492.

19. JELLINEK, E. H. Motor neuron disease—a challenge to medical ethics, *Journal of the Royal Society of Medicine,* 79, 1986, 684-5.

20. CAREY, J. Motor neuron disease— a challenge to medical ethics, *Journal of the Royal Society of Medicine,* 79, 1986, 216-220.

21. BRITISH MEDICAL ASSOCIATION. Risks of medicine and surgery, In: BMA Guide, *Living with risk.* London: BMA, 1987, 123-133.

McNEILL, B. et al. On the elicitation of preferences for alternative therapies, *New England Journal of Medicine,* 306, 1982, 1259-1262.

22. SURGEON GENERAL OF THE UNITED STATES. *Healthy people. Report on health, promotion and disease prevention.* Washington, DC: US Department of Health and Human Services, 1980.

23. FREEMANTLE, B. Fully informed consent? A patient's view, *Journal of the Medical Defence Union,* 7 (2), 1991, 40-42.

24. TURNER, B. Professions, knowledge and power, In: B. Turner, *Medical power and social knowledge.* London: Sage, 1987, 130-156.

25. ROYSTON, V. Personal view, *British Medical Journal,* 295, 1987, 665. SPENCER-JONES, J. Telling the right patient, *British Medical Journal,* 283, 1981, 291-2.

26. OSMOND, H. God and the doctor, *New England Journal of Medicine,* 320 (10), 1980, 555-8.

27. PENDLETON, D. Doctor-patient communication: a review, In: D. Pendleton and J. Hasler, *eds. Doctor-patient communication.* London: Academic Press, 1983, 5-53.

28. GANN, R. The people their own physicians: 2000 years of patient information, *Health Libraries Review,* 4, 1987, 151-155.

29. MONGIARDI, F. The needs of relatives of patients admitted to the coronary care unit, *Intensive Care Nursing,* 3, 1987, 67-70.

30. TATE, P. Doctor's style, In: D. Pendleton and J. Hasler, *eds. Doctor-patient communication.* London: Academic Press, 1983, 75-85. WHITEHORN, K. Public expectations, In: G. Teeling-Smith *ed. Health education and general practice.* London: Office of Health Economics, 1986, 15-17.

31. MOORE, J. et al. Why do people seek treatment by alternative medicine? *British Medical Journal,* 290, 1985, 28-29.

32. COLLINGS, L. et al. Value of health information in the general practice setting, *British Journal of General Practice,* 41, 1991 (in press).

33. DEPARTMENT OF HEALTH AND SOCIAL SECURITY. *Promoting better health.* London: HMSO, 1987.

34. CLOSE, A. Necessity or luxury? *Nursing Times,* 87, 1991, 36-38.

35. COLLINGS, L. *and* KNIGHT, S. Patient information collections in general practice, *Health Libraries Review,* 7 (3), 1990, 166-168. VARNAVIDES, C. K. et al. Health library for patients in general practice, *British Medical Journal,* 288, 1984, 535-537.

36. SECRETARIES OF STATE FOR HEALTH IN WALES, NORTHERN IRELAND AND SCOTLAND. *Working for patients.* London: HMSO, 1989. Cmnd. 555.

37. CABINET OFFICE. *Citizen's Charter.* London: HMSO, 1991. Cmnd. 1599.

38. KEMPSON, E. *Informing health consumers: a review of consumer health information needs and services.* London: College of Health/The British Library, 1987.

39. NATIONAL HEALTH SERVICE MANAGEMENT EXECUTIVE. *Implementation of the health information services.* London: NHS Management Executive, 1992 (HSG(92)21).

CHAPTER EIGHT

COMMUNITY ARTS

Paul Catcheside

Community Arts

During the course of discussions about a restructuring of Liverpool City Libraries and Arts Department I wrote a paper for staff in which I posed the question 'What business are we in?' In it I commented that:

> It seems to me that like Smiths and Boots we are in a different business to the one we started out in. I think that we are in the business of communicating ideas...It doesn't just involve promoting books and literature, but in supporting a whole range of manifestations of imagination through the arts.[1]

I do not claim that this thought is original, and indeed the rationale of a link between libraries and the arts is set out in the Association of Metropolitan Authorities (AMA) paper *Libraries and cultural policy,* which states that:

> By providing access to a wide range of materials in a variety of media and the opportunity to participate in a diverse programme of cultural activities, the public library service gives people the opportunity to pursue their own artistic, literary and intellectual interests. In so doing it enriches the lives of individuals and the community of which they are part.[2]

Both of these statements imply a formal commitment to the arts on the part of public libraries. In this chapter I intend first to examine briefly the nature and extent of this commitment within the library profession through the literature and practice since the Second World War. I will then go on to scan the current position. For this I draw upon the current literature, in particular Peggy Heeks' significant report *Public libraries and the arts: an evolving partnership,*[3] and the Association of Assistant Librarians' (AAL) excellent handbook;[4] and upon the responses I received to a letter sent to all chief public librarians in Great Britain and Ireland. (This letter is reproduced at the end of this chapter (Appendix 1), and I must thank all those chief library officers and others who responded in a very full and helpful manner. This survey was aimed at being brief and to the point so as to elicit a response, and indeed an overall response rate of 66 per cent was achieved. The survey therefore provides a useful 'snapshot' of the practice of arts in libraries, and complements Heeks' rather more attitudinal survey.)

Arts and Libraries, 1945 to date

Many libraries have practised promotion of the arts since before the Second World War when lectures and music recitals were held regularly in more progressive metropolitan and municipal libraries throughout the country, and when Manchester pinned its colours firmly to the mast by including in its new Central Library a Library Theatre under the direct control of the City Librarian. This tradition continued in municipal libraries post war, and was recognised on the international scene by André Maurois in his drafting of the Unesco Public Libraries Manifesto in 1949:

> The public library is a natural cultural centre for the community, bringing together as it does people of similar interests. Space and equipment are therefore necessary for exhibitions, discussions, lectures, musical performances and films, both for adults and children.[5]

However, outside the few pioneer authorities, the British library world barely recognised the possibilities of the libraries and arts relationship, and the Bourdillon Report encapsulates this lack of imagination in its sparse reference to arts activities which states baldly:

> We draw attention to the role of the public library as a centre of cultural life.[6]

The possibilities were however set out in enthusiastic detail by Harold Jolliffe, one of the small band of committed librarians in his writings about the practice of arts activities in the libraries of Swindon.[7, 8]

The library world's general lack of commitment was commented upon by Alex Wilson in 1969 at a conference on Libraries and the Arts held at the College of Librarianship, Wales when he gave his opinion that:

> The public library contribution to the arts is traditional, but usually somewhat half-hearted . . .
>
> Those public libraries which undertook arts activities . . . had arrived gradually through the personal enthusiasm of the chief librarian attempting, in an improvised way, to fill some of the vacuum in local cultural life with, if he is lucky the support or otherwise merely the consent of his committee.[9]

The comments of Wilson and other contributors to the Aberystwyth Conference seem to have drawn attention to the need for a more formal commitment to the arts on the part of public librarians, and in 1975 the Department of Education and Science (DES) published a valuable guideline as Number 5 in the Library Information Series. This report surveyed the range of possibilities of provision and co-operation and suggested ways in which public libraries could use these to help form 'the total pattern of facilities for the arts in the area'. The report sets out in its conclusion:

> What seem to us powerful arguments in favour of using public libraries as major centres for cultural activities in the communities which they serve. The 3 principal arguments can be summarised as: the character of a library's primary function and the natural affinity between reading and other cultural activities; the public image of the library; and the ubiquity and accessibility of public libraries (Para. 82).[10]

Excellent and challenging though this report is, it does not seem to have elicited a great response from the public library world, perhaps because at this time much of that world was wrestling with the problems of forming new public library services out of the varied conglomerations of library authorities brought together by the local government reorganization of 1974.

It was another five years before the Arts Council of Great Britain and the Library Association began working together to try to improve the situation, and in 1982/3 they produced a number of useful guidelines before the partnership ceased to function. Even these, however, were promoted with less than enthusiasm by the Library Association, and Geoffrey Hare—a contributor—commented:

> Like perhaps the majority of the papers produced for the Working Party, mine have not seen the light of day since its suspension, although I know that the Library Association reported to a subsequent meeting of the Working Party that (and I quote) 'it did not support in its current form the publication of the (Arts Exhibitions) paper.'[11]

Pat Coleman had also written one of the papers for the Arts Council/ Library Association[12] (though this paper is also extremely difficult to get hold of), and it was she who, as in community librarianship, challenged librarians to address the deficiencies of provision. Thus in 1985 Sheffield City Libraries hosted a conference on 'Libraries and the arts: in action or inaction?'.[13] This conference led to the presentation of a paper on 'Libraries, the Arts, and the Library Association' to the Library and Information Services Council by an informal group convened by Stuart Brewer. This paper in turn led to the establishment of the Library Association's Working Party on Libraries and the Arts, and the commissioning of the survey *Public libraries and the arts: an evolving partnership* which was undertaken by Peggy Heeks.[14]

Heeks is unimpressed by the lack of systematic support for library involvement in the arts, one symptom of which is the paucity of literature on the subject. She comments:

> The contribution from printed sources was small: compared with other aspects of librarianship documentation of arts activities is poor.

She concludes that 'comparatively few people have addressed the public library/arts relationship'.

Heeks' study contains a more detailed account of the history of the project, but from this brief summary readers will see that it was 20 years since the Aberystwyth Conference, and 14 years since the DES Guidelines before any formal action was taken by the library world to consider the situation *vis a vis* libraries and the arts. Even now it does not appear that—despite the enthusiastic work of individual librarians, and the promptings of energetic chief librarians in the field—the public library profession has taken on board the need to adopt a policy of whole-hearted involvement in the arts.

A more hopeful note is provided by the AAL's *Marshalled arts: a handbook for arts in libraries.*[15] This invaluable work consists of essays by librarians and arts practitioners on the philosophy and practice of different aspects of arts work, and of the organization and results of specific projects. As John Dolan commented in his review:

> What comes through, from Belfast to the Isle of Wight, from the amateur's oils to ballet, is the complete span of arts with which libraries can link.[16]

Definitions

Before looking at current practice in arts in libraries, I wish to look first at the definitions of the two terms 'the arts' and 'community arts', in order to examine the relevance of these activities to libraries.

The majority of librarians, it seems from the responses I had to my letter, take a liberal view of the arts, and it is such a view that Heeks adopts as according 'well with the views expressed in the course of this study'. She quotes the definition of 'the arts' set out in the constitution of the Council of Regional Arts Associations (CORAA):

> The term 'the arts' includes, but is not limited to, music. . ., dance, drama, folk art, creative writing, architecture and allied fields, painting, sculpture, photography, graphic and craft arts, industrial design, costume and fashion design, motion pictures, television, radio, tape and sound recording, the arts related to the presentation, performance and exhibition of such major art forms, and the study and application of the arts to the human environment.[17]

This is the view I have taken for my survey, though some librarians would clearly go further and use instead the term 'culture' as used as a basis in *Public libraries and cultural activities:*

the term 'cultural centres' was deliberately adopted in preference to 'arts centres'. Culture is usefully ambiguous, denoting both a total lifestyle (the anthropologist's usage) and also a consciously-adopted set of values and pattern of behaviour.[18]

This definition would clearly incorporate the role of the library in promoting local studies, and the use of local history in the recreation of individuals' memories in creative writing, or in graphic and photographic arts. However, this definition could encompass the whole of the library's role, and is far too broad to be used for a defined area of that role, so for this chapter I have restricted myself to the CORAA definition set out above. This discussion should, however, serve to remind us that there are overlaps between the arts, and between other aspects of service, and that arts in libraries must be seen as part of the total philosophy of the library service, not just as the 'add-on' to which several librarians alluded in their survey responses. As J. B. Priestley wrote (quoted in Oldham's policy document): 'Art is not really like the icing on the cake, it is far more like the yeast in the dough'.[19]

The next definition to consider is that of 'community arts', and to see if that is different in the library context to 'the arts'. Certainly many librarians refer to an element of bringing art as excellence to local communities, and this idea is best developed in the chapter by Michael Messenger in *Marshalled arts.*[20] He sets out the practice of Hereford and Worcester County Library which is largely based upon an opportunistic use of library openings and other events as a focus around which to build arts festivals. These consist in large part of professional artists performing to local audiences, and Messenger argues cogently for the value of this access to 'high art' which rural and small town residents might otherwise not have. While the County's policy statement also relates to the approach of 'provision for' rather than 'participation in', Messenger's article speaks also of writers in residence, and of local art exhibitions. Clearly

Messenger sees the 'high art' provision as part of a total arts policy which involves participative activities. The impossibility of separating the two is referred to by many librarians in their responses, and certainly was brought home to me in the 'Writing and Liverpool Libraries' programme, where local creative writers have been considerably inspired and aided by nationally and internationally acclaimed poets and novelists performing or talking about their own works—particularly where locally-based writers were included in such programmes.

The Greater London Arts Association defines community arts as follows:

> The community arts begin with the 'community', not the 'art'. In effect it is potentially the most sophisticated of all forms of arts marketing, responding directly to market (community) demand.[21]

However, this definition does not seem as useful to me as that adopted by the AMA:

> The basic philosophy of Community Arts is to encourage people to become actively involved in the arts so that they discover their own creative potential. This is identical to the philosophy of public libraries.[22]

This view is fundamentally the one argued by Patrick Conway in *Marshalled arts*,[23] and is the one that most survey responses take. Eighty-four out of the 119 responses detail participative arts as a major area of their activities, and several librarians saw this as the main focus of their library's support for arts activities.

Several libraries adopt policies which define their roles as supporting community arts (though at least one response questioned the validity of community arts as an oudated term). Thus in Cheshire,

> 'Community arts' is not a separate, isolated art form, it employs all art forms. As a term it describes a philosophical standpoint and a practical working method. The arts are a powerful tool for expression, communication, personal and social growth, education and enjoyment, and as such are not the preserve of the few but of value to all. This means that access to resources, expertise and opportunity should be available on a much wider basis than at present.[24]

In Eire, Donegal County Library is more aggressively political in its definition of 'cultural democracy':

> An arts promotion service must 1) work towards the control and direction of their own cultural life by individuals, by individual communities, and by people of the County as a whole. 2) support the right of each citizen to engage in contemporary and traditional arts individually and/or collectively. 3) Support the creativity and freedom of the artist. 4) Support the right of each citizen to participate in decision making in cultural affairs. 5) Safeguard the cultural heritage of the County for all the people.[25]

Perhaps the view that most librarians seem to take is best summed up in the response from Lancashire, which states:

> We feel strongly that arts activities fill a gap in the market as well as providing for better use of key public facilities. It is my view that our work is more friendly, approachable and, dare I say it, less elitist than many such programmes supported by the Art Establishment...

Current Practice: the Heeks Report

Peggy Heeks based her study on a detailed questionnaire which elicited an 84 per cent response from library authorities, and on five case studies: Clwyd, Gateshead, Kent, Renfrew, and the South Eastern Library and Education Board in Northern Ireland. She reported that she found the situation was far from satisfactory:

> There are some perturbing features about the nature of public library involvement in the arts: the too frequent belief that the arts are someone else's business; the way progress depends too often on personal enthusiasm unsupported by elected members; the lack of consistency and continuity in the events organised.[26]

Indeed, provision for library involvement in the arts—as demonstrated in the survey I carried out for this chapter—is rather like the situation for the arts generally as described in Tim Challans' contribution to a National Arts and Media Strategy:

> ...in adjacent authorities it is possible to have no support for the arts in one, significant but limited provision in another, and a full-blown cultural policy in the third.[27]

In her 'End thoughts' Heeks comments that:

> the evidence gathered in the study shows three phases of library/arts

involvement: co-existence with other agencies; co-operation with other agencies; and commitment to co-ordination of effort. Very roughly we can say that a third of United Kingdom libraries...are at each of these stages.[28]

The study concludes with a chapter headed 'Agenda for development', and Heeks lists a number of items of 'outstanding business' together with suggestions about how to address this business—'Definitions; Structures; What Business are we in; Traditional roles; Current issues; Moving to new models.' I do not intend to summarise her recommendations and suggestions, for the study itself is essential reading for any librarian involved, or wishing to be involved in arts and libraries, or indeed, following Conway's persuasive arguments for any public librarian.[29]

Current Practice: Reflections Based on Survey Responses, Summer 1991
In the summer of 1991, I sent out a letter requesting information on practice and principles within their library service to all chief librarians in the UK and Eire. Responses were received from:

20 Metropolitan Boroughs
31 English Counties
6 Welsh Counties
16 London Boroughs
2 Welsh Districts
30 Scottish Districts
4 Northern Ireland Education and Library Boards
10 Irish libraries

The overall response rate was 66 per cent (only 33 per cent for Eire), and despite the general nature of the questions which makes detailed analysis impossible, this survey provides a good snapshot of the situation at that moment, and gave me useful information about the policies and practices of individual libraries. As one would expect, the responses echoed the findings of the Heeks report.

i) *Departmental structures*

One difference between Heeks and my survey was that I specifically addressed the question of the role of libraries in the arts. Heeks' question on departmental structures does not necessarily relate to libraries in those authorities where the library service forms one section of a wider department or directorate (the terminology is confusing in British local government for a 'department' can vary from being a unit of service, an autonomous administrative unit responsible for a service area, a subsidiary administrative unit responsible for a service area, or an agglomeration of administrative units into a larger multi-service unit. For clarity I shall refer to the last as 'directorates'). Thus her statement that, 'In 74 per cent of authorities the library department carried out an arts responsibility' is not accurate. From her questionnaire it is only possible to elicit that 74 per cent of the departments/directorates responsible for libraries are also responsible for the arts, and this does not mean that the library service itself is involved in the arts. In some cases, particularly in responses from Scotland, it is clear that libraries play no role in the arts, despite being within the same broader directorate as the arts service. Sometimes this is because of a lack of suitable premises, and in others there is a rueful note suggesting that departmental politics are leading to a deliberate exclusion of libraries from this area of activity. Heeks herself is aware of this possibility:

> However it frequently became clear that the different strands within such directorates were working on parallel lines, not in concert. We are reminded here of Alex Wilson's comments on many arts/library/museums directorates: 'the individual services jog along side by side without exciting new development or even integration'.[30]

The only 'rule' that can be drawn about the relationship between library involvement in arts activities and departmental structures is that where libraries and arts responsibilities are directly joined either in one independent department, or in one section of a directorate, then there is almost invariably an active involvement of libraries in the arts. In other structures—autonomous library departments, or a separate library section within a directorate—the situation ranges from taking an enthusiastic lead on the one hand to total exclusion on the other, and this seems to depend either upon the enthusiasm and drive of the chief officer, and/or upon the organizational politics of the local authority.

ii) *Levels of involvement*
Eighty-three British libraries, 76 per cent of the respondents, had either a regular programme of arts activities, or sufficiently frequent activities to be considered a regular involvement in the arts (50 per cent for Eire).

In one respect this figure is highly misleading, for it is clear that virtually every library service within the UK offers a range of children's extension activities which they do not define as arts activities, and yet which form the most significant exposure of many children to arts activities outside the school. I make the point strongly that in ignoring the significance of the arts in such activities librarians are undervaluing and underselling their own service, and this may result in a public and political perception which undervalues the service.

The programmes of activities reported range across a formally co-ordinated and structured programme such as Bedfordshire's performing arts at Leighton Buzzard, 'Wordlink' at Bedford, and fine arts at Luton; the organization of regular festivals—Buckinghamshire's and Leicestershire's annual literary festivals; and varied arts programmes integrated with the programmes of other venues and facilities—Edinburgh's, and Richmond's, Sutton's and Westminster's varied activities. An interesting variant of central co-ordination is provided in Suffolk where the County Arts Officer publishes a list of events provisionally organized for the coming year, indicating target audience, space and facilities needed, dates available, etc. Local libraries then bid for the events, making their case in competition with other local librarians within the County.

Some authorities do not organize activities centrally, but promulgate policy statements which encourage local library participation in, and organization of, arts activities—Cheshire, Berkshire, Wakefield and Waltham Forest take this approach.

In some authorities responsibility for arts activities is built in to local librarians' titles (e.g. Area Cultural Co-ordinator in Manchester), or job descriptions (e.g. Liverpool include arts activities and venue development within all community librarians' job descriptions).

Further along the scale is the permissive role which is best summed up in the response from Somerset which states that 'activities are determined by the facilities which are available and the willingness of our staff to undertake these ventures out of hours and in their own time'.

Of the 25 per cent of libraries that do not offer arts programmes, some are developing policies, as in Gwent, or are 'keeping the door open' as North Yorkshire described it. While other libraries do not participate in the arts through circumstances, or the absence of a policy, only one library service, Wiltshire, referred to a definite policy of not involving libraries in arts activities: 'the policy is to encourage self-help via grants—which have to be justified in terms of financial resources and perceived County value.'

On the other side of the scale, two authorities reported a considerable drop in arts activities owing to their financial situation. Sheffield state that:

> a direct provision of community arts activities has had to revert by and large to individual programming and offered by community library staff. The Community Arts Section which latterly became the 'Opening the Book' Unit was wound up during 1990.

Derbyshire comment that:

> Derbyshire Library Service has in the past provided a whole range of arts presentations in libraries, however, due to the effects of poll tax capping there is no arts budget in the current financial year.

iii) *Policy statements*

A number of libraries accompanied their response with a copy of their policy documents. Some of these were well-argued and detailed—as with Bedfordshire's which moves progressively from a mission statement, through a set of general objectives, to specific methods to achieve those objectives, for example:—

7. *Education and Training*
The Leisure Committee recognises that investment in education and training is vital for an ongoing and healthy arts programme in the future.

Objectives and methods.
7.1 Offer opportunities for potential audiences to experience a wide variety of art forms.
7.1.1 Establish a diverse programme of workshops, concerts, exhibitions etc.
7.1.2 Introduce children to a wide variety of arts forms through specialist activities at Leisure Services sites and service points.

Berkshire has a detailed document of 'Mission Statement and Service Aims' for the Library and Information Service, which approaches arts in libraries from the libraries' viewpoint. The section 'Culture and the Arts' will form the basis of that Department's response to the County Council's newly-adopted arts policy.

Other policy statements follow one or other of these patterns—either a corporate arts policy which includes the library's role, or into which the library's departmental policy fits; or a departmental policy which makes specific the library's objectives in arts involvement.

It must be commented that of the 83 library respondents with arts activities, 54 (65 per cent) did not mention a policy document. Since I did not specifically ask if such a document existed I do not know whether other authorities have policy documents, but in view of my request for such documents I can only presume that they either did not have policy statements, or did not see them as being important.

It is also noticeable that there is a strong correlation between libraries with a well-established policy statement and those libraries which have the most active involvement in arts activities.

Several other authorities are at present preparing, or have just prepared policies—in the case of Hillingdon bringing in the arts consultant 'Comedia' to undertake the task of drafting the policy (given the variation in the standard of policy statements, this seems an idea worth considering if arts expertise is not present within an authority). Those authorities in the process of preparing a policy statement appear to be often those where the chief librarian wishes to establish the arts as an area in which libraries should be involved as a matter of course, and who wish to expand or to protect those activities.

It must be said, however, that neither of the correlations I observed are exclusive, and Lambeth—a Borough with well established support for the arts—comment: 'arts policy is regarded as being a too constraining notion.'

iv) *The purpose of arts in libraries*
I suggested in discussion of definitions that librarians appear to take a liberal view of the arts. It is clear from the responses that they also tend to take a community-oriented view of the arts, but this is often seen as including the provision of 'high art' through the library service. Many libraries simply see the two aspects of arts provision as merging into one another, and complementing one another. As Wakefield comment:

> We are proud of our integration with our communities, and our ability to adapt to local needs, and we perceive this as our greatest strength.

Lancashire's response expresses this even more clearly:

> We do not really distinguish between the arts in general and community arts. This is not just because we have consciously decided not to deal with the 'high art' principle, but because the wider definition fits better with our concept of libraries as a community service.

Like most libraries, Gwynedd see their role as part of a wider picture, and specifically state that a major part of their role is to provide a stepping stone for local creative artists-

'through which the "artist" exhibits as he grows in stature, often outstripping our facilities and our public platform'.

A further motive for the provision of arts activities is to encourage people to use 'mainstream' library services, and many librarians make this point. I suspect that several see arts activities purely in this light, and not as a worthwhile provision *per se.* There is certainly an arguable case for this position, though like Patrick Conway[31] it is not a view I take. In my experience in Liverpool where an arts programme has been brought in over the last few years, many field librarians and clerical staff hold this view, and are reluctant to become involved in arts activities where they do not see a direct return in conventional library usage measures.

I suspect though that most librarians, myself included, have mixed motives in being involved in arts activities, and this is well summarised in Kensington and Chelsea's response:

The events and performances are aimed at:

a) bringing a new public into the library in the hope that they will become regular library users;

b) offering the arts as an extra service to existing library users;

c) encouraging people living in each area to participate as artist/es in the activities.

v) *Arts services offered*

In the remainder of this chapter I intend to glance briefly at the forms of library participation in arts activities, drawing attention to some of the more unusual or instructive examples. This list is by no means comprehensive, and must be considered alongside Heeks and Hinton.[32]

It is a truism that is sometimes overlooked that every public library provides an arts service simply through the lending of creative literature, and of material to inform and support individuals in their arts activities. The wider range of materials often lent by libraries extends this service, and several libraries make the point that they maintain collections such as play sets and music scores which directly support the work of organizations in music and drama. Surrey mention particularly their Collectors' Library as supporting fine arts.

Virtually every library maintains a local 'what's on' noticeboard, and several organize this information into a local diary of events. Lists of local societies are held at almost every library, and several libraries go beyond this to publish, or co-operate in publishing, a list of local arts and other organizations. A smaller number collate and publish a regular list of arts activities in the area.

Library buildings are themselves a resource, and frequently these are used to support arts activities in a variety of ways. Many libraries have purpose-built or adapted meetings/exhibitions rooms—Manchester has several of the former, and Liverpool of the latter—which are used, either free of charge, or for a nominal fee, by local arts groups. Sometimes this facility is rather more than just an open space—as at the Mitchell Library in Glasgow where there is a formal gallery facility. Three libraries in the Isle of Wight are also provided with gallery facilities. In Dun Laoghaire (Eire) music practice rooms, including a piano, are incorporated. In Skelmersdale (Lancashire) the library was planned with an integrated arts centre, and the Community Arts Worker for West Lancashire is based there. Similarly, the Community Arts Project is housed in Haltwhistle Library in Northumberland. In Leigh (Wigan Metropolitan Borough Council) the Derby Rooms and Turnpike Gallery offer a high quality venue for both community and 'high arts' activities.

Of course, the absence of separate rooms does not prohibit arts activities, and exhibitions of local artists and organizations take place in many libraries. It may in this case be difficult to stage other activities, and Kerry County

Library (Eire) refer to the curtailment of dance and drama occasions. Gateshead, seeing the limitations of facilities in libraries, decided to accept the challenge and work extensively out in the community. Of course, provision of space is a valuable resource, but use of this resource need only involve the library in little more than acting as a booking agency. However, those libraries with a regular pattern of arts activities go beyond this and proactively organize arts events and activities.

Of the responses I received, by far the greatest number of libraries have a strength, as you might expect, in literature related activities. This finding appears to contradict Heeks finding that only 19 per cent of librarians felt that literature should be the main arts responsibility of public libraries.[33] In my survey 69 (58 per cent) of the responses detailed literature-based activities and events. West Sussex commented that their arts events 'lean heavily towards literature', and this leaning is borne out in several other libraries by the arts programmes and lists of events organized. Indeed, many libraries which organize nothing else do organize literature-based events.

These activities include promotion of purposive reading through schemes like 'Well Worth Reading' (written up at length, most recently in Kempthorne,[34]) and focus on various types of literature (crime fiction at North Tyneside, feminist books at Liverpool). Several libraries take part in local literature festivals (Cardiff in South Glamorgan, Bedfordshire, Leicestershire, South Tyneside, Surrey), others have storytelling as a specialism, organizing workshops or festivals (Havering). Many libraries mention authors' visits as a regular occurrence.

Support for creative writing is detailed by several libraries. The most comprehensive scheme was that formerly operated in Sheffield, 'Opening the Book'. Elements of this are reflected most extensively in Liverpool ('Writing and Liverpool Libraries') and Bradford ('In Your Own Write').

There are writing development officers in Bedfordshire, Humberside, and Northamptonshire (in association with East Midland Arts). Writers in residence are present in libraries in Cheshire, East Lothian, Perth, Staffordshire, Glamorgan, and (in association with schools) in South Tyneside. Hamilton and Cheshire, amongst others, support writers' groups. Aberdeen has writing advice desks. Paisley organize writers' weekends.

Several responses mention drama being staged in libraries—by the Northumberland Theatre Company, or Wigan's Pit Prop Theatre, or many other community based drama groups.

All this list, as I suggested earlier, ignores the substantial provision made for children within the field of literature.

Reviewing this literature-related activity I must confess to being puzzled by Peggy Heeks' 19 per cent figure, which I must regard as unreliable. What is of serious concern is that Alastair Niven bases on this figure part of the argument of his Arts Council Discussion Document on literature.[35]

Activities involving ethnic minority cultures are widespread: Bradford's Caribbean Week; Blackburn's Asian Writer in Residence (Lancashire); the Temba Black Theatre's residency in Gloucestershire; a multi-cultural project in Cardiff (South Glamorgan) funded by an urban programme grant; Westminster's Community Dance Week; the Islington Festival, and so on.

Disadvantaged people form the focus of some libraries' activities:—Bradford's 'leisure for life'; Havering's targeting of the elderly, handicapped, single parents, and deaf children; Lambeth's general policy of support for the disadvantaged, and Strathkelvin's and Derbyshire's concentration on the elderly.

Children's activities, as I have said, have not usually been detailed in the responses I received. Arts activities for young people that are mentioned are the teenage literature promotion 'Culture shock' in Northamptonshire, the many activities focused on JILL in Renfrew, Trafford's promotion of 'family-type events' and children's activities focusing on workshops and discussions of works of art, and the conversion of Old Trafford Children's Library which 'has recently had a major conversion to incorporate a "whole world" theme which has been done in conjunction with the Art and Architecture Award by the RSA and some funding from North West Arts'. Sandwell used arts development funding to train librarians in working creatively with children.

A number of other specializations are listed by libraries, Welsh and Irish libraries, and to a lesser extent Scottish libraries, indicating that a major focus of support was their national culture, language, and literature. (Dyfed issue a most attractive magazine of library arts activities in Welsh entitled *Nod*—meaning 'target'). This includes publications and activities focusing on local history, and this is a field in which many libraries throughout the UK are active, and one which I do not intend to detail.

Music recitals are organized by Lancashire, Liverpool, Westminster, Western Education and Library Board, and North Yorkshire ('Live Music Now'). Picture loans of works of art purchased from local artists are offered by East Kilbride and Roscommon (Eire) libraries; and Kirkcaldy take part in FACET—the marketing of arts of the disabled in Scotland.

A wide variety of workshops and talks or demonstrations by artists are organized, amongst which the most unusual are stained glass, and map-making in Devon, and a banner-making project in Strathkelvin. Angus organize guided walks, talks, and trips on local history and culture, while Midlothian operate 'literary buses' to the homes of noted Scottish writers.

Many of the arts activities are organized in conjunction with a network of groups. Some of these networks are formalized, as in the Arts Associations in several Scottish towns, which are in fact associations of local arts organizations, not agents of the Arts Council as are English Arts Associations. Some English and Welsh libraries work with similar bodies, e.g. the Gloucestershire County Arts Forum, Redbridge Arts Council (whose two workers are employed in the library), Waltham Forest Arts Council. Several libraries also take part in locally-organized community and arts festivals—Wexford, Wolverhampton, Edinburgh, Chichester, West Sussex, Gateshead, and so on, Sunderland organized thematic festivals ('Festival of the Air', 'Waterfront Festival').

A number of libraries also give grants directly to local arts organizations (Wiltshire, South Glamorgan, Wandsworth). Some sponsor exhibitions or prizes (Barking and Dagenham, Hillingdon, Isle of Wight, Knowsley, Midlothian); others will offer advice and support.

A small number of library departments also lend equipment to arts groups (Aberdeen, Salford). Northumberland County Library organize a free transport service to the Hexham Arts Centre from their rural mobile library routes.

More 'off the wall' activities seem to be rare, though Chris Meade (formerly of Sheffield, now Principal Arts Development Officer in Birmingham) argued strongly the need for more unstructured and imaginative approaches to arts work in an address to a day school, 'Arts in action: a practical guide to promoting art through libraries' organized by the Community Services Group—North West and the Merseyside Public Libraries Training Co-operative on 16th May 1991.

Conclusions

From this brief extract from the survey responses I received it is clear that there is a wealth of enthusiasm and energy going into arts activities in libraries. However, I must echo Peggy Heeks' concern at the scarcity of policy statements, and of formal structures involving libraries with arts activities and policies both within their own council, and within the community. In particular, I have to voice my concern at the failure, over 20 years and more, of the Library Association to give a clear lead in emphasising the importance of the arts to libraries.

Wilson spoke of a new profession emerging—that of arts administrator.[36] This profession is now well-established, and because of the direct community involvement in the arts is assuming a high-profile, and consequently significant role in the local authority. This high-profile role is not a comfortable one for a chief librarian to espouse and undertake, and many librarians shy away from so political a field. However, if chief librarians are not willing to take on such a role I believe that the gradual recession of power from chief librarians, which seems to me to characterize post-reorganization local government, will continue. This powershift has seen a diminution in the value placed upon the library service by councillors, and a consequent lessening of the proportion of resources awarded to libraries. This question may well become even more significant if the proposed local government restructuring returns several libraries to unitary district councils—councils who may already have an arts officer, and certainly will have a leisure services officer already in post. The librarian may well be in competition with such an officer for the directorship of a wider leisure services department. If the librarian is unwilling to take on a broader view of the role of the library, then he or she will stand little chance of being appointed to such a directorship. It is not only for reason of belief therefore that librarians should embrace the significance of the arts in the library's role, but from the baser motive of the maintenance of the status and importance of the librarian, and hence of the service he or she manages.

In the final analysis, the question for librarians is posed by Anthony Sargent in a discussion document on the national arts and media strategy:

Whether libraries are just places to borrow elderly books, or are places to dream, to be inspired, and to unlock the imagination from its daytime prison.[37]

References

1. CATCHESIDE, P. *What Business are we in?* (A paper addressed to staff as part of the discussion over departmental restructuring). Liverpool: Liverpool City Council, Libraries and Arts Department, 1990.

2. ASSOCIATION OF METROPOLITAN AUTHORITIES. *Libraries and cultural policy: a discussion document.* London: Association of Metropolitan Authorities, 1990.

3. HEEKS, P. *Public libraries and the arts: an evolving partnership.* London: The Library Association, 1989.

4. HINTON, B. *Marshalled arts: a handbook for arts in libraries.* Newcastle-under-Lyme: AAL Publishing, 1990.

5. UNESCO. *The public library manifesto,* 1972 edition. In: *Guidelines for public libraries.* Prepared for the IFLA Section of Public Libraries. Paris: K. G. Saur, 1986. (IFLA Publications 36).

6. MINISTRY OF EDUCATION. *Standards of public library service in England and Wales.* London: HMSO, 1962. (The Bourdillon Report).

7. JOLLIFFE, H. *Arts centre adventure.* Swindon: Swindon Borough Council, 1968.

8. JOLLIFFE, H. *Public library extension activities.* London: The Library Association, 1962.

9. WILSON, A. Practical implications of a permanent programme, In: D. Gerard, *ed. Libraries and the arts: a symposium of papers and discussions at the Seminar held in the College of Librarianship Wales, September 1-6, 1969.* London: Clive Bingley, 1970.

10. DEPARTMENT OF EDUCATION AND SCIENCE. *Public libraries and cultural activities.* Joint Report by the Library Advisory Councils of England and Wales. London: HMSO, 1975. (Library Information Series No. 5).

11. HARE, G. Visual arts in a library setting, In: Sheffield Conference, *Libraries and the arts: in action or inaction. Proceedings of the Sheffield Conference, 1985.* Sheffield: Sheffield City Libraries, 1987.

12. COLEMAN, P. *Libraries and community arts.* London: Arts Council of Great Britain/Library Association Working Party, 1983.

13. SHEFFIELD CONFERENCE. *Libraries and the arts: in action or inaction. Proceedings of the Sheffield Conference, 1985.* Sheffield: Sheffield City Libraries, 1987.

14. HEEKS, P. *Public libraries and the arts: an evolving partnership.* London: The Library Association, 1989.

15. HINTON, B. *Marshalled arts: a handbook for arts in libraries.* Newcastle-under-Lyme: AAL Publishing, 1990.

16. DOLAN, J. Review of *Marshalled arts: a handbook for arts in libraries, Public Library Journal,* 6 (3), 1991, 77.

17. COUNCIL OF REGIONAL ARTS ASSOCIATIONS. *Constitution.* London: Council of Regional Arts Associations, 1988.

18. DEPARTMENT OF EDUCATION AND SCIENCE. *Public libraries and cultural activities.* Joint Report by the Library Advisory Councils of England and Wales. London: HMSO, 1975. (Library Information Series No. 5).

19. OLDHAM METROPOLITAN BOROUGH COUNCIL. *Next..........Arts development in Oldham, 1990-92.* Oldham: Oldham Metropolitan Borough Council, Leisure Services Department, 1989.

20. MESSENGER, M. Even more than bread, In: B. Hinton, *ed. Marshalled arts: a handbook for arts in libraries.* Newcastle-under-Lyme: AAL Publishing, 1990.

21. LONDON STRATEGIC POLICY UNIT. RECREATION AND ARTS GROUP. *The nature of community arts.* London: Greater London Arts Association, n.d.

22. ASSOCIATION OF METROPOLITAN AUTHORITIES. *Libraries and cultural policy: a discussion document.* London: Association of Metropolitan Authorities, 1990.

23. CONWAY, P. Community arts—outmoded concept or of value to library workers in the 1990s, In: B. Hinton *ed. Marshalled arts: a handbook for arts in libraries.* Newcastle-under-Lyme: AAL Publishing, 1990.

24. CHESHIRE COUNTY COUNCIL. *Strategies for community arts development in Cheshire: a summary.* Chester: Cheshire County Council, n.d.

25. DONEGAL COUNTY COUNCIL. *Programme for the development of the arts.* Letterkenny, Co. Donegal, Eire: Donegal County Council, 1989.

26. HEEKS, P. *Public libraries and the arts: an evolving partnership.* London: The Library Association, 1989, 66.

27. CHALLANS, T. A review and prospects, In Arts Council, National Arts and Media Strategy Unit. *Local authorities and the arts: discussion document 16.* London: Arts Council, 1991.

28. HEEKS, P. *Public libraries and the arts: an evolving partnership.* London: The Library Association, 1989, 71-2.

29. CONWAY, P. Community arts—outmoded concept or of value to library workers in the 1990s, In: B. Hinton *ed. Marshalled arts: a handbook for arts in libraries.* Newcastle-under-Lyme: AAL Publishing, 1990.

30. HEEKS, P. *Public libraries and the arts: an evolving partnership.* London: The Library Association, 1989, 15.

31. CONWAY, P. Community arts—outmoded concept or of value to library workers in the 1990s, In: B. Hinton *ed. Marshalled arts: a handbook for arts*

in libraries. Newcastle-under-Lyme: AAL Publishing, 1990.

32. HEEKS, P. *Public libraries and the arts: an evolving partnership.* London: The Library Association, 1989.
HINTON, B. *ed. Marshalled arts: a handbook for arts in libraries.* Newcastle-under-Lyme: AAL Publishing, 1990.

33. HEEKS, P. *Public libraries and the arts: an evolving partnership.* London: The Library Association, 1989, 29.

34. KEMPTHORNE, B. Still well worth reading about: well worth reading— the third chapter, *Public Library Journal,* 6 (6), Nov/Dec 1991, 157-161.

35. NIVEN, A. *ed. Discussion document on literature.* London: Arts Council, 1991. (Arts Council National Arts and Media Strategy).

36. WILSON, A. Practical implications of a permanent programme, In: D. Gerard, *ed. Libraries and the arts: a symposium of papers and discussions at the Seminar held in the College of Librarianship Wales, September 1-6, 1969.* London: Clive Bingley, 1970.

37. SARGENT, A. Views from a big city, In: Arts Council, National Arts and Media Strategy Unit. *Local authorities and the arts: discussion document 16.* London: Arts Council, 1991.

Appendix 1

 City of Liverpool

Neville Carrick, B.A., L.A.,
Director, Libraries and Arts Department
Brown, Picton and Hornby Libraries,
William Brown Street,
Liverpool L3 8EW.
Direct Line: 051-225 5419
Fax: 051-207 1342   Telex: 629500

When calling or telephoning please ask for Mr. P. R. Catcheside

Your ref
Our ref   G25/PAD/JB
Date   16th December, 1991

Dear Colleague,

Community Arts in Libraries

I am writing the chapter Community Arts in Libraries for the planned CSG manual on Community Librarianship.

I am anxious to include as wide a variety of experiences and approaches as possible, and would be grateful if you could answer the following few questions for me.

1) Do you have a programme of arts presentation in libraries?
2) Is your programme aimed at:
    a) Bringing arts to local audiences?
    b) If so what kind of arts?
3) Is your programme aimed at encouraging local participation in arts activities?
    If so what kind of arts?
4) Does your library have a particular strength/specialism in community arts? If so can you please send details and a contact name so I can follow up the information.

I would be glad to receive copies of policy documents and programmes relating to your arts activities.

Yours sincerely,

P. R. Catcheside,
Principal Assistant Director.

CHAPTER NINE

FICTION SERVICES

Deborah Goodall and Margaret Kinnell

Fiction Services

Introduction

It is perhaps surprising to find a chapter on fiction services in a book primarily concerned with considering the information needs of community groups. It is certainly challenging to try and shift the emphasis when looking at community information services, that is, to focus on the 'community' rather than the 'information' aspects of the service. The aim of this chapter is to illustrate that public library fiction services can, and do, make a positive impact on the local community, particularly, but not exclusively, on those members who have special needs. As Margaret Drabble recently argued,

> Novels are not, as all who read and write them know, a frivolity, a luxury, an indulgence. They are a means of comprehending and experiencing and extending our world and our vision. They can exercise the imagination, they can widen our sympathies, they can issue dire and necessary warnings, they can suggest solutions to social problems, they are the raw material of the historians of tomorrow.[1]

Of all public library services the community information service is one which most reflects the ethos of the library authority, and this was also evident when a selection of library authorities were surveyed to provide background information for this chapter on their fiction services to special groups. Whilst one or two, rather apologetically, felt that they could not provide anything of interest:-

> . . . although we do a great deal of special services work with all of the groups

> ... I'm not sure that we have anything currently which quite matches your description ... [2]

—most seized the opportunity to reassess their services from another point of view and were able to identify appropriate services and projects. For example, there were Sheffield's Write Back and Opening the Book initiatives, which were seen as 'focusing on support for creative writing ... and making... an innovative contribution to libraries' support for and promotion of fiction.'[3]

The main problem facing fiction services in community service terms is that they are generally considered as separate, if not mutually exclusive, services. This dichotomy is compounded by the fact that most fiction stock tends to be distributed to special needs groups in the community as part of the general library service, and thus does not necessarily come under the direct supervision of the community (information) librarian, but rather fiction provision is managed through a number of differing and disparate channels. In essence, fiction services to special needs groups are no different to 'ordinary' fiction provision, excepting a difference in format, that is books in large print or on audio cassette, and/or service delivery, because so-called 'special needs groups' still have the same variety and depth of fiction needs as everyone else in the community.

So, rather than describing the approaches taken by individual library authorities, fiction services will be considered in this chapter essentially in terms of provision for specific community groups, together with some examples of community-wide initiatives.

Adult Literacy Services
Fiction has an undeniable input into adult literacy services, particularly as such services should be responsive to customer needs regarding materials. There is a continuing need for assistance to those who have problems with adult

literacy and basic numeracy skills; one estimate is of approximately two million adults with literacy problems.[4] A number of librarians surveyed noted the difficulties in finding good suppliers of relevant fiction at an appropriate level and subject interest to serve the needs of those with little confidence and poor reading skills, though the range has increased in the last few years.

In Staffordshire, Hanley Library has produced a resources guide, incorporating an index, to Adult Basic Education (ABE) fiction, which is aimed at staff, public, and ABE tutors and pupils.[5] The guide is divided into three main sections: beginner readers, developing readers and advanced readers. Books are entered into a particular section according to criteria such as word density, language, print size, length of book and illustrations, and a brief description is also provided. What is particularly useful is that to facilitate the effective identification and choice of suitable reading materials, a representative sample of print and language taken from each book is also included as an integral part of the guide.

An innovative approach to raising the profile of reading and improving literacy in the community, targeted towards those groups who are over-represented amongst the total numbers of people who lack reading skills, is currently being planned by Birmingham City Council.[6] The action research project, entitled Skills for Life, which forms part of a Community Care Special Action Project on Reading, aims to raise the profile of reading in the City. The justification for this project is that, despite the advances in visual communications, the printed word remains the main form of communication and instruction and so the key to acquiring other skills is the ability to read. There was a feeling that, although the current concern with literacy is valid, it has tended to focus upon methods of teaching (particularly for children), rather than tackling the wider and more pervasive problem, that is, the motivation for reading: people increasingly feel that they are 'too busy to read'.

As a way of tackling these problems, and encouraging people to simply make time for reading, an innovative promotion, entitled Why Read?, is being planned for 1992. Essentially, the message of the promotion is that reading is a fundamental skill for life and a unique pathway to information and imagination. It will be aimed particularly at teenagers and adults in the workplace and at home, using visually striking leaflets, posters and 'taster' booklets which will be piloted in projects with local firms and users of Council services. For example, promotional material giving answers to the question 'why read?' could suggest all the reasons and possibilities whether informational, recreational or educational and could include people of influence—pop stars, sports personalities, community leaders, politicians—giving their reasons. There are plans to appoint a Reader in Residence, and it is also hoped to regenerate the reading habit by taking the campaign out into factories and companies. One way to do this could be by encouraging firms to sponsor 'lucky bags' of reading chosen by, say, a famous personality. After reading the contents of the bags each recipient would be encouraged to respond and give feedback, either by writing or through discussion, about the experience. Bags could be swapped, and eventually groups could put their own bags together, to be exchanged and discussed.

As well as developing new ventures along the lines of those suggested above, there are plans to further promote work which is already being undertaken in Birmingham, for example, the Library Services' Early Literacy Projects and Parents' Reading Groups. A new service which has recently been introduced is Words on Wheels, a mobile library which promotes the value of reading to children under five and their parents and carers. As well as displaying books, toys and educational games for young children it also provides information for parents and carers, and offers activities such as story sessions, workshops and talks.

What is most attractive about Birmingham City Council's initiative is that it is Council wide. Although the Library Service will inevitably play a leading role, it is hoped that this wide-ranging approach will ensure that all Council services promote the necessity, value, and pleasure, of reading to the whole community.

Children and Young People

Encouraging the reading habit in children has always been a primary concern of public library services. And it has been shown, unsurprisingly, that young people who read are more likely to be members of their public library, with parents who are also library users.[7] Linking children's reading to active library membership is therefore an important means of helping to promote reading. However, there has been increasing concern recently at the standards of reading being achieved in schools, and this concern is mirrored in a fresh debate on the role of children's library services. The welcome decision of the Library and Information Services Council to set up a Working Party on Library Services for Children and Young People should enable important questions to be addressed, questions to do with existing provision and future needs, and the impact of educational change on the role of children's library services.

Children aged between 0-sixteen account for around 20 per cent of the population and therefore constitute a significant proportion of the community; their individual needs for fiction differ tremendously, as they display a wide variety of different characteristics, abilities, interests and needs. Importantly, they also depend on parents and other carers in their early years so that any library service for children needs to work not only with children directly, but also with and to the adults responsible for them. As is demonstrated in the Library Association's Guidelines, *Children and young people*, it is therefore essential that when selecting and providing fiction for children a considered selection policy is formulated and agreed, to meet the needs of individual children, categories of children—including the *whole* community, not users alone—and to answer the enquiries of parents and others.[8] Reading fiction is an important means to developing the reading skills which children require if they are to succeed at school—so that developing and implementing effective book selection is a prime function of a public library service for children. In a recent study of five library services, it was found that each of the library authorities had developed selection procedures unique to their situation, however a common problem was the lack of policy on collection building as an adjunct to the selection of individual titles.[9] There was found to be a need for collections as a whole to be properly planned, for stock purchase to be co-ordinated between service points and to ensure that stock revision was a continuing exercise.

The importance of providing and promoting fiction for children and young people through public libraries has been further highlighted by two reports on readership which looked forward to the 1990s and showed how print-runs and spending on books have declined in real terms since 1981. The Scottish Arts Council's *Readership report*[10] and the Young Report on *Book retailing in the 1990s*[11] stress that libraries have an important role in fostering a reading culture, at a time when as one teenager said, 'it is so tempting to watch TV instead of sitting down reading a book'.[12]

Many of the published studies of children's library services have focused on methods of promoting books to children and young adults, rather than the less glamorous yet essential problems of identifying needs, and developing and managing collections for children in order to ensure there is something worth promoting. This is not however the case when looking at public libraries' own in-house interests in investigating their children's services. In a British National Bibliography Research Fund study of research initiatives undertaken by public libraries, educational institutions and the book trade, we found a commendable range of studies being undertaken by public library services to improve the management of their services for children. Sadly, most of these studies go unreported in the professional press. Two examples are Gloucestershire's development of 'Teen-extra' sections in libraries and Northamptonshire's feasibility study of the better use of the public library service by schools, undertaken by a teacher seconded to work with the library service. Other work included the monitoring of separate teenage provision by Warwickshire Libraries; a study of the books, magazines and newspapers read by 11-16 year-olds by Dorset Library Service; an investigation of the attitudes and reading habits of 13-16 year-olds when starting up teenage provision County wide by Nottinghamshire Libraries; and a study of teenagers' patterns of library use by Knowsley Libraries. The large number of frequent, small scale investigations by public librarians to gauge local needs and interests was a particular feature of our study and highlights the clear commitment of public libraries to identifying and providing for young people's reading needs through innovative projects.[13]

It is doubly unfortunate that so little is generally known of these local initiatives. First, there is clearly a need to pool knowledge so that other librarians may benefit from the findings of in-house management studies and, secondly, it is vital that public library services are given credit for the work they are doing and are publicly recognised as partners in national initiatives. The need for a higher profile for public library services is exemplified in two recent national promotional campaigns for literacy and reading with young people, neither of which featured the role of public libraries in their initial book trade publicity. The 99 by 99 Campaign aims to ensure that, by 1999, 99 per cent of children leave school with adequate literacy, and Children's Book Week for 1992 aims to 'promote reading as an enjoyable pastime for children, rather than to promote literacy *per see...*'. While promotion to and by schools was clearly noted, there was no mention of liaison with public library services in these press notices.[14]

Despite such a lack of publicity for their innovative work, there continues to be considerable concern by public librarians at the transition from children's reading to adult fiction—the point at which many readers are lost to public libraries. Provision for teenagers is a vexed question; whether or not to offer separate collections, or even separate libraries, to encourage reading continues to be a live issue. The experience of JILL, the teenage service provided by Renfrew Library Service, would seem to suggest that a clearly targeted, specialist service for young people does indeed encourage greater use and meets both the information and reading needs of a higher proportion of teenagers.[15]

Amongst those library authorities sampled when writing this chapter we also found an interesting number of options described. For example, Croydon provided Young Adult Plus collections in either the children's or adult sections of the library[16] and in Coventry a small, but separately and attractively shelved, Teenage Section gives young adults a definite focus to their reading. In both cases, these sections consist mainly of fiction but also include some non-fiction on relevant topics such as careers, fashion and sport. Not surprisingly, most libraries noted the popularity of paperback stock for this type of collection.

A recent pilot project in Lincolnshire has involved stocking graphic novels in the teenage section of Boston Public Library to ascertain whether this will boost teenage issues and the number of teenage members.[17] The service was publicised in the local press and on posters inside the library and use has been monitored by questionnaires, issue counts, records of new teenage borrowers, etc.

Services to Hospitals, Homes and Day Centres

One of the most significant areas of growth in public library services in recent years has been to hospitals, residential homes and other similar institutions. From 1974-84 there was an increase of 6,717 service points, and from 1985-89 a further rise of 49.5 per cent. In Dyfed, one interesting further development was the setting up of bibliotherapy sessions with the Probation Service, using library service facilities.[18]

According to Leicestershire Libraries and Information Service's publicity material, it would appear that their services for homes and day centres etc. are prompted by a realization that the enjoyment and mental stimulation provided by using libraries, reading books, listening to records and to cassettes is something most people take for granted.[19] But many, due to age or disability, may be unable to make full use of a library. Consequently, by taking library services out to hospitals, homes and day centres, opportunities are provided for direct access to library resources and library staff, for encouraging reading, for stimulating interest in new ideas or pursuits, and for improving the quality of life of clients.

This client group is very varied, including elderly people, people with visual or physical handicaps, people with hearing impairment and people with learning difficulties. Despite the variety of needs the supply of fiction to these target groups is invariably covered by the general stock in libraries, though the method of distribution varies. Services to homes and day centres, sheltered accommodation and to hospitals are commonplace and probably the most traditional and valuable way of getting fiction out into the community.

For example, Lincolnshire's deposit collection service (numbering between 30-400 items) includes 'large print, fiction and non-fiction, jigsaws, talking books, adult literacy books and reminiscence materials'.[20] Despite the wide range of materials offered, 90 per cent of the issues are for fiction material (in all formats). And even though the nature of the fiction is fairly standard it is pleasing to see that there is some concern for the effectiveness of the collections and the quality of the bookstock left in the homes, for example, romances are not just bought 'by the shelf' but consideration is given to particular authors who are known to be popular.

The actual provision of such services usually involves professional staff meeting their clients to discuss services available and to complete a profile form outlining personal requirements. Now, an emphasis is also placed on making contacts with the staff in homes, for example, to encourage greater awareness of the services offered and more useful feedback on use.

There are many aids to enable people with disabilities to continue to read and library services can act as a link between readers and the appropriate aid. A product guide which offers valuable advice in the selection of equipment is published by Oxfordshire Health Authority[21] and further information on services to people with disabilities can be found in *Library services to housebound people*.[22] Some authorities are aiming to develop a more proactive fiction service which increases clients' choice and access to fiction via booklists of recent additions, newsletters incorporating book reviews, and lists of authors who write in a similar style. In Warwickshire, the 'bulk loan collection' is actually provided by the Community Services vehicle; this allows more tailored collections to be provided which, although they are slightly smaller (between 50-150 books) than when provided by a branch library, can be changed on a monthly basis.[23]

Leicestershire Libraries and Information Service also offers to arrange library visits for groups to attend library clubs or open evenings, and activities such as reading aloud sessions in homes and centres and display material. Plenty of advice and support is provided for staff in centres and homes, including a regular newsletter—*Link-Up News*—

which promotes use of the Home Library and highlights other available resources.

Many authorities use their mobile library service to serve this client group. Such services require specialist staffing and specific bookfunds, and, ideally, a dedicated vehicle, if they are to respond fully to the needs of this client group. Regarding access, mobile libraries such as Coventry's are equipped with a steplift to enable disabled access, whilst larger authorities such as Staffordshire and Warwickshire have 'special services vehicles'.

Warwickshire's Community Services vehicle, which serves a mixture of sheltered housing and rest homes, is a good example. It has its own bookfund and is staffed by a qualified librarian and a driver-assistant—the authority's ethos being that everyone should have access to a professional librarian. The closed environment and captive audience, many of whom are very intensive readers, enable the staff to achieve some positive and personal promotion, helping readers choose books, and encouraging them to try new and contemporary authors. Although there is not much space on the vehicle for displays, the users certainly appreciate the friendly 'corner shop' nature of the service. The stock tends to be mostly fiction (about 80 per cent), and mostly large print (about two-thirds). Issues, not surprisingly, are heavily weighted towards fiction—about nine out of ten books.

Housebound Readers

"I can't get out of the house, but I can travel around the world in a book."

The housebound readers' service is for people who are confined to their own homes and who do not have anyone to go to the library for them. It is often provided in partnership by volunteers from organizations such as the Women's Royal Voluntary Service (WRVS) and Age Concern, as well as local community groups, and obviously the social contact is an important aspect of the service.

However, as the Library Association's *Guidelines for library services to people who are housebound* state:

> Staffing provision should start from the premise that users of housebound library services require access to trained staff in the same way that general library users do, and this should not be denied to them simply because this level of service might be difficult or expensive to provide.[24]

Equally, housebound services should not operate in isolation from the rest of the library service, and the materials available to other users, including for example ethnic minority language books, should be made available to the housebound.

In Leicestershire, the housebound service is enhanced by the *Library Link* newsletter which is produced four times a year. It contains lists of recent titles in large print and books in cassette format, information on benefits, details of activities, reviews and feature articles etc.; this gives an added professionalism to the voluntary service.

In Staffordshire, as well as providing the traditional personal delivery service, the housebound service is enhanced by monthly 'get togethers', or Library Clubs, held in libraries and with transport provided by the WRVS or other volunteers. Although not specifically aimed at fiction provision, the majority of books borrowed at these sessions is fiction. In Warwickshire, the service is supplemented with a free request service.

Partially Sighted

Again, a traditional focus, but also an increasingly well-served group in the community. As well as large print books, pleasingly supported in Essex by a large print Large Print Books catalogue,[25] increasing use is made of talking books which are stocked in libraries, distributed in mobile libraries and special services vehicles and also through the post. The range of literature available on cassettes has increased to include popular fiction, and material in Indic languages, as well as the classics. In Warwickshire, the talking bookstock is promoted through the talking newspaper which includes a selection of additions to stock and also some reviews.

Many library authorities have a Kurzweil reading machine or a closed-circuit television system which magnifies print and images. In Birmingham, this equipment is used frequently by the Eye to Eye group who meet regularly in Balsall Heath Library, which is also embarking on providing talking magazines, Braille labels on talking books, and producing a supplement to a talking newspaper. Again, examples of simple, yet effective, ways of improving services to a special needs group.[26]

Services to Prisons

Often overlooked in considering services to the community, services to prisons play a vital part in the rehabilitation of some of the most difficult members of society. The needs of prisoners largely reflect those of the population at large, and the range and level of library stock should therefore be equivalent to that of a good public branch library. However, as the Home Office requires that the Prison Education Officer should have managerial responsibility for the library service, the link between libraries and education is clearly defined and there is naturally a strong educational emphasis in the stock and its use.

The role played by fiction is considerable, through support for basic education, and the encouragement of recreational reading. The public library service provides invaluable professional advice and support for prison libraries, support which includes the regular exchange of collections, particularly important where there are small collections of 5,000 items or less.[27] The range of demand for materials can be very wide and a flexible request service is needed, so that, for example, if a book arrives when a prisoner has been moved to another establishment it is sent on via the local public library service. Books become a lifeline to the outer world, just as they do for housebound readers, and the prison library service enables prisoners to maintain their contact with society.

The Prison Libraries Group Study School for 1991 had as its theme 'Window on the world' and explored the development of the arts in prisons and the contribution of library services. The role of reading is central to this concern, with fiction provision and the encouragement of creative writing by prisoners an important means of encouraging this. For example, Lewes Prison has a writer-in-residence to foster creative work by prisoners.

Fiction in the Community

The section on Literacy discussed Birmingham's focus on the value of reading in the community, and this community-orientated approach to fiction provision is also apparent in other authorities. Sheffield's Opening the Book festival was made possible by the work that had already been done with Sheffield people through the Write Back scheme, established in the mid-Eighties with the appointment of Community Arts Co-ordinators.[28] This scheme embraces new approaches to publication and to public support for creative writing.

Originally, the scheme started with Write Back boards so that readers could share their reviews of books and poems; stories, plays, articles and even cartoons were also encouraged. Now, Write Back libraries offer writers and readers an important point of contact and also continue to provide practical support in the form of word processors for use by the community, plus free leaflets and lists of local magazines and writing groups. As well as actually publishing books by local people, Write Back produces one-off publications by photocopying manuscripts and encourages writers to produce multiple copies of their work by offering cost price photocopying facilities. Work is also displayed on Write Back boards in various Sheffield libraries. This community ethos was also apparent in the mission statement for Opening The Book. 'A unique festival of reading and writing' organized chiefly by Sheffield Libraries, it was built upon the developmental work undertaken by the Community Arts Section to open up libraries as places of creative activity, in that the festival aimed, among other things, to 'increase the self confidence of people in Sheffield in how they read and communicate' and to 'offer ways to bring together isolated readers'. It is interesting to note the emphasis on the reader—a report on the festival defines its uniqueness as stemming from the way that Sheffield Libraries, as a library authority, 'were able to raise the status of the reader as well as the writer'.

It is also possible effectively to target sections of the community. In Warwickshire, a literary competition for people over 60 ran from September 1991 to February 1992.[29] The competition themes focused on reminiscence-type topics such as 'market day' and 'my corner shop' which would encourage creative writing based on real life situations and memories. The event was organised by Warwickshire Library Service and Age Concern, and so allowed the library service to achieve a long-term goal of working with voluntary and statutory organizations, and not in isolation. Obviously, there are benefits with funding if promotions are shared, but there are also opportunities to share experience and make contacts.

Another recent initiative is Writing in Merseyside. This is a writers' directory with a difference: there is no logical sequence, or subject index, but rather it aims to raise awareness of facilities and resources and generate enthusiasm—to 'provide inspiration as well as information'. The directory was first published in 1986 as a result of co-operation between Liverpool Libraries and Arts, the University of Liverpool and Canning Street Adult Centre. It is reported that 6,000 copies were distributed free via libraries and colleges, and its impact was tremendous with people joining classes and existing workshops and going on to become tutors.[30]

225

Clearly, the library service played a major role in this project and in 1988 a Writing Liaison Officer responsible for Writing Activities in Liverpool Libraries (WALL) was appointed to exploit the potential for broader community development of the library service. The Writing Liaison Officer acts as a 'catalyst for community arts in libraries' who can determine the needs of writers and potential writers and provide appropriate services and facilities such as access to word processors, cheap photocopying and opportunities to reach an audience, etc. Writing workshops have also developed, together with programmes of events and successful publications, showing the value of links between writers and their local community through libraries.[31]

As noted in Chapter Eight, many library authorities have made literature promotion a particular strength, often in conjunction with local arts associations and in co-operation with other organizations. One of the best documented is the Well Worth Reading fiction promotion which involves co-operation between library authorities, bookshops, library suppliers, publishers, the media and the regional Arts Association. Dorset, Hampshire and West Sussex were given a pump priming grant of £10,000 by Southern Arts and they also struck deals with other organizations to keep their campaign going over the three years following their first funding. The story of how the initial promotion became a national, commercially viable enterprise which marketed reading lists to other library authorities makes fascinating reading.[32] It serves also to emphasize that community-orientated fiction services require professionalism of a high order and adequate resourcing if they are to produce publicity materials that compete effectively with other media. Well Worth Reading's latest promotions are Better Read Than Dead and Voices from Europe—their fourth marketing drive. One difficulty, however, is the inevitable distance between the campaign initiators and the local community when a national fiction promotion is mounted.

There will always be the need for librarians to complement nationally produced publicity with locally relevant materials and events. The Leicestershire Literature Festival is an excellent example of a successful, locally led arts event which brought authors and the community together and developed links with special needs groups such as writers with physical disabilities and students enrolled in Leicestershire's adult basic education scheme. As well as lectures and 'meet the author' sessions, workshops encouraged creative writing and other activities. Again, sponsorship from local organizations was important, while the commitment from library staff throughout the county was essential to the smooth running of a complex series of events.[33]

Fiction In and For the Community

It is appropriate in concluding this chapter to return to Margaret Drabble's argument that fiction is important to the community, and that as a means of comprehending our world and our vision, novels serve a significant function within our culture. Serving the community's best interests has always been the role of public library services; their function in the promotion of fiction reading continues to be significant, with fiction accounting for around 60 per cent of all books issued. We have attempted to show how special groups within the community are at present being served through public library fiction services and to indicate the significance of developing such services.

References

1. DRABBLE, M. Foreword, In: M. Kinnell ed., *Managing fiction in libraries*, London: Library Association Publishing, 1991, vii.

2. Personal communication with Martin Palmer, Area Librarian, Essex County Libraries.

3. Personal communication with Alan Beevers, Executive Director, Sheffield Information 2000.

4. ADULT LITERACY AND BASIC SKILLS UNIT. *Literacy and*

numeracy: evidence from the national child development unit. London: ALBSU, 1983.

5. Personal communication with Pat Phelps, Leader, Fiction Group, Staffordshire Libraries, Arts and Archives.

6. Personal communication and interview with Chris Meade, Principal Officer, Arts Development, Birmingham City Council Library Services.

7. CARTER, C. Young people and books: a review of research into young people's reading habits, *Journal of Librarianship*, 18 (1) Jan, 1986, 1-22.

8. LIBRARY ASSOCIATION. *Children and young people: Library Association guidelines for public library services.* London: Library Association Publishing, 1991.

9. LEWINS, H. Fiction for children in libraries, In: M. Kinnell ed. *Managing fiction in libraries*, London: Library Association Publishing, 1991, 63.

10. WORKING PARTY OF THE LITERATURE COMMITTEE OF THE SCOTTISH ARTS COUNCIL. *Readership report.* Edinburgh: Scottish Arts Council, 1989.

11. YOUNG, A. *Book retailing in the 1990s.* London: Booksellers Association, 1987.

12. WORKING PARTY OF THE LITERATURE COMMITTEE OF THE SCOTTISH ARTS COUNCIL. *Readership report.* Edinburgh: Scottish Arts Council, 1989, 5.

13. KINNELL, M., PAIN-LEWINS, H. and STEVENSON, J. *Book acquisition and use by young people.* London: BNB Research Fund, 1989. (Report No. 39).

14. *The Bookseller* 3 Jan, 1992, 5.

15. NEILL, L. and JOHNSON, I. Information for unemployed teenagers, *International Review of Children's Literature and Librarianship*, 6(2) 1991.

16. Personal communication with Adie Scott, Principal Librarian, Croydon Libraries.

17. Personal communication with Alison Hodson, Librarian, Special Needs Groups, Lincolnshire County Council Recreational Services (Libraries).

18. KINNELL, M. *All change? Public library management strategies for the 1990s.* London: Taylor Graham, 1992, 116.

19. Personal communication with Stephen Hoy, Leicestershire Libraries and Information Service.

20. Personal communication with Alison Hodson, Librarian, Special Needs Groups, Lincolnshire County Council Recreational Services (Libraries).

21. SOUTHGATE, T. N. (comp) *Communication*, 7th ed. Oxford: Oxfordshire Health Authority, 1990. (Equipment for Disabled People Series).

22. RYDER, J. *Library services to housebound people.* London: Library Association, 1987.

23. Personal communication with Desmond Heaps, Head of Community Services and Maggie Hooley, Assistant, Warwickshire County Council.

24. LIBRARY ASSOCIATION. *Guidelines for library services to people who are housebound*. London: Library Association, 1991, 7.

25. Personal communication with Martin Palmer, Area Librarian, Essex County Libraries.

26. Personal Communication with Martin Flynn, Area Librarian, Balsall Heath Library, Birmingham City Council Library Service.

27. LIBRARY ASSOCIATION. *Prison libraries. Library Association guidelines for library provision in Prison Department establishments*. London: Library Association, 1981.

28. Personal communication with Martin Palmer, Area Librarian, Essex County Libraries.

29. Personal communication with Desmond Heaps, Head of Community Services and Maggie Hooley, Assistant, Warwickshire County Council.

30. WALLACE, P. The right stuff? Writing in the community— a Liverpool Libraries initiative, *Community Librarian*, 7, Spring 1991, 2. Writing in Merseyside. A multi-agency response to a community need, *Public Libraries Journal*, 6, 6, 1991, 129.

31. Personal communication with Phil Taylor, WLO, Liverpool Libraries.

32. KEMPTHORNE, B. Still well worth reading about: Well Worth Reading —the third chapter, *Public Libraries Journal*, 6 (6), 1991, 157-161.

33. Personal communication with Stephen Hoy, Leicestershire Libraries and Information Service.

CHAPTER TEN

INTER-AGENCY CO-OPERATION

Owen McDowell

Inter-Agency Co-operation

Introduction

Co-operation among organizations providing information to the community has now become an established practice across many sectors. Public libraries, academic institutions, advice centres, voluntary groups, business organizations, statutory services and the mass media are in regular contact with each other as part of their efforts to satisfy the increasingly sophisticated demands expressed by a modern society. This trend has accelerated over the past few decades for a number of reasons. The specialization of information provision has created an environment within which no single organization can satisfy most needs—a user accessing one agency will often have to be referred to another. However, what is particularly interesting is the extent to which many organizations are progressing from basic awareness and referral liaison to more ambitious forms of joint working, those activities which enable them to collectively offer an enhanced service to the community. This chapter examines why and how this has happened, and it will look in detail at three case studies which have occurred in one city. It concludes with some thoughts as to how the trend of inter-agency co-operation could develop over the next few years.

The Value of Co-operation

While the trend towards co-operation reflects both local and national influences it is worthwhile examining the benefits that individual organizations can gain by this form of practice. The first is the opportunity it offers for agencies to widen their perception of the information needs of the community. Because each individual organization has its own 'information culture'—namely, its own policies and practices governing the acquisition, organization and dissemination of information—it may often be the case that users can only gain partial satisfaction of their needs. For example, an individual of Asian origin might visit the local library to find a reference book which describes British nationality and immigration law, but if that person wanted advice about how to appeal against a decision by the Home Office he or she would need to see an advice centre or lawyer. Co-operation between libraries and these agencies may bring together these two aspects of information dissemination—written materials and advice provision—so that the user is not faced with a fragmented response. Hence, the library may provide an advice centre with a collection of reference materials so that they can be used to their full potential. In this way, agencies benefit from their different approaches to meeting the needs of the community, rather than remaining blinkered by a narrow information culture.

The second benefit of co-operative working is the potential it offers for increasing the level of resources available for information provision. It has become standard practice for funders of new initiatives to insist upon inter-agency co-operation as a condition for obtaining resources. A notable example of this occurred in 1991 with the introduction of the National Disability Information Project by the Department of Health. The project allotted funds of almost £3 million to help establish pilot, local 'Federations of Disability Information Providers' across the country. These Federations were proposed by the management consultants, Coopers and Lybrand, in a study commissioned by the Department in 1988.[1] They consist of voluntary groups, local authorities, health authorities and other agencies involved in the provision of information to people with disabilities on such subjects as services, welfare benefits and housing needs. The principal aim would be to identify deficiencies in services and develop initiatives to tackle them. Bids for funding were invited on a competitive basis, and over a hundred local consortia applied. A condition for success was a commitment to inter-agency collaboration, at both the organizational and resource levels. Those bids which were able to meet this requirement were among the twelve that were successful. The National Disability Information Project is one of many sources of funding for new initiatives in information provision which insist on a commitment by applicants to co-operative working, and areas of the country with a low level of collaborative working will lose out on new resources in the future.

Forms of Inter-Agency Co-operation
Beyond the level of day-to-day liaison between information providers there are three types of inter-agency co-operation. The first may be termed 'networking', whereby two or more agencies may develop stronger links in order to improve the services each offers its users. Examples include meetings between agencies, and talks and visits which provide each organizaton with a more comprehensive view of the work of the other. These contacts may lead on to initiatives which enable the agencies to enhance their services with respect to quality of information resources or dissemination methods. A good instance is that of a Citizens Advice Bureau (CAB) or advice centre being given space in a public library to run a regular advice session. Both parties benefit from the former obtaining free or low-cost premises and the latter being able to offer a broader range of information service for the public. Another example is the regular exchange of information via a current awareness mailing, newsletter or, at its most basic, a 'Have you seen this?' note. Generally, these sorts of contacts enable agencies with common

interests to share their existing resources and dissemination methods for mutual benefit, and in many cities and towns these activities are so common that the participants may view them as natural extensions of their individual organizational work.

The second form of co-operation is project-based working. At this level a number of agencies may decide to go beyond mutual enhancement of existing services, in order to produce new information resources or devise new dissemination mechanisms. A common example of this is a directory of community organizations aimed at a particular locality or at a selected social group. Another example includes information technology applications, such as the creation of a database of information for people with disabilities, to be accessed via computers located within key voluntary and statutory agencies. Other examples are local authority and advice centre welfare benefit take-up campaigns, which use a variety of publicity methods to target those who are unaware of their rights. What all these projects have in common is the overt identification of a gap in exisiting information provision followed by joint initiatives to remedy this deficiency by setting short-term targets. Should these be achieved the organizations may well go on to undertake new projects to sustain the improvements in provision.

The third form of co-operative working is at the most ambitious level, that of the strategic planning of library and information services within a particular locality. Nationally, the catalyst for this strategic form of co-operation has been the concept of the Library and Information Plan (LIP) which was advocated by the Library and Information Services Council in their 1986 report, *The future development of libraries and information services: progress through planning and partnership.*[2] The Report, commonly cited as FD3, suggested that, if library and information services are to be maintained and resources fully exploited, it is necessary for provision to be co-ordinated at a local level.

In particular, FD3 stressed the need for agencies not only to augment informal co-operation by planned relationships, but also to contract within a LIP to maximise possible use of resources. The LIP itself is a management plan with a duration of three to five years which brings together all library and information services in a given area: the public library, academic libraries, other library and information services within the public, industrial, commercial, professional and other sectors in the private sphere. The plan is drawn up following a review of the services these sectors currently provide and discussions as to what they want to achieve. As a planning tool the LIP enables organizations to review their services in the light of users' needs, it allows services to rely on the undertakings given to them by the other parties to the plan, and it acts as a framework within which new developments in information provision can be fostered.

Since FD3 was published the concept of the LIP has been realised in many parts of the country. The first LIP was drawn up to plan library and information services provision in the county of Cambridgeshire, and by the early 1990s there were over twenty LIPs across the UK. The process by which a LIP comes into existence varies according to the particular circumstances existing within a locality. FD3—and a subsequent report[3]—described a model process which consists of the following stages:

(a)   an assessment of the current needs of local users for library and information services;

(b)   an examination of the goals of existing services, on an individual and co-operative basis;

(c)   a statement of objectives and recommendations for the LIP; a strategy is drawn up to specify strategies to meet these objectives;

(d)   implementation and review of progress made under the LIP.

Funding for the drawing up of many LIPs created in the

1980s came from the Office of Arts and Libraries and the British Library Research and Development Department, usually with assistance from local organizations. Since the end of the developmental stage for the LIP concept in 1989 the resources for LIPs—consultants, staffing, premises and other costs—have had to be found from local authorities and other sources alone.

In 1991 a review of the LIP concept commissioned by the Library and Information Co-operative Council[4] concluded that progress in most areas had been very positive. The main drawback that some LIPs had experienced was a lack of resources to progress the implementation of strategies to meet declared objectives. However, the key ingredient of co-operation between library and information services is being given a new emphasis by the LIP, and whilst its effectiveness can only be measured in the long term it is likely that the momentum of co-operation will continue at a steady pace.

A City in need of Information

For other parts of the country the name of Sheffield remains synonymous with the production of steel. However, the collapse of this industry during the 1980s has rendered this image obsolete, and the City has striven to adopt a new identity to present to the world. As with other cities struggling with change brought on by the post-industrial society, the political and business leaders of Sheffield have set themselves the challenge of establishing the City as a centre for leisure, the retail trade and tourism. Millions of pounds have been spent on state-of-the-art sports stadiums in an effort to attract world class competitions, such as the European Swimming Championships which will take place in Sheffield in 1993. Other developments, such as the huge Meadowhall 'leisure shopping' complex—built on the site of a steelworks—draw millions of visitors every year, as does the beautiful Peak District National Park which lies to the south west of the City.

For the City's population of over 500,000 the rapid economic changes of the past two decades have had both positive and negative consequences. Sheffield is in many ways succeeding in modernising its image and facilities to cater for the demands of its people. For many, it retains the character of being both a major regional centre and, at heart, a collection of villages with names like Ecclesfield, Stocksbridge, Totley and Frecheville. Less romantically, however, the 'steel shock' of the 1980s is still causing reverberations as the City struggles to replace what was a labour intensive industry. The rate of unemployment in the City remains too high and the numbers dependent on social security and other benefits is above the national average. The latter is due partly to the large proportion of people over the age of 60, but there are areas in Sheffield which are particularly disadvantaged, with poverty affecting those of all ages. Certain groups, such as the Afro-Caribbean and Asian communities, face more significant barriers in the way of employment opportunities and quality housing.

With regard to the City's information infrastructure one is presented with a range of agencies which serve a variety of interests. The public library service developed a high profile among the population during the 1980s with exciting innovative work in the arts and information spheres. By the 1990s, however, funding problems facing the local authority have jeopardised both the range of its activities and its branch network serving over thirty districts. The University and the Polytechnic both have major libraries, and Sheffield is the base for the national headquarters of the Government's Health and Safety Executive. Many business organizations have library and information sections, and there is a high level of networking between many of these and the public sector through the Sheffield Interchange Organization, which was established in 1932. The voluntary and community sector in the city is composed of thousands of groups, including over forty advice centres and Citizens

Advice Bureaux. Finally, there are the local mass media which include local newspapers, two radio stations and two outpost offices of the regional TV stations in Yorkshire.

It can be seen that the information infrastructure in Sheffield exhibits the characteristics typical of a major regional city in the 1990s. In 1989 the Sheffield Library and Information Plan[5] found that there was a great willingness among agencies to work in a co-operative way, whether through established formal structures such as SINTO or through other styles of working, as the following case studies show.

Networking in an Inner-City Area

The district of Upperthorpe, Netherthorpe and Kelvin in Sheffield has a population of approximately 16,000. The community faces many problems: a high rate of unemployment, acute poverty and under-resourced social services. The district's housing consists of large council estates, maisonettes rather than houses, and it is dominated by the Kelvin complex, one of the architectural delights of the 1960s which rapidly became a concrete and metal nightmare for many of the tenants who lived in it. During the 1980s the pressures facing the area intensified with the implementation of Care in the Community policies, which place people with mental health problems in the community rather than accommodating them in mental hospitals.

As a 'less popular' area for housing, the district experienced an influx of such individuals, and this created concern among statutory and voluntary services. The Housing Department initiated a research project to investigate the effectiveness of care in the community policies and to find out how it and other agencies could ensure that they were meeting the needs of those with mental health problems in the area. The resulting report, in late 1989, drew upon the experiences of individuals and agencies to suggest that many people with difficulties were failing to obtain the help they needed, either because the level of services in the area could not cope with the level of demand or because there was an insufficient degree of co-ordination between services to ensure that individuals were referred to the right places. While there were severe resource constraints restricting the scope for expanding services, the report recommended that the Housing Department needed to provide more information about its services to people with mental health problems and that there was a need for links between mental health services and other services—such as advice centres and community organizations—to be strengthened. These links would facilitate the delivery of services and support to individuals who might otherwise fail to obtain all the help they required.

In 1990, following distribution of the report, a meeting of statutory and voluntary agencies working in the district took place to discuss how links between them could be developed. The agencies represented included the Housing Department, Social Services, the local advice centre, the Community Nursing Service and Upperthorpe Community Library. The need for those organizations to become more aware of what each did was recognized as urgent. A suggestion was made to produce an 'Inter-Agency Mental Health Information Pack' which would help meet this need. The pack would be circulated to all relevant organizations in the area to create more effective referral and communication links. The information-gathering for the pack was carried out by a student on placement with the Care in the Community Team within the central Housing Department, with assistance from the local library and other agencies. A questionnaire was drawn up and sent to over thirty organizations serving people in the district and this requested the following information:

organization's name;
contact person;
address;

telephone number and operating hours;
organizational structure;
function;
services available for other agencies;
referral processes;
and publications produced.

This material was reproduced in a standard format in booklet form with a length of 50 pages, and it was printed by the Housing Department. The information it contains is an invaluable guide to statutory and community services which can offer help to people with mental health problems in the district. As well as listing the many functions of the Housing Department and Social Services it describes the activities of over twenty community organizations, including advice centres, church community centres, tenants' associations, an Afro-Caribbean centre and the Samaritans. Reaction to the pack from agencies has been extremely favourable, and the local library has undertaken to update it at regular periods.

There are a number of factors which make this local project particularly interesting. The first is the extent to which a research project was able to persuade many agencies in an area to work more closely together and exchange more information about themselves. It may have been that such co-operation would have developed even without the research work, but it would undoubtedly have taken longer to do so. The second factor was the consensus that had developed as to the importance of information as a binding agent between organizations to help them meet the needs of a target group. Here, the value of information as a method of achieving a shared goal was demonstrated. The collection of information was carried out by individuals from different agencies working together, and, within modest means, a valuable information product was produced as a method of improving services for a vulnerable group and, ultimately, for the benefit of all the community.

The City-wide Debt Information Project
In Sheffield, as in other parts of the country, the numbers
of individuals with personal debt problems became a major
social issue by the late 1980s. Redundancy, unemployment,
break-up of relationships and changes in social security rules
were creating significant levels of hardship for thousands
who were having difficulty paying mortgages, rent, fuel bills
or consumer credit debts. For many of those on welfare
benefits their debts intensified with the introduction in 1988
of the Government's Social Fund, which replaced the
previous system of grants for clothes, furniture and other
items with a loan scheme. Those on higher incomes faced
the consequences of the rapid rise in consumption which had
been fuelled by looser credit controls.

The City's advice centres were finding it harder to cope
with the rising demands for assistance from those in
difficulty. The vast majority rely on volunteers for staffing,
and this imposed a limit upon their ability to be able to
undertake debt advice work. Such work is labour intensive,
usually involving contact being made with an individual's
creditors to press for a reduction in levels of debt
repayments, and benefit checks to maximize incomes. One
specialist unit in the city, the Citizens Advice Bureaux Debt
Support Unit, had been established in 1988, but its role was
to act as a training and consultancy service for other
agencies—not a drop-in advice service.

In 1989 the Sheffield Libraries and Information Services
Department offered to help the Debt Support Unit initiate a
project designed to meet some of the needs of those with debt
problems in the city. Several years earlier the Birmingham
Settlement, a debt advice agency, had established a telephone
helpline in that city to advise individuals. Experienced
advisers staffed the 'Housing Debtline', and two self-help
information packs were produced, one for home-owners, the
other for tenants. It was agreed that the Sheffield project
would incorporate these features as a means of helping

243

individuals to obtain information that would assist them. 'Sheffield Debtline' was launched by a major publicity campaign that publicized the service by exhibitions, posters and leaflets which were funded by the City Council. The Community Information and Enquiries Section in Libraries and Information Services distributed the publicity materials and organized publicity through the local press and radio stations. The City's central and local libraries promoted two Sheffield Debtline self-help information booklets alongside books on coping with money problems. Many users were directed towards the Debtline for help; and within a year the service had dealt with 1206 calls. By the early 1990s the number of enquiries grew rapidly, particularly in response to the onset of the recession.

This example of inter-agency co-operation is notable for a number of features. The project was clearly created to meet a growing information need from the community which could not be met by existing services. The telephone helpline and self-help booklets were designed to offer much of the information that was required as a means of developing a speedy form of provision. Secondly, the public library network in the city was employed as a comprehensive access point to the debt information, a method which could not have been created by the Debt Support Unit on its own. Thirdly, the project showed how a public library service can help overcome the disadvantage many community organizations may face in providing a sufficient level of resources to fund a major information project. The staff time and funding for publicity materials allocated amounted to a significant resource for the Unit, and in return the public library benefited from the enhanced profile it acquired among its users and the wider community.

Strategic Co-operation: the Sheffield LIP
The commitment of the Sheffield information infrastructure to co-operative working was demonstrated by the adoption

of a Library and Information Plan in 1989. The Plan incorporated the results of a survey of over 130 information-providing organizations in the City. This revealed that there were 'areas of excellence' such as high quality resources and staff skills within the sector and a climate favourable to forward planning. The weaknesses within the infrastructure included an under-resourced voluntary and community sector, inadequate provision for the needs of black and ethnic minorities in the City, and few formal links between libraries and other information services. The Plan laid down a three-year strategy for the period 1989-1993 which would seek to tackle these and other weaknesses by increasing the level of inter-agency awareness, develop initiatives to improve provision across all sectors and raise the profile of the information infrastructure within the City. A Board for Library and Information Services in Sheffield (BLISS) was established in June 1989 to oversee the implementation of the Plan, which would be progressed by sectoral standing committees covering business information, health information and research, information technology, legal information, media resources, training and staff development and the voluntary and community sector. In 1990 BLISS appointed an Executive Director on a three-year contract to co-ordinate day-to-day implementation of the LIP, which has become known as 'Sheffield Information 2000'.

The challenge facing any strategic initiative is that of creating any significant improvements in information services for users. In Sheffield—as elsewhere—the challenge is probably greatest in relation to the voluntary and community sector. As the Sheffield LIP noted, the sector suffers from a low resource base which hinders the development of a quality information providing role. Its major funding sources are the local authority, charitable trusts, local businesses or fund-raising appeals, with little scope for the generation of income by the sale of products or services. By the early 1990s pressures upon all of these sources were creating new difficulties for many groups, particularly those facing rising demands from the community. In the case of advice centres, rising levels of unemployment and homelessness meant more individuals were contacting them for advice about claiming benefits or seeking assistance under the Housing Act. The burden of coping with this level of casework meant it was harder for centres to disseminate information in the form of local benefit take-up campaigns and other initiatives.

In recent years research has been conducted into the information needs of voluntary and community groups. In 1988 a survey of groups in the East and West Midlands revealed that these needs, in order of priority, included funding information, awareness of other groups, training, research, local government, the media, management of staff and resources, central government, public libraries and computer technology.[6] While such detailed research has not been conducted in Sheffield these findings complement those of the survey conducted for the LIP. Other needs include the ability of groups to acquire, organize and disseminate information for the use of its members, users and the wider community. Within many groups—and other organizations in other sectors—the absence of a developed information culture meant that these activities were being undertaken in an *ad hoc* manner, with a resulting impact on their effectiveness.

In attempting to tackle these issues, BLISS, working with the public library service, invited representatives from a number of groups to join its standing committee for the voluntary and community sector. During 1991 the committee embarked upon two initiatives, the production of a poster listing useful helpful contacts for groups and the organization of a training day. The poster displays the telephone numbers of a variety of statutory and community agencies under the headings of general help, funding, training, transport, premises, the law and the media. Graphics give it a lively and attractive appearance, and it has received a favourable reaction from many quarters. The training day, 'The ABC of Information', was organized in response to the perception that many groups wished to enhance their ability to use information to support their work. The day brought together nearly 40 community groups and staff from the public library to exchange experiences as to how materials would be acquired, how they could be organized and how they would be disseminated, both within a group and externally. Discussions and exercises brought out the ways by which groups could organize an effective classification system using key words, how noticeboards, newsletters and meetings could be used to circulate information, and the potential offered by computers, including database and desk-top publishing methods. The course opened up new territory for both the voluntary sector and the public library, particularly with regard to the latter's development of information services for groups. Further initiatives will seek to build upon this solid foundation for co-operative working, including more training courses and the creation of an information support network, similar to initiatives such as the Lambeth Umbrella Group in the 1970s.

The priority given by Sheffield Information 2000 to the needs of the voluntary sector was a response to the scale of the problems facing most community groups in the city. The LIP has certainly produced tangible benefits by bringing together organizations with complementary attributes in forums which produce useful information resources or support mechanisms. No one involved on the voluntary sector committee would claim that its work can overcome all the severe difficulties confronting groups but by helping to improve their ability to access and utilize information the Committee can alleviate some of them.

Conclusion
It is clear that the trend for inter-agency co-operation will

continue to gather momentum as a variety of organizations recognise the benefits that can accrue to them and their users. However, while welcoming this trend, it is submitted that the potential for achieving these goals may be greater if co-operation were to proceed in a particular direction, that which addresses the issue of unequal resource levels among information agencies. The difficulties facing the voluntary and community sector have been described in this chapter, and while the root causes lie outside the library and information sphere, it is right that this sector receives special attention. The range and level of information needs expressed by modern society are being increasingly directed towards voluntary and community groups, such as advice centres, self help groups, community services and groups catering for black and ethnic minorities and for people with disabilities. Their ability to satisfy these needs is hindered by their limited access to resources, but it has been shown in this chapter how other, better resourced organizations can help them to overcome many of the hurdles. This does not necessarily mean that other agencies should seek to provide groups with grants, though this should certainly be considered if it is possible. Rather, it means that many organizations can help out by offering training in information skills, assist with the production of information packs and publicity materials, advise on new technology applications, and much more. In this way the imbalance between agencies offering information can be partly corrected for the benefit of those sections of the community which face disadvantage and for the general benefit of the community as a whole.

The obvious question is how can the issue of inequality be raised within the information infrastructure of a particular locality? The answer to this relates to the role of the public library. In the case of the LIP it often has the function of compiling the plan within a given area as, in the words of FD3, an 'honest broker' between libraries. It has the responsibility to negotiate equally and openly with all these services as a review of what they currently do and what they want to achieve. Yet, as FD3 noted, the public library was chosen for this role because Parliament granted it statutory authority to do so. Under the Public Libraries and Museums Act, 1964, section 7 (2) (c), a library authority in England and Wales has the duty of:

> securing, in relation to any matter concerning the functions both of the library authority as such and any other authority whose functions are exercisable within the library area, that there is full co-operation between the persons engaged in carrying out those functions.

The concept of the LIP provides a particular approach to the carrying out of this duty, but what is clear is that public libraries in areas without a LIP should still be expected to play such a role. The role should ideally involve the promotion of inter-agency co-ordination and the advocacy of initiatives which alleviate inequalities between agencies. There are many examples of this happening across the country, but it may be reasonable to assume that it does not occur to the extent it should. It is the case that there are significant obstacles in the way of many public library services playing a strong co-ordinating role. In rural areas the level of information infrastructure may be relatively low, with little scope for initiating co-operative working. For public libraries everywhere the issue of financial constraints is making it more difficult for them to devote staff time and other resources to this role. Nevertheless, there is a danger that, as the trend for inter-agency co-operation accelerates, public libraries in many parts of the country may be left behind as others strive to combine resources to meet the needs of the community. In one sense this observation is another contribution to the continuing debate as to what role the public library should play in the twenty-first century. What is clear is that central and local government need to empower public library services to act as catalysts for inter-agency co-operation, both within and outside LIPs, and to enable them to strive for a rich network of information services which will be able to satisfy the needs of all sections of the community.

Acknowledgement

The author acknowledges the assistance provided by Alan Beevers, Sheffield Information 2000, and Carol Philpotts, Sheffield Libraries and Information Services.

References

1. COOPERS AND LYBRAND. *Information needs of people with disabilities, their carers and service providers. Final Report.* London: Department of Health and Social Security Priority Care Division, 1988.

2. OFFICE OF ARTS AND LIBRARIES: *The future development of libraries and information services: progress through planning and partnership.* London: HMSO, 1986. (Library Information Series No. 14).

3. CAPITAL PLANNING INFORMATION. *A draft outline Library and Information Plan manual.* London: British Library Research and Development Department, 1988. (British Library Research Paper 43).

4. CHILDS, S.M. *The Library and Information Plan concept: a review of some key issues.* London: Libraries and Information Co-operation Council, 1991.

5. CAPITAL PLANNING INFORMATION: *Sheffield Information 2000: the Sheffield Library and Information Plan 1989-93.* Sheffield: Pavric Publications, 1989.

6. DEACON, D. *and* GOLDING, P. *The information needs of voluntary and community groups.* Leicester: University of Leicester Centre for Mass Communication Research, 1988.

CHAPTER ELEVEN

STRATEGIC MANAGEMENT

John Davies

Strategic Management

Introduction

By any yardstick you may care to use, local authorities are big business. Annual turnover in county and metropolitan authorities runs into hundreds of millions of pounds. Local councils have the power to touch positively (or negatively!) on the lives of every one of their local residents because of the huge and diverse range of their service provision. They provide, and have a need to transmit, vast quantities of information to the communities they serve. One of the tragedies of modern local government, however, has been the rigid departmental and professional boundaries within which it has too often sought to respond to local needs. Increasingly, the issues and challenges faced by information providers have no respect for these traditional boundaries. The very nature and purpose of information cannot be bounded by such structures and departments. Ways have to be found of managing across these barriers, of striking new balances and forging new partnerships, not just within local authorities but also outside with other agencies such as community and voluntary groups, the police and health services who are equally active in local communities. The strategic management approach offers an exciting way forward in the search for ever more effective community information services.

What is Strategic Management?

Management thinking has always been prone to the vicissitudes of fashion. The path of management practitioners is often littered with bright ideas and worthy intentions, but these are often incapable of meeting the exaggerated claims made by their proponents. Strategic management is much in vogue at present—the Local Government Management Board even has a project team dedicated to the subject[1]. John Stewart has defined strategic management as 'changing the organization to enable it to meet changing needs and to express changing values'.[2] The Local Government Management Board's *Strategies for success* notes that:

> Strategic management is an important step towards making the complexity of change more manageable. It is about sorting out what is significant, deciding how it needs to be handled and ensuring that it is. It has some core elements but there is no simple recipe to be followed. It does need a disciplined and carefully thought out approach; but there is no simple set of systems, routines or procedures that will deliver a resolution.[3]

Each organization and each local authority has very different needs, operates within its own political and managerial culture and responds to a unique and distinct local environment. Strategic management has to be crafted within each authority, taking account of its own peculiar circumstances.

Good operational management in local government has a capacity that should not be underestimated—it can carry out effectively predetermined tasks, it can adjust to change through innovation and adaptation. Its ways of working, however, follow predetermined patterns based on its structure, processes and culture. Professor Stewart has argued that problems are perceived and certain responses are favoured by that way of working. The resources available set limits to the organizational capacity of the local authority and the departments within it. Normal ways of working tend to be self-reinforcing. Whilst capacity for adjustment tends to be determined by the normal way of working that is itself related to the past pattern of activities. Many problems will not be adequately perceived by the organization if they are not related to existing activities, or, if perceived, will be approached through the perspective of existing activities. New activities, if undertaken, are therefore too often conditioned by the past ways of working.[4] This has characterized many of the responses local government has traditionally made towards informing its communities. It has tended to tackle issues and problems through single departments, through existing committee and departmental structures and through existing ways of working. This approach has prevailed even though information provision should have little regard for these narrow and rigid boundaries.

The role of strategic management is to enable each local authority to identify problems, respond to emerging values or to undertake activities that are beyond the capacity of conventional ways of working. Strategic management must add value to what the organization does. It must have a capacity not limited to the normal way of working and must be capable of changing the normal way of working. It has important implications for the way we should deliver our information services to our communities in the future.

The Key Elements of Strategic Management.
The Local Government Management Board's *Strategies for success,* based on analysis of case study experience and the practice of strategic management in local government, provides an invaluable guide to the strategic management approach.[5] Their best practice methodology has been followed in looking at how one local authority—St. Helens Metropolitan Borough Council (MBC) has taken up the information service strategic challenge.

Strategies for success emphasizes three key characteristics of strategic management:

First, strategic management can offer a perspective beyond

the normal way of working. It can:

- be **long term** where operational management perspective is **short term**;
- expose **choices** where operational management reinforces **continuities**;
- be guided by **political values** where operational management expresses **professional concerns**;
- be grounded in the **environment** if operational management is grounded in the **organization**;
- look at the **network of community organizations** if operational management is limited by **organizational boundaries**;
- see **inter-relationships between tasks** if operational management is **centred on specific tasks**.

Secondly, strategic management identifies issues to be dealt with, choices to be made, values to be expressed or activities to be undertaken which lie beyond present organizational capacity because of current structures, processes or culture or of the existing allocation of resources.

Thirdly, strategic management is concerned with changing organizations to establish new ways of working where the existing set-up is deficient. Strategic management does not carry out the strategy; it builds an organization capable of carrying it out by:

- changing organizational structures (e.g., decentralization, creating new service links/new departments);
- changing the process through which the organization works
  (e.g., creating strategy task groups, inter-agency teams);
- building the culture through processes of socialization (e.g., developing shared values and beliefs through team working);
- giving leadership in the emphasis given to certain themes

(e.g., providing clear direction and priorities);
- altering the balance of resources and not merely financial resources (e.g., encouraging flexible use of staff and budgets).

Strategic management applied to information service development should be:
- **selective in action**, it addresses only those aspects of information provision that require change;
- **wide ranging in review** because it requires understanding of the environment, political values and organizational capacity required to provide effective information services;
- **changing in focus** because its rationale is changing the organization to encompass new ways of working to provide community information which, once accomplished, removes strategic management's concerns and becomes part of operational management;
- **linked to organization development** which is the means through which it acts by creating new organizational approaches to problems and issues in the information field;
- the **expression of political purpose** which must guide organizational response to a changing environment of which information provision is an often neglected key;
- **dependent upon communication** since, through communication, organizational change to benefit information services gains meaning—a strategic plan is an exercise in communication for strategic management, not an end in itself.

The Strategic Management Approach and Community Information—A Case Study Approach

The value of the strategic management approach to community information development can best be illustrated by its application to an actual local authority setting. It would be wrong to pretend that this single authority case study of St. Helens MBC is typical of all. It is not. It does, however, seek to illustrate how the strategic management approach has brought added value to the work of informing local communities in St. Helens. New organizational structures and processes and attitudes have provided better responsiveness to community needs, better integration, improved corporate and inter-agency working and better use of staff and building resources.

St. Helens is a unitary Metropolitan Borough Council on Merseyside with a population of almost 190,000. The original Borough grew up around three manufacturing industries—coal, glass and chemicals—which have had a dramatic effect not only on the physical landscape of much of the Borough, but also provided it, until recently, with its major sources of employment. These industries also styled and fashioned a number of fiercely proud and independent local communities based around old coal mines and glassworks. By contrast, the post 1974 Borough contains some of the richest agricultural land in the region with open space accounting for some 48 per cent of the Borough's land area. In 1984/85 St. Helens MBC totally reorganized its organizational structures, processes and culture in order to make its services more responsive to local needs, to unlock the potential of its workforce, to adopt a strategic approach to the future management of its affairs and to involve the community in the provision of services.

Taking stock through strategic review
The starting point in St. Helens for strategic management was strategic review—a process of taking stock in which members and officers engaged in a total appraisal of the local authority's environment, political priorities, public expectations and aspirations and organizational capacity. This process of taking an holistic view of the organization

and looking at total needs, problems and opportunities, strengths and weaknesses, is on-going and must permeate the whole approach to local authority service provision. It is within this framework that community information services in all their many forms have developed in the Borough's libraries, area and neighbourhood offices, community centres, schools and colleges, community and voluntary group premises.

(a) Environmental analysis.
The object of analysis of the environment in which the total authority operates is to identify significant factors that could affect the work of the authority and which may require new initiatives from the local authority and its partner agencies and organizations. Factors such as demographic change, emerging social problems, patterns of mobility, changing lifestyles and changing legislation are vital in helping to determine the nature and focus of information service developments.

(b) Focusing on community concerns, attitudes and aspirations.
Information services to local communities must be set against a backdrop of frequent market surveys, community consultation exercises, monitoring of complaints and suggestions, user panels and listening to front line staff. Information workers must be allowed ample opportunities to develop and nurture strong community links through work with local community groups, other local agencies and local authority departments. Questions must continually be posed about what are the information needs of our local communities and how do we find out about them? In St. Helens this feedback is often obtained in conjunction with other community based departments such as Education, and Personal Services (Housing and Social Services). Sometimes this has taken the form of community

SUTTON NEEDS YOU

TO SHAPE IT'S FUTURE
Come and share your views at a
COMMUNITY ACTION DAY

FIGURE 1.
SUTTON SHAPES ITS FUTURE

conferences in neighbourhoods, when a whole range of issues raised by local people have been the focus of workshop forums over a number of days. Through one such initiative, 'Sutton Shapes its Future', emerged the desire on the part of the Sutton Neighbourhood Forum to develop with the local library and community centre a community information database for their area. This was successfully accomplished using students and new technology from the local community high school to develop the database. Other initiatives to emerge from this particular community conference were the formation of a Credit Union, a play forum, an environmental forum and an action group for the elderly.[6] These are vital activities for information workers to be involved in to help them shape their service development and heighten their strategic awareness.

Recently, a new technique of 'Rapid Appraisal' has been tried in the Thatto Heath community, by the Neighbourhood Planning Group. Rapid Appraisal is a method and a process for getting information about a set of problems in a relatively short time. A team is formed from people with direct responsibilities for local services. Team members review the existing records and sources of information, interview key people from the community and make direct observations, then, together as a team, and with community participation, they formulate community priorities for action. Carried out in conjunction with St. Helens & Knowsley Health Promotion Unit, the study looked at community identity and relationships, the socio-economic environment, housing, physical environment, health problems, local services and facilities, and health services. The results, whilst not indisputable facts, are important community perceptions and are the basis for further investigation and/or action. They reveal much of importance in relation to the development of information services in the particular area in question, e.g., negative attitudes towards health, lack of provision for young people, low regard for school education, poor information exchange between local agencies, lack of community meeting places, poor awareness of services, lack of awareness of employment, educational and training opportunities.[7]

(c) Political aspirations and priorities.
Information service providers must be aware of how their service can help to contribute strategically to the political priorities of the authority. In St. Helens, priority has been given in recent years to the improvement of front line services, to decentralization, to enhanced corporate working, to extending community use of all buildings, to strengthening care services, to regenerating the Borough, to developing a partnership approach wtih local people, local groups and agencies and directing additional resources to target groups and target areas. Library and information services in St. Helens, as part of the authority's leisure services department, have played an effective part in the delivery of action programmes in all of these key areas. This has resulted in improvements to the resource base of the service and all party support for maintaining and developing the existing library network and its associated services against a backdrop of poll tax capping and severe resource constraint.

(d) Analysis of organizational and community capacity.
Organizational and community capacity is a critical factor in determining the extent to which a local authority can bring about the necessary strategic changes. In the present restricted financial climate in which local authorities are operating, capacity often has to be built and developed within the existing resources of finance, staff and buildings rather than through incremental growth. This calls for a flexible, imaginative and innovative approach to the challenges faced by the authority. Importantly, too, this should result in a recognition of community capacity—the rich vein of

resources of local people—that can link into and help support the authority's own aspirations for positive change.

In St. Helens, strategic management has sought to match capacity to aspiration. It has involved a recognition of the importance of unlocking the staff resources of the authority. This has been achieved by the creation of greater opportunities and incentives for working together across traditional departmental boundaries to provide better integrated local responses to issues and problems. Information provision to communities is a complex process involving not just library and information staff but also teachers, social workers, community development staff, housing staff, planners, public relations staff, environmental health officers, play and recreation staff, youth workers and elected members. Informing our communities takes place not just through libraries, but also area offices, community centres, leisure centres, family centres, residential homes, schools and colleges, maintenance depots, parks. A strategic approach must recognize the role that ALL these staff and resources play in information dissemination so that the whole resource can be effectively harnessed. Too narrow a focus will result in lost opportunities, in often costly duplication of effort and poorly informed and frustrated customers. Managing information provision as an authority service rather than a single department concern is one of the great strategic challenges for information workers to take on. It can be greatly assisted, as many authorities have found, by shared use of strategically located buildings to create 'one stop shops' providing a full range of information and services to local communities under the same roof or on the same site.[8]

Partnerships can also be forged with a wide variety of other information agencies outside the local authority to similarly enhance the delivery through a single location of imaginative and innovative information services. In St. Helens, a partnership between the Community Leisure

Department, the Personal Services Department and the St. Helens Council for Voluntary Services provides, through the Central Library, the Disability Advice and Information Service known as DASH.

The aims of the service are:

- to collect and collate information on all aspects of access and assimilate this into an Access Guide for use by local disabled people;
- to provide an information and visiting service for disabled people and their carers;
- to raise the awareness of the local community to the needs and problems of people with a physical or mental disability which prevents them having a full interaction with their environment.

Support from the Department of Health Consortium on Opportunities for Volunteering, several charitable trusts and the Mayor of St. Helens Appeal has been forthcoming. It has enabled the service to provide collections of books and pamphlets on matters affecting disabled people, and aided access to all the resources and services of St. Helens Community Libraries. New equipment has been purchased to help disabled people access the Wavelength database, with information especially for disabled people. Minicom systems for the deaf, Braille printing machines and closed circuit TVs for enlarging small print have also been acquired.

The service provides information and advice on solving everyday problems, helpful aids and services, learning and education, leisure activities, money and benefits, employment, housing, and access to buildings and services. During its first year, 55 volunteers were recruited—many of whom were themselves disabled. DASH volunteers help disabled people at the DASH centre, at their homes or at day centres and old people's homes. They help people to use equipment to access information more easily and will deliver information to people's homes and show how to use DASH equipment independently. DASH now employs its own

Disability Advice
and Information
St.Helens

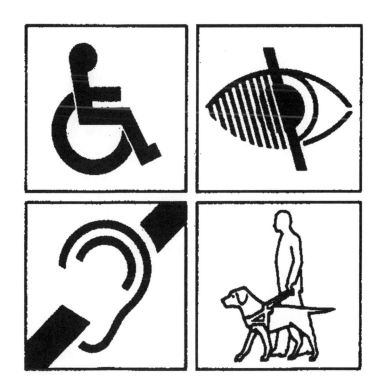

FIGURE 2—DASH LOGO AND SIGNS

disability information officer. It has improved and developed information services for disabled people within the Borough beyond recognition.

Major developmental benefits can accrue to local authorities that recognize the importance of community development and the power of local communities to assist in the strategic approach.[9] The Association of Metropolitan Authorities (AMA) has defined community development as:

> The involvement of people in the issues which affect their lives. It is a process based on the development of an equal partnership between those involved to enable a sharing of skills, knowledge and experience. Community development can take place in both geographical neighbourhoods or area based communities as well as communities of interest, related to factors such as age, gender, race, disability etc., as people identify what is relevant to them.

The AMA policy guidelines on community development have recognized that the community development approach:

> will be put to best effect by the local authority if it is seen as a strategic approach within which all Council departments have a role to play and through which a local authority can be not just reactive and responsive to local expressed views and issues but proactive in helping to stimulate and encourage groups of local people to organise collectively, participate in local issues and help formulate and provide services that are best suited to meet their needs.[10]

Figure 3 illustrates how this strategic approach can operate.

In St. Helens, the community development approach has involved four basic elements:

1. presenting and communicating policies and services of the Council to the people of St. Helens;
2. developing policies and services in response to feedback from local people;
3. the co-ordination of services in achieving authority objectives;
4. the promotion of partnerships between the authority and voluntary organizations and groups.

Information staff in St. Helens have gained considerable benefit from working within the Leisure Department, alongside the authority's Community Development Team.

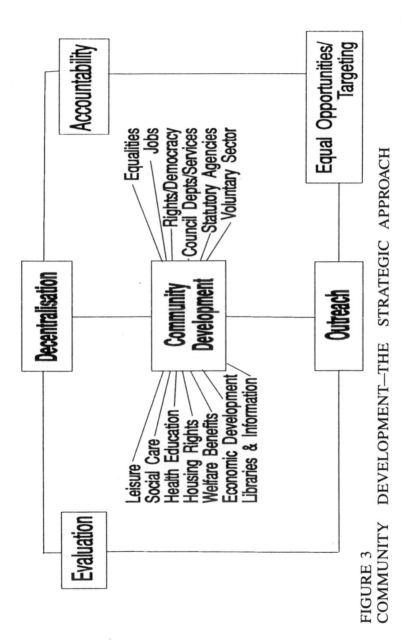

FIGURE 3
COMMUNITY DEVELOPMENT—THE STRATEGIC APPROACH

Indeed, four of the six team members are based in library buildings and many library staff have been trained in the community development approach along with social work, education, housing and leisure colleagues. The approach and process of community development has important implications for the strategic management of information development, recognizing as it does the inestimable value of working with communities in an enabling and partnership role. It helps people to achieve things for themselves, through suggestion, education, organization building and through the provision of information and advice. Locking in to this 'community capacity' is a critical factor in the strategic management approach to information provision since communities are a huge, and often untapped, resource in the information process.

Making Choices
The strategic review process provides the raw material upon which choices can then begin to be made and directions set. Strategic issues emerge as relationships in apparently unrelated areas are identified, significant change and continuing trends are focused upon, and incompatibilities between problems and capacity are realized. Whilst issues are considered in their broadest context and with an open mind, the practical implications for operational management begin to figure in the equation. How this process works in practice is well illustrated in St. Helens by the development of a Mental Health Awareness Programme.

Within St. Helens itself and on its boundary with Warrington, lie two major psychiatric hospitals. Rainhill hospital is one of the largest psychiatric hospitals in Europe, housing over 3,500 patients at its peak, and Winwick hospital is a giant Victorian establishment with over seven miles of corridors. Both were, as part of the new policy of 'care in the community', beginning to decamp their residents into local communities. Mental illness has always aroused public fears and suspicions and officers, elected members and public alike were becoming increasingly aware of the scale and the impact of the new policy on St. Helens, given the presence locally of two such huge institutions. The need for greater public awareness and understanding of mental illness and mental handicap was never greater, as more and more local people began to have contact with mentally ill people within their communities.

The agreed strategy was to embark upon an information campaign to increase public awareness of the needs of mentally ill people and the reasons behind the care in the community policy. St. Helens community libraries were chosen as a focal point for this awareness campaign because of their information role, their strategic locations in communities, the volume of their use and, significantly, their friendliness and familiarity. The project transcended the boundaries of one department involving as it did social work, housing, education, leisure, health authority and voluntary sector staff. Par excellence, a problem identified as a strategic issue required a strategically managed response.

In 1988, a task group consisting of representatives from local authority departments, St. Helens and Knowsley Heath Authority and a host of voluntary agencies operating in the field of mental illness and mental handicap put together the Borough's first Mental Health Awareness Week based at Thatto Heath Community Library—the area nearest to Rainhill Hospital. A major informational display was produced taking up most of the library; this informed the public of the historic development of the care of the mentally ill and explained the difference between mental illness and mental handicap and the care and support services now in use. Teachers' information packs were produced and all secondary schools in the area were involved in a week of education and information including visits to the exhibition, project work on mental health topics, videos and talks by staff from social work teams, residential establishments and

St.Helens Borough Council

25th February - 2nd March 1991

ECCLESTON COMMUNITY LIBRARY

Information, advice, counselling, displays, videos, exhibitions, books, Public Forum.

Caring for people - Making it happen

FIGURE 4
MENTAL HEALTH AWARENESS LEAFLET FRONT

the Health Authority. Public surgeries and forums were held on topics such as schizophrenia, depression, coping with learning difficulties and Alzheimer's disease. An open public meeting on mental hospital closures and care in the community was held at Thatto Heath Community Library, chaired by the Council Leader with a panel of social workers and Health Authority consultants and staff answering questions.

Public, school and professional interest in this information initiative was enormous and has led to four more mental health awareness weeks being held in other parts of the Borough. One week at Newton le Willows Community and College Library attracted over 3,000 visitors and participants from local schools and colleges, the local community, local groups and the Health Authority. This pioneering information project has since been utilized in many local authorities up and down the country. It illustrates the pivotal role which information provision and its providers often play in strategic issues and how the strategic approach to problem solving can operate to maximum advantage all round, given the right balance of sensitivity and conviction from all staff and members involved. A narrow focus through one department working in isolation would have had none of the dramatic effects which cross-departmental and cross-agency co-operation engendered.

Strategic choice and direction
At the heart of strategic management lies choice: choice about what is important, what to concentrate energy and resources on, what changes to make. To make an issue strategic implies giving it priority in terms of political emphasis and management focus. It implies selectivity in order to match capacity with aspirations. This selectivity within local authorities is likely to be guided not just by local needs but also by the political process. It is also linked to the overall aims and objectives of the authority and its

political priorities.

In St. Helens, community information development has been significantly shaped by the agreement to give priority in the development of services to seven key target groups:

Young people;
The disabled;
Under-fives
The unemployed and low waged;
The elderly;
One-parent families;
People with a mental illness.

Figure 5 illustrates how the strategic development of information services in St. Helens has been influenced by this target group emphasis. All the examples involved a multi-agency response to issues identified through detailed exploration of data obtained by techniques of environmental analysis and the exploration of public attitudes described previously in this chapter.

The information Directory for one-parent families in St. Helens—the first guide produced in the Borough for people bringing up children alone—is a good example of strategic direction influencing information development. The Directory grew out of the Council's desire to improve services and the support network for one-parent families. It was the product of work between single parents, the local Council for Voluntary Services, Gingerbread and the Leisure Department's information and community development staff. The Directory contains details of organizations providing information and support on benefits and taxes, child care, education, employment and training, emotional and family support, health, housing, leisure and legal advice. [11]

Making Changes
Strategic management must build an organization capable of carrying out agreed strategies. This frequently involves

FIGURE FIVE

MAKING A STRATEGIC CONTRIBUTION:
HOW INFORMATION SERVICES HAVE
DEVELOPED
TO ASSIST KEY TARGET GROUPS IN ST. HELENS

Disabled —	Formation of DASH (Disability Advice and Information Service, St. Helens)
Under-fives —	New childminder/play group directories are produced. St. Helens Play Forum—an information exchange network for all those involved in play provision—is set up.
One-parent families —	Directory of Services for One-Parent Families is produced.
Unemployed & low waged —	Sutton Shapes Its Future community conference leads to the creation of a Credit Union.
Young people —	Youth Information Project produces a new newspaper for teenagers. Women and Young Girls Resource Centre is established.
Mentally ill —	Mental Health Awareness Weeks are held throughout the Borough.
Elderly —	'Keeping in Touch' informational newsletter for housebound elderly is produced.

ST.HELENS METROPOLITAN BOROUGH COUNCIL
Community Leisure Department

Community Services Library
Newsletter
Issue No 8

FIGURE 6
COVER OF 'KEEPING IN TOUCH'

strategic organization changes embracing structural changes such as the creation of new departments or sections, for example, for services to under-fives, policy planning, or leisure. Organizational processes and ways of working are also likely to be changed in order to focus organizational attention on an issue or to create new devices and mechanisms to bring officers together from separate disciplines or departments. This can often also involve working in partnership with community organizations and other agencies such as the police, health authorities and government departments.

In St. Helens MBC a variety of mechanisms have been employed since the restructuring of the authority in 1985 in an attempt to engender greater corporate working and to offer a better strategic perspective for members and officers. A Community Services Committee that brought together Leisure, Education and Personal Services members and officers was utilized initially, but ultimately abandoned as too bureaucratic. A Management Board consisting of committee chairs, chief officers and the Council leader and deputy also operated for a two-year period but failed really to get to grips with the strategic tasks in hand.

The most successful strategic vehicle for developing change and creating imaginative corporate innovation in service development has proved to be the Community Strategies Task Group, consisting of the chief officers and senior managers of the Leisure, Education and Personal Services departments together with their committee chairs, the Council leader and deputy and other senior politicians. The Group's aims have been to develop strategic policy initiatives for the Policy and Resources Committee with the objective of maximising the impact of the community service departments, promoting joint working between officers and members of the Education, Leisure and Personal Services departments and advising on all aspects of community development. It has tackled issues such as the development of community schools, the establishment of a framework for the environment, providing for children with special needs in mainstream schools, and has developed the authority's key target groups, created a play strategy, a community development approach, a Pastime Keycard scheme for Leisure and Education opportunities, and identified health issues to tackle on a corporate front.

As a forum it has consciously steered away from allowing detailed financial deliberations and weighty single department reports to dominate its work. It has concentrated instead on the exploration of ideas through discussion and debate and establishing experimental approaches and task groups to address emerging strategic issues. Task groups have been formed utilizing staff from the three community service departments, and library and information staff have played a full part in the main task groups and many of its working groups. The work of the Community Strategies Task Group has enabled information staff to gain an understanding, involvement and, importantly, ownership of the strategic approach to the management of service provision and development. It has helped to ensure that the authority's culture is receptive to change and encourages and supports inter-departmental co-operation and working in partnership with local communities, voluntary sector groups and other agencies such as the Health Authority and the police. It has had a significant impact on many aspects of the work of informing St. Helens' communities, as the examples of community conferences, target groups and Mental Health Awareness campaigns bear testimony. Experimentation with mechanisms to create and extend the strategic perspective in the development of community information services is a key element in the strategic management approach.

Evaluation and monitoring of performance
At its heart, strategic management is continuous in the sense

that it is always on the look out for change which cannot be dealt with in the normal way. It must therefore continually seek to learn from what is happening and to adapt the work of the organization to better fit the changing environment. Targets and clear objectives have to be set and progress similarly measured and checked to ensure that operational issues are not crowding out the achievement of strategic aims. Training and development opportunities for staff and communication systems all need to be linked to this evaluation system to ensure that staff are given support to develop the diversity of skills and experience that the strategic approach will demand in ways of working. Information staff will best rise to the challenges facing them if they are equipped and willing to respond strategically and corporately to the needs of their communities.

In St. Helens, the Community Strategies Task Group regularly reviews the progress of all its initiatives, departments have performance measures that are reported regularly to service committees, and all departmental managers take part in performance appraisal and have personal action plans that they are expected to deliver. In this way the culture of the authority has become task, performance and action centred. 'Checking out' has helped ensure that the work of informing communities in St. Helens is continuously subject to discussion, debate, evaluation and adjustment. Projects do not assume lives of their own but are expected to account for and justify their existence on an on-going basis in terms of their impact on, and outcomes for, local people. Thus the Mental Health Awareness campaigns, for example, are all subjected to detailed before-and-after research to assess not simply the numbers attending exhibitions, forums and teaching sessions but also the impact on perceptions and awareness of the issues involved in the target audiences involved.

Conclusion

Strategic management has much to offer the information worker in local government, in voluntary groups, in health authorities, in government agencies and in other areas. Sadly, all too often, existing departmental and sectional obsessions discourage a strategic view of information service provision from taking place. The key steps, elements and processes of a more holistic, catalytic and strategic approach to community information management and development—the thinking and the planning, the doing and the delivering, the evaluating and the developing—all have an important contribution to make towards enhancing the effectiveness of informing our communities. Figure 7 illustrates conceptually what the strategic management approach to information provision must involve and what this chapter has argued strongly in favour of.

Local groups, according to recent research, need more than anything else five support mechanisms from local authorities. These are: resources, facilities, opportunities to meet other groups, training and INFORMATION.[12] The strategic management approach based on experience in St. Helens and elsewhere offers an imaginative and exciting approach to focusing management activity on the issues that really count for both the organization and for the communities served.

A recent joint statement of the Association of Metropolitan Authorities, the Association of District Councils and the Association of County Councils, commenting on the proposed review of local government structure, functions, finance and management endorsed the following principles of local government:

> Citizens have rights within the system of government: to know; to speak; to be heard; to be given explanation; to choose; to be accorded accountability; to vote; to be given service of acceptable standards; to redress . . .[13]

Information provision is fundamental to all these principles. We owe it to our communities, to our local groups, to our

AN HOLISTIC APPROACH

FIGURE 7
THE STRATEGIC MANAGEMENT OF COMMUNITY
INFORMATION DEVELOPMENT: WHAT IT MUST
INVOLVE

customers, to manage this provision effectively, responsively
. . . and strategically.

References

1. HARRIES, S. Pushing for Change—is the strategic approach the answer?, *Municipal Journal* 47, 23-29 November 1990, 26-27.

2. STEWART, J. Considerations on strategic management in local government, *Local Government Policy Making,* 17(4) March 1991, 64.

3. CLARKE, M *and* STEWART, J., *Strategies for success.* Local Government Management Board, 1991, (MS 0120), 13.

4. STEWART, J Considerations on strategic management in local government, *Local Government Policy Making,* 17 (4), March 1991, 62-64.

5. CLARKE, M. *and* STEWART, J. *Strategies for Success.* Local Government Management Board, 1991, (MS 0120).

6. ST. HELENS METROPOLITAN BOROUGH COUNCIL COMMUNITY LEISURE DEPARTMENT, *Sutton shapes its future: Action Day Report*, February 1990.
(obtainable from Community Leisure Department, St. Helens MBC, Century House, Hardshaw Street, St. Helens, Merseyside. WA10 1RN).

7. McKENZIE, M *and* CRITCHLEY, M., *Thatto Heath—a rapid appraisal survey.* December 1990.
(obtainable from Community Leisure Department, St. Helens MBC, Century House, Hardshaw Street, St. Helens, Merseyside. WA10 1RN).

8. GASTER, L. Defining and measuring quality: does decentralisation help, *Local Government Policy Making,* 17 (2) September 1990, 15-23.

9. COMMUNITY DEVELOPMENT FOUNDATION AND NATIONAL COALITION FOR NEIGHBOURHOODS *Taking communities seriously—a policy prospectus for community development and local democracy*, London: CDF, 1990.

10. ASSOCIATION OF METROPOLITAN AUTHORITIES, *Community development and the local authority*, London: AMA 1990.

11. GREEN, A *and* LEAVESLEY, S *eds, Information for one-parent families in St. Helens*, St. Helens: St. Helens MBC, Community Leisure Department/St. Helens Gingerbread/St. Helens Council for Voluntary Services, April 1989.

12. NATIONAL COUNCIL FOR VOLUNTARY ORGANIZATIONS, What local groups need—their efficiency and effectiveness and the role of local authorities, *NCVO,* October 1990, 10.

13. JOINT LOCAL AUTHORITY ASSOCIATIONS STATEMENT, 22nd March 1991.

CHAPTER TWELVE

STAFF DEVELOPMENT

Alan F. MacDougall

Staff Development

Introduction

Reference has been made in many of the chapters of this work to the requirement for 'training', but that word is being gradually replaced by the more accurate term 'staff development', which although it includes training, suggests a more wide-ranging proactive approach.

It would indeed be surprising if the need for training were not mentioned, but to what extent do those in positions of responsibility actually devise, implement and evaluate programmes? The evidence in the literature suggests a large number only pay lip-service to the requirement for staff development and training—it is reported that its application is somewhat unsystematic, unco-ordinated and uneven.[1,2] This chapter therefore focuses on the framework and options which a manager of community information would need to consider for a systematic implementation of staff development and training.

This volume clearly illustrates the variety, range and scope associated with the provision of community information; it has been discussed under the headings of arts, culture, children, fiction and the environment, to instance only a few. Since all these activities can vary in their staffing requirements from one person in a voluntary capacity, to several hundred salaried employees in large library authorities, it would be impossible to present a comprehensive and prescriptive package which could be used as a model for staff programmes in community information. Instead it would be more useful to consider the principles which would be used in the evolution of a programme to more closely reflect the needs of the individual organization in question. It is therefore worth emphasizing, from the outset, that there is no unique set of training requirements for all staff involved in community information, but as circumstances vary from organization to organization so the programme will vary, marginally or significantly, from one to another. As has been made clear elsewhere in this volume, it is possible to identify differing needs from two libraries within the same authority yet only separated by a few miles.

This, then, highlights the essential pre-requisite to effective and successful staff development and training: it must be related to the specific needs of the community to be served—it cannot exist in isolation. It is quite remarkable that so-called training and developmental programmes are still being created in a vacuum, that is, often formulated, and outwardly vindicated, by *ad hoc* dispatch of staff to the occasional course without any recourse to the needs of the organization, its clientele and importantly, the individual. David Tozer, however, in his chapter on environmental information identified the difficulty of defining the needs of the public, and its various sectors, while Kevin Harris made reference to the arrogant assumption of some information providers that they know better than their clients. The problems are further compounded by Paul Catcheside's finding that there is little evidence of good policy statements which would enable the trainer to identify needs, in relation to community arts provision by libraries. Further, in the chapter on Strategic Management by John Davies, there is an eloquent plea for the creation of a strategic policy which would help to give, an informed perspective on future activities.

Therefore information providers who are underpinned by

a policy statement, a mission statement, or a strategic plan, will be able to move smoothly to the next stage of translating those defined needs to the requirements of a developmental training programme. However, there will be many community information staff who do not have this management information, yet wish to provide some form of staff development programme. This is where the first difficulty has to be overcome; the lack cannot be ignored since it will be necessary, at the very least, to identify some form of organizational mission statement (often existing but not readily identifiable) and from this to develop the organization's objectives through appropriate discussion. The absence of written statements may seem surprising, but it should not be forgotten that community information could be serviced by small and voluntary organizations existing on large amounts of goodwill but relatively small amounts of expertise.

Assuming there is some basic concept of what the organization is doing, and should do, (if there is none then there is perhaps a need to query its continued existence), how then can this be translated into a staff development programme? Again, it has to be emphasised that the following cannot be all-encompassing since the local environment will dictate differing solutions. For example, the finest developmental model in the world would have to be modified in the context of one-person information units since a preponderance of external training programmes, which involve leaving the library or unit without cover for days or weeks at a time, may be deemed to be counter-productive, as equally would be a programme costing large amounts of money where there could never be any possibility of matching financial support.

The Need
It could be argued that there are three important areas of need to be addressed which provide a framework for further

thought, namely: knowledge, skills, and attitudes and awareness. These are now considered in turn:

Knowledge

It is perhaps an obvious point, but there is a need for staff to have a sound basis of knowledge associated with community information. Presumably it would also involve a combination of specialized understanding of the particular subject field together with more general aspects as appropriate, for example marketing, publicity and promotion amongst others. It would be presumptuous of the author to identify each of the specialized areas of knowledge required for community information, but perhaps it would be apposite to suggest that the community librarian reviews and then lists those areas of specialist expertise which are deemed to be essential within the objectives of the service. These would then provide the basis upon which to draw up a section of the training and development programme.

Skills

There is a need to develop the ability to handle concepts and translate them into reality, and a genuine requirement to develop the skills of each individual to their maximum capability. In former years this may have been viewed in a more restricted light to be activities such as filing, indexing, and so on. In recent times there has been more of a premium placed on the skills associated with the use of new technology, inter-personal skills or, more generally, on proactive management skills. This is not to suggest that in all environments such developmental training will be required since many organizations will still be low-tech through choice, or lack the resources necessary to upgrade their operation. Again, it is up to the community information officer to select a list of the skills which would be required within the particular organization. The choice will be dependent on how the needs of the organization are supported.

Attitudes and awareness

The possibilities afforded by new technology will allow great potential for the development of increasingly sophisticated database creation, analysis and dissemination. Further, modern-day requirements for innovation and change are accelerating. In this environment it becomes even more important to encourage attitudes which foster creativity and flexibility. A list of requirements suited to the organization could once again be compiled.

The above gives a framework in which the training needs for community work can be considered; it does not pretend to be profound since individual needs will vary from organization to organization, and, from individual to individual. Tozer, in his chapter, made the point that he required access to accurate, easy to handle information and the ability to exploit and act upon it. This is no doubt applicable to all; however, the means to effect that end and the individual training requirements will differ.

The decision is therefore left to the manager to decide on the precise content required to meet the training objectives. It is worth spelling out the difference at this stage between aims and objectives, which are frequently used synonymously. Aims are usually general statements of intent, whereas objectives are precise and concrete statements of what will actually be achieved. To illustrate this within the training context, it could be advanced that one of the aims could be 'to increase knowledge of activities of the local community', while the objectives might be 'to be aware of publications produced by the community' and 'to contact all local community officials'.

After due deliberation and consultation, having identified objectives, and defined the appropriate policy, it will be necessary to plan a training and development programme to meet the needs of the organization. It is important to stress that this is not a finite operation—the programme will need to be reviewed continually and updated as necessary.

The Developmental Programme
Awareness that people matter is an over-riding concern when devising a programme. Too often a programme will primarily address the mechanistic element of providing the end-product, that is solely the community information. As part of that process the human interface is often not sufficiently nurtured. This can be illustrated with reference to Hicken and Kay,[3] who listed staff training in community information as: classification schemes; meaning of community information; step-by-step instruction in filing and retrieval of information for the user; awareness of additions to stock; without mention of the needs of the individual. Appraisal schemes may have a role to play here, and although it is outside the scope of this chapter, it is nonetheless flagged as an area which might usefully be studied. Gibbs' contribution[4] is a useful starting point.

Before concentrating on the content of the programme itself it is also worth bearing in mind that staff development is no longer concerned with a top-down approach in which the individual received training. The emphasis now is on the individual being able to have ownership of their own work and ideas and being given the environment and framework in which to develop. Ownership is vitally important. Re-activeness, having things done to and for trainees, is now being replaced by pro-activeness, that is, how the trainee can develop and make a contribution to the organization.

During 1992 the Library Association launched a major initiative aimed at securing a prominent place for continuing staff development.[5] It has declared its intention to produce guidelines for continuing development for employers and employees as well as a commitment to the concept of a formal record of progress. Such an initiative should have significance for those involved in community information since the employers' guidelines will create an appropriate climate and support system for continuous staff development. The guidelines for employees will develop and maintain intellectual and personal development throughout the individual's working life. The Library Association is keen to point out that this includes personal responsibility for taking action to improve skills and update knowledge in relation to current employment and anticipated future work. The formal record of continuous development aims to reinforce the principle of continuous improvement in work performance as the responsibility of the individual. Such a scheme will help to overcome the objection that employees often wait for the employer to take the initiative, and will also harmonize the legitimate ambition of the individual with that of the organization.

Types of Training

There is an enormous array of training initiatives which can be used to assist in staff development. It is suggested that there are two main types of training which need to be addressed, namely, induction and continuing development.

Induction

It is worth stressing that an induction programme would need to be systematic, well-planned and introduce the new employee to the major components of their work in community information as well as an acquaintance with the overall organization and environment. A checklist of induction processes is a useful aid which can be kept by the employee. Induction is normally completed within the first six months of employment although the timescale will vary depending on size of library or unit, nature and sophistication of the job and previous experience or knowledge of the employee.

Luccock provides a list of questions which will help to

elicit the type of training needs of new recruits.[6] They are:
1. What knowledge, skills and attitudes are required to achieve a satisfactory level of competence in this job?
2. What will the new starter need to know about the organization and library in order to carry out his/her duties effectively?
3. What are the most appropriate methods to be used in this training?
4. What resources are required to carry out the training? (i.e. competent training staff, materials such as checklists, sufficient finance and time for courses and programmes, adequate facilities in terms of space, etc.)
5. What will be the timescale of training?
6. How will the training be monitored and evaluated? Who will do this?
7. How will the whole process be established and communicated to all staff involved?

By these means it should be possible to begin to bridge the training gap. The minutiae of induction training have been written about at length by Luccock and it is therefore recommended that the reader consult that work. Finally, it should be emphasized that there is no artificial divide between induction and development training since one should merge into the other.

Developmental Training
Developmental training, however, needs more skill to maximize it to its full potential since there are a whole range of existing or possible activities, ideas and concepts which could be blended into a rounded programme. It should also be noted at this stage that this chapter deliberately concentrates on the training and developmental aspect rather than the formal educational qualifications which in their own right could command a chapter. Suffice it to say that formal courses in library and information studies could form a useful complement to training initiatives, especially as

increased opportunities now exist for part-time and distance learning.

Methods of Training

The following internal and external training options are offered as a menu for further deliberations:

Internal

1. One-to-one training ('sitting next to Nellie' syndrome). This can be an excellent way of learning if the two partners have the right attributes. If they have not, then it can be a recipe for disaster, but in a small working environment there might be little alternative choice.

2. Guided reading may be a useful alternative or supplement. The medium should be widened to include videos, television, CDs, etc.

3. Job rotation within a planned training support environment.

4. Secondment, job exchange and visits can, with care, be a useful form of development.

5. Encouragement to prepare reports, attend working parties, committees, give lectures within and outside the organization.

6. Attendance at in-service courses.

The advantages of internal training and development have been summed up by the Library Association Working Party[7] which advocated:

1. The type of training can be related directly to the library's needs.

2. The timing and content of training can be controlled and geared to the precise training needs and availability of employees.

3. Management retains control over the number and types of staff who attend the course (e.g. should the course members be of the same background and seniority, or should they be mixed?)

4. The wide range of professional and technical expertise available within the library can be utilized more fully.

5. Overall, the library gets better value for money in terms of more effective training.

6. Common training needs—i.e. those not confined to one branch or department, can be met centrally.

However, it was acknowledged that there were also problems which have to be borne in mind, for example:

1. Administrative difficulties must be overcome—i.e. a trainee within the library must be as free from outside pressure, such as telephone calls, as would be the case on an external course.

2. The type of training must be suitable for internal organization.

3. The training must be cost-effective—i.e. viable in terms of potential costs per trainee.

4. Employees may feel inhibited when their training involves their colleagues.

External

This can be a valuable form of training and development where expertise is lacking within the organization, but, as the Library Association stresses, its main problem is that it can be an *ad hoc* activity bearing little relation to a current problem or systematic training scheme, and thus the wrong people can be trained, at the wrong time, by the wrong method. As mentioned earlier this sort of activity often passes for training and development. Its successful application must be monitored closely. Again, the Library Association Working Party suggested some good advice. Before sending someone on an external course, all alternative methods should be explored. There are only two valid reasons for sending someone on an external training course:

1. The need to improve performance in a current job

(and a belief that this can be achieved).
2. To equip the trainee with the attitudes, knowledge and skills for a future job.
The course selected must meet the individual and organizational needs, and form an integral part of the individual's development programme.

Mechanisms
The above indicate some of the types of training and development that could be entertained, but how does one capitalize on these to best effect? At the present time there is a plethora of training opportunities being offered by professional bodies such as the Institute of Information Scientists, ASLIB, and the Library Association and its sub-groups, for example, the Community Services Group. The courses run by these groups are often inexpensive and it can pay to evaluate such courses by keeping a central log of their general quality and relevance. Naturally, each staff member in attendance should provide an evaluative report for other members of staff. Consideration could also be given to importing the whole of a short course to the organization. This can be cost-effective, especially where the costs can be defrayed by inviting people from outside the organization, who in effect subsidise the course. Also, in recent times university and polytechnic departments of library and information studies have been more to the fore in offering continuing education courses and these should not be overlooked as a source of training, indeed some departments will offer to bring courses to the institution.

In addition to the employment of professional bodies and library and information studies departments there has also been an increase in recent years in professional training consultants who are prepared to provide appropriately designed training for libraries of all kinds. Their costs can be expensive but this has to be set against the potentially beneficial outcome.

Finally in this section, the recent popularity of training co-operatives should not be overlooked. The subject has been investigated at some length elsewhere.[8] Briefly, the current examples of co-operatives, both formal and informal in nature, are outlined, and the varying demands of how institutions can be accommodated within the parameters of a co-operative arrangement are demonstrated. Such bodies can offer a valuable opportunity to arrange exchange of experience seminars; workshops; exchange of staff; joint seminars; visits; social meetings; design of training packages; creation of joint training video collections; training the trainers, and so on. Co-operatives can be a useful creative environment in which training and staff development can be fostered both for trainers and trainees. However it is not advocated as an idyllic solution since experience demonstrates that they are only likely to flourish where there is encouragement and backing at the highest level.[8] At present it would appear that there are opportunities to develop and create more training initiatives arising out of the recent trend to formulate Library Information Plans (LIPs) for districts and regions.

Evaluation and Validation
Having identified the needs, set the objectives, established the policy, planned the training and staff development scheme and implemented it, it is all of little use unless the scheme's effectiveness is assessed and evaluated. Immediately one is faced with a potential problem since the term 'evaluation' is used differently according to the circumstances. It can be used in the context of value for money, whilst 'validation' could be used as a method of determining whether training was serving a real need in meeting training objectives. In this chapter evaluation is used to cover both interpretations. Casteleyn has dealt with the subject admirably[9] and therefore the reader is advised to consult her work for a detailed consideration—here it will

suffice to outline the main points.

Evaluation is designed to assess cost effectiveness and provide the framework to improve it. It must be a planned and systematic process; the odd one-off subjective comment is not acceptable. As Casteleyn points out, almost all evaluation falls into two categories: one is summative evaluation which adds up and gives evidence of the results of training; and the other is formative evaluation which yields information to develop a course. The evaluation process can then be divided into four sections:

1. The organizational level: has the training course improved the performance of the organization?
2. The application level: has the course made the trainees more effective at their work and can they apply what they have learnt?
3. The learning level: what did the trainees actually learn on the course and did these skills match the objectives of the course?
4. The reaction level: how did the trainees and lecturers react to the course?

The methods of evaluation can involve questionnaire analysis, testing observation, oral valuation—all these can be followed in greater detail in Casteleyn's work.

Conclusion

A chapter of this length can only outline some of the main features of training and development. It has sought to advocate that the training and development needs of those engaged in community information will not be significantly different from any other specialist group. The same parameters exist, the same problems prevail, and the same range of potential solutions can be posed. Consequently the message from this chapter is a plea for a systematic and planned approach to the training and developmental needs of staff, whether it be for a staff of one or a thousand. It is of little value to arrange the occasional course in the hope that it will meet the needs of the staff. It is imperative that the organizational needs are identified and that the library objectives are set to respond to those needs. A strategic policy/plan is essential. The training is then set against the library objectives, implemented and evaluated.

It is no longer acceptable to consider only the needs of the institution in isolation, since the needs of the individual have also to be considered. Further, the climate is now such that the trainee is encouraged to propose how they might develop, whereas previously it was considered acceptable for the management to provide top-down only training.

Finally, this chapter has deliberately contained no reference to professional and non-professional since the above statements apply equally to all staff and not just one group. Training is for all!

References

1. PRYTHERCH, R. ed. *Staff training in libraries*. Aldershot: Gower, 1985.

2. MACDOUGALL, J., LEWINS, H. and TSENG, G. *Continuing education and training opportunities in librarianship*. British Library Research Paper 74. London: British Library, 1990.

3. HICKEN, M. and KAYE, R. Training in community librarianship. *In:* Prytherch, R., ed. *Handbook for library training practice*. Aldershot: Gower, 1986, 129-166.

4. GIBBS, S. Staff appraisal. *In* Prytherch, R. ed. *Handbook of library training practice*. Aldershot: Gower, 1986, 61-81.

5. LIBRARY ASSOCIATION. Encouraging career-long personal growth. (Library Association Council debate on Continuing Professional Development reported by Chris Brockhurst). *Library Association Record, 93* (12) 1991, 832-833.

6. LUCCOCK, G. Induction training. *In* Prytherch, R. ed. *Handbook of library training practice*. Aldershot: Gower, 1986, 3-36.

7. LIBRARY ASSOCIATION. *Training in libraries. Report of the Library Association Working Party on Training*. London: Library Association, 1979.

8. MACDOUGALL, A.F. and PRYTHERCH, R. eds *Co-operative training in libraries*. Aldershot: Gower, 1989.

9. CASTELEYN, M. Evaluating training. *In* Prytherch, R. ed. *Handbook of library training practice*. Aldershot: Gower, 1986, 90-128.

CONCLUSION

PAST TO FUTURE—
THE PUBLIC LIBRARY'S CHANGING ROLE

Pat Coleman

Past to Future—
The Public Library's Changing Role

Introduction

In Birmingham Library Services we have found two words which encapsulate the complete range of services we aim to provide. These two words are 'information' and 'imagination'. Some aspects of service fall clearly into one area—either 'information' or 'imagination'—but most impinge on both. Our aim is to meet the needs of people in local communities; needs for entertainment, learning, ideas, company, stimulation, help, support, etc. How we meet these needs is of secondary importance to whether we are successful or not. Looking back over the past twenty years of developments in public library services it seems that today we are more flexible, less isolationist, better able to concentrate on the ends rather than the means and to recognize that information and imagination are not always too far apart.

In Chapter One, Bob Usherwood described some approaches to Community Information services. Community Information began or was first described during the early to middle 1970s and was an important element of the Community Librarianship movement. Indeed, for some librarians, Community Information and Community Librarianship were synonymous. Both developments arose as a reaction against the prevailing approach to the provision of public library services, which was perceived to be largely irrelevant for many potential users, and too heavily influenced by the views of professional librarians rather than by an analysis of the needs of communities.

I can remember, as a newly appointed librarian, criticising the contents of the Quick Reference collection in an inner city library in Manchester which included such gems as *Crockford's Clerical Directory* and *The Public and Preparatory Schools Yearbook*, both several years out of date having been passed on from another library higher in the pecking order for the receipt of new reference books. My reaction was to replace the whole collection with box files labelled 'Health', 'Housing', 'Welfare Rights', etc. which contained as up-to-date and comprehensive a range of leaflets on the specially selected topics as I could gather together. The majority of library users undoubtedly found the contents of the boxes as inaccessible as they had the Quick Reference Section it replaced, for what I soon realized was that most people who are faced with problems 'to do with their homes, their jobs and their rights'[1] want personal help and advice—which most librarians were and are not equipped to provide.

During the late 1970s and early 1980s the big debate was about whether librarians could or should give advice. Both sides of the argument were fiercely promulgated, but eventually the position was accepted which I believe most librarians would adhere to today. This is that people with problems need help and the type of help they require will range along a continuum from information, through referral and advice, to practical assistance and advocacy. The skills of librarians are most likely to prove useful at the information and referral end of the continuum.

The nature and content of Community Information was also a matter for great debate. The Library Association guidelines *Community information: what libraries can do*, already quoted by myself and Bob Usherwood, describe what Community Information is not, for example public information and local information, as well as defining very precisely what it is. Interestingly, I can remember similar debates in the 1970s and 1980s about the term 'Community Arts'. Here, the nature of the artistic experience is the essential feature. Community Arts involve professional artists as animateurs who enable ordinary people to become involved directly in performance and through that to discover their own creative potential. Arts in the Community, on the other hand, are simply traditional arts activities taking place in a community base. On reflection, what the proponents of Community Arts and Community Information were concerned to do, was to empower people to take control themselves—in order to interpret information directly and to use it to take action to solve their problems, and to employ and develop their creativity for their own personal satisfaction and enjoyment and for that of their community.

Today, we are more concerned with providing services based on the collection, organization and dissemination of resources than with undertaking a more broadly based community development role. Paradoxically, this has led to a wider range of approaches to 'informing communities' as the nature of the response is tailored to the specific circumstance. During the 1970s, librarians were among the only professionals who were 'patch' or community based. Inevitably, therefore, those librarians who were concerned about increasing the relevance of their services to local communities, particularly in inner urban areas, found it relatively easy to develop the public library as a focus for general community activity. As a result of this there was considerable criticism that these librarians were engaging in social work rather than performing their role as librarians. There is no doubt that some of the activities engaged in by librarians in the cause of community librarianship were not entirely appropriate. However, the 1970s were, rightly, a period of experimentation. The knowledge base developed by library authorities about the nature of 'community', and the experience of working in and with communities, prepared librarians to become leaders in the provision of community based services during the 1980s. It is interesting to note that in those countries which seek to emulate what they see as the best practice of British public library development, for example, in Scandinavia, Germany, France and Ireland, community librarianship and community information are of considerable interest.

During the course of the last twelve years in this country, many more public services have decentralized and yet others have developed a community role for the first time. Librarians now need to work together with other professionals serving the same community (some of whom may have a specialist information or advice remit) in an integrated way. In order to achieve this successfully, the librarian's response must focus on using our unique skills and resources.

Public understanding and appreciation of the importance and utility of information does not appear to have improved to any great extent in the last twenty years. Results of a recent survey undertaken at Oxford University revealed that up to 50 per cent of people eligible are not claiming the Family Credit to which they are entitled.[2] This is a benefit specifically targeted at low-income families in work with dependent children. When questioned about the reasons, while most were aware that it was available they assumed it did not apply to them or that the amounts were so small it was not worth bothering, while others had claimed, been turned down and failed to realize that they could appeal or apply again. This is very reminiscent of similar surveys during the 1970s. Also reminiscent is the revelation that claimants of Family Credit must complete a sixteen-page form! Consequently there remains a very real role to promote the value of information generally, to target particular aspects of information to people and groups who will benefit from using it, and to refer people on for specialist help to claim what is due to them.

Whilst it would be impossible to catalogue all the kinds of information that librarians need to provide to communities, it is possible to point to certain areas of information provision in addition to those covered in detail in previous chapters which should now form a vital part of the library's information role. These include:

Health

Awareness of the importance of diet, the perils of smoking, the threat posed by Aids and the propensity of some groups in the community to have higher risks of falling victim to certain medical problems have increased the significance of Health Information in recent years. Reference libraries have always been patronized by individuals seeking to diagnose their problem using medical dictionaries and directories. Today the emphasis is more on the provision of public information about health, often linking in with local and national campaigns. There is also the opportunity to work closely with public health staff in Regional Health Authorities and with those employed in Education Departments to teach public health in schools. Many local authorities are now running their own public health campaigns, either for their staff or for the community more generally too. The Public Library Department has potentially a very important role to play in the provision of public health information and grants may be available to build up special collections of resources in particular areas, for example, on Aids.

Jobs, Careers and Training

With unemployment levels remaining high throughout the country and particularly so in some communities, the importance of Job Information remains critical. Information required falls into two categories: first, information which describes different jobs, qualifications required, training and courses available and the practicalities of applying for jobs—the application form, curriculum vitae, interview, etc.; and second, information about specific jobs and the available training opportunities. Some libraries formed a relationship with the Training Agency which has continued through its successors the local Training and Enterprise Councils (TECs), to provide training information through a system called TAP (Training Access Points). This is a local computerized database giving details of training opportunities available, which is intended for people to consult directly themselves in libraries and other community venues. TECs are very keen to work with public libraries as they recognize the value of their widespread network and community base and also the skills of librarians in collecting and organizing information to maximize access. The other important local provider of job and careers information with which libraries should develop a close working relationship is the Careers Service, which now has an important role with adults as well as school leavers, although current proposals to take this responsibility away from local authorities may make this more difficult.

Educational Information
In many ways this area overlaps with that of job and training information but it is far broader and covers information about any aspect of educational opportunity including evening classes and leisure oriented courses. There is a mass of information available at a local level, most of it often appearing at a single point in the year before the start of the academic year in September. Librarians are the only people with the skills to organize such a mass of information effectively. They also have an independence which is important when, increasingly, direct educational providers are in a competitive situation and need to attract as many recruits as possible for their own courses. Librarians need

to form relationships with those who can provide educational guidance, for example, educational providers in colleges and universities and the Careers Service, in order to supplement their information providing role.

'What's On', Events and Activities

This was a traditional area of public library information provision which became under-valued when the emphasis turned to Community Information. It is important not to lose sight of how important this is for several reasons. First, with their high level of use and role as the focal point of community life, all libraries are the obvious places in which to display 'What's On' information. Second, involvement in and attendance at events taking place locally helps to give people a sense of community and to meet and form relationships with people with similar interests or concerns. Third, it is important to recognize how positively people feel about public libraries and that this extends to activities which appear to be recommended by libraries. So, in terms of activities which some people might feel quite hesitant about, for example, certain kinds of arts or educational events, positive promotion by and through the library can make a real difference to people's commitment.

Local History

This is another traditional area of library activity which in recent years has begun to be viewed rather differently with the recognition that previously employed methods of collecting and disseminating local history have had a rather narrow focus. The history of some communities has hitherto been ignored or misrepresented, for example that of black and some working class communities, and dissemination has been largely to so-called 'expert' local historians and academics. There is an important role for public libraries in redressing the balance with such a tremendous interest in local history, currently, amongst people of all ages and backgrounds. It is an area where the process of dissemination can go hand in hand with collection. Local history lectures, workshops and discussion groups can identify new information for collection and preservation and local history collections in individual libraries can be a focus for exhibitions which invite people to contribute their family history, photographs and memorabilia in order to make them more comprehensive. The interest in and study of local history has an important role to play in cementing relationships within individual communities, since a community which is secure in the knowledge of its past is more likely to view its future with confidence too.

Europe
As the law and regulations governing many aspects of life in the UK become ever more closely influenced by decisions of the European Commission (EC) which apply across all European States, there will be an increasing need to inform people about the EC's role and remit. At present the bulk of information available in libraries about Europe is aimed at specialist audiences, for example in business and industry. European Information Centres are often located in academic libraries or Chambers of Commerce and, as a result, are not easily accessible to the general public. Already, the Social Charter and laws on citizenship have the potential to affect particular community groups quite significantly, and consequently it is important that some priority is given to responding to this new area of information need.

Child Care
The Children Act is a recent piece of social legislation which covers almost every aspect of child care law and emphasizes that the child's welfare and safety are of paramount importance. The Act has many implications for public libraries including the provision and promotion of materials for children covering appropriate culture, languages, race

and religion, consideration in the design of libraries and regulations governing the organization of events.

Most important for present purposes is the requirement on local authorities to provide information for children, parents, carers and professionals working with children on their rights and obligations within the legislation. In some local authorities, for example, Birmingham and Sheffield, it has already been decided that this provision is best made through the public library.

Literature and Reading
This is one of the most obvious areas in which public libraries can provide information but for many years no really purposive attempts have been made to do so. Librarians who are used to working with and amongst books can often fail to realize the lack of confidence which many people feel about making a choice about what to read. As a result they resort to the shelves where they found something good last time, or the 'Returned Book Bay' which, in effect, is someone else's recommendation. It is not only failure to recognize need which has resulted in librarians' failure to make provision in this area but, in some cases, a philosophical antipathy to presuming to dictate what individuals ought to read. But many people are anxious for guidance and, in the absence of recommendations from librarians, turn to other sources, for example, newspaper reviews, awards listings and media advertising. Well thought out booklists and exhibitions by librarians can help people choose the books which will satisfy their personal need for information or imagination. And it is important to recognize that in some cases imaginative literature can be the best way through which to help people to acquire information and understanding, for example, about physical or mental illness, or life in another country.

In order to inform some groups of people with special needs or so-called communities of interest, public libraries have to take positive action to ensure that information is presented in a format and on a basis which will make it accessible to them. Twenty years ago this was viewed as the library making special provision to serve groups of people who were disadvantaged, or 'positive discrimination', and one of the most famous reports ever published about public library services, *The libraries' choice,* described initiatives undertaken by libraries in order to achieve this. In the 1990s we would say that it is not people who are disadvantaged but communities which experience disadvantage because of our failure as service providers to offer them the same standard of service as other users. Consequently, we need to take positive action to rectify matters. Some of the communities we need to respond to on this basis include:

Black and Minority Ethnic Communities
People with Physical Disabilities
People with Learning Difficulties
People who are Mentally Ill
Women.

In some cases the action required will be to provide informational materials which take account of the specific circumstances of individuals and groups. In other cases the language in which the information is provided or the level of comprehension required to interpret it are the significant factors. People with certain kinds of physical disabilities will be unable to access print and will either require material to be provided in alternative formats or special equipment to be provided to help them use print. In some cases the information required by people will not be available and here there is a potential role for the library as publisher of leaflets and directories. Some people, in particular those with learning difficulties or experiencing mental illness, may think a library has nothing to offer them and that they would not be welcome there. They will need special encouragement and support from staff to help them to see the situation differently. Along with elderly people, these latter groups are the ones most fundamentally affected by current policies on Community Care. Previously used to having their lives ordered and controlled in institutions, many will have to look after themselves with the minimum of preparation. They will need all the help that any library can give them.

In providing information for people with special needs, public libraries will have many opportunities to work with other public and voluntary sector agencies and to apply to sources of funding other than the local authority. Through Section 11 of the Local Government Act of 1966, for example, local authorities have been able to apply for 75 per cent of the costs of providing services to ethnic minority communities where they form a substantial proportion of the local authority's total population. Funding used to be open-ended, but from 1992, it is provided only on a fixed term project basis. The criteria for grant aid have also been refocused to emphasize projects which will assist people from ethnic minority communities to have access to services and facilities provided for the majority population. The potential role of public libraries as providers of information is specifically mentioned. Under these new arrangements, Birmingham Library Services have received a grant to employ four staff to provide an information service for elderly Asian people.

In the area of providing information services for people with disabilities, there are many voluntary organizations with which the public library can work closely. Rather than provide specialist information services directly from the library, it is far preferable for library staff to use their skills to improve and support the information services which these organizations normally already provide. The National Disability Information Project funded by the Department of Health and described in the Chapter on Inter-Agency Co-operation is an excellent project because it encourages organizations to 'play to their strengths'. Public libraries should be involved in all of the twelve successful pilots and help to establish and structure the information database and determine the pattern of the information service leaving the voluntary sector organizations, Social Services and Health Authority to concentrate on advice-giving, counselling, practical assistance and advocacy.

Local authorities in urban areas are usually eligible for grants for services, equipment and building work through some aspect of Central Government's Urban Programme. Revenue projects are time-limited to a maximum of five years but it can be a very helpful way of starting off new schemes and services. Some examples of projects funded in Birmingham which have an information remit or element within them include:

- a member of staff to work with patients with mental illness about to be discharged from institutions to help them appreciate how to use the library for information and leisure;
- a member of staff to collect and disseminate information about the history of the black community in the city;
- two members of staff to work with parents of children under five in two areas of the city to develop an awareness of the importance of books and reading for their children;
- staff and resources to provide job information;
- a special vehicle to take local history resources and information out from the Central Library through the city;
- a special vehicle to take exhibition collections of children's books and information about reading to health and community centres in parts of the city where children are unlikely to be encouraged to read and use books;
- funding for a number of open learning collections—one specifically aimed at child minders covering all aspects

of child care and others focusing on business opportunities and basic skills;

● a project to provide information about opportunities for volunteering by establishing information points operated by the Volunteer Information Bureau in five libraries;

● grants to help with access to buildings and within buildings including installing ramps and automatic doors, induction loops, Kurzweil readers, and an ambulance with a tail lift to bring elderly people and people with limited mobility into libraries.

Finally, there are some other relevant areas of information provision in which there have been developments in public libraries in recent years. The first is that of Public Information systems. In a number of local authorities the Public Library has been the department which has developed and co-ordinated the provision of information about the authority, for example, committee structures and names, departmental structures and service responsibilities and related information, such as tourist attractions and bus timetables, and made it available through computer systems such as Viewdata or Hypertext. Similar systems are in a more advanced stage of development in other parts of Europe, for example Minitel in France and Italy and there is some interest in developing networking between systems across Europe,

Business Information is another traditional area of public library provision, most usually associated with major reference library services, in which there have been notable developments in recent years with the encouragement of individuals to start their own businesses. Some who have tried this, or are interested in trying, are from interest groups not traditionally associated with the business sector. Business sections in public libraries have responded by providing more information of interest to small businesses, by developing links with organizations specifically established to support and encourage this area of economic development and by investigating different ways of reaching these non-traditional users with their services.

Open Learning is one of the most exciting developments to reach public libraries for a very long time. Through its increasingly widespread introduction, the role of public libraries in the whole area of support to adult learning has undergone a transformation. Open Learning really does bring the idea of the public library as the alternative 'people's university' up to date. Many of the topic areas covered by open learning packages provide specific aspects of information. Because of their accessible approach they enable people to take in quite complex information with relative ease. The interest in Open Learning is very widespread and, here again, there is great scope for co-operation—and joint working—between librarians and their colleagues in the education sector.

Conclusion

The present approach to the provision of information by public libraries is more diverse than it has ever been. Most librarians have moved away from a narrow definition of Community Information to one which would be more accurately termed 'information for the community'. In order to inform communities effectively librarians need to adopt a very flexible approach, using all the resources at their disposal wherever they happen to be in the library's stock: reference or lending, non-fiction or fiction, book, leaflet, video or computer disc. They should also concentrate on networking with other professionals serving the same community before determining what the exact nature of their role should be. It may be that the librarian's specialist skills of information collection, organization, retrieval and dissemination are best utilized to support others to provide direct public service. This service may not necessarily be provided in the library, either, but in another more appropriate community venue.

Public librarians should seek to promote themselves as the information specialists in the local authority. There are plenty of opportunities to demonstrate that information is a key aspect of many currently important issues in local government. Although money is not easily available through mainstream library budgets for new services, there are other funding opportunities which librarians should be aware of and constantly seeking to exploit.

In order to fulfil the role outlined here librarians will need to develop a level of confidence in their skills and abilities which is, unfortunately, sometimes lacking. But we should do it and we can.

References

1. LIBRARY ASSOCIATION: *Community information: what libraries can do*. London: Library Association, 1978.

2. *The take-up of Family Credit*. Oxford: Department of Applied Social Studies and Social Research, Barnet House, Wellington Square, Oxford, 1992.

3. DEPARTMENT OF EDUCATION AND SCIENCE. *The libraries' choice*. London: HMSO, 1978. (Library Information Series No. 10).

100416792

Printed in Great Britain by J. H. Brookes (Printers) Ltd., Hanley, Stoke-on-Trent.